Hands-On Data Engineering

with R, Python, and PostgreSQL

Second Edition

Michel Ballings
Dirk Van den Poel

Table of Contents

Preface

In 2008 Michel started his PhD under Dirk. As Michel worked on data science projects he started a list detailing how to accomplish certain tasks in R to use as a reference when the need would arise. We then started using this list as course materials in our classes. In 2014 Michel became a professor allowing him to make equivalent lists for Python and PostgreSQL. Every year since 2018, we had the idea to publish these lists in a book. However, the book never seemed finished. There were always new developments in the field, and there were always new chapters to add. We therefore kept on iterating on the book as we used it as course materials in award-winning data engineering classes in business schools.

Over the years we have received many requests to publish our materials. In 2022 we decided to publish our book containing the lists, in contrast to trying to finish the book and coming to the conclusion, yet again, as is the case every year, that there is more to add. By doing so we not only satisfy the requests to share our materials beyond our universty students but we also gather feedback from a larger group of people so that we can iterate faster on improving the content.

We note that the book is typically consumed in a classroom setting with an instructor talking through the material. As a result the book may be concise at times. When that is the case, please let us know and we will elaborate where necessary. We look forward to your feedback and plan on releasing updated versions of the book every two or three years taking into account your comments.

Email michel.ballings@gmail.com to provide feedback or ask questions. We would also appreciate you helping us spread the word by reviewing the book on Amazon.

Chapter 1

Preliminaries

1.1 Data Engineering in Development Operations

Development Operations (DevOps) is a set of practices that aim to maximize the probability that a data science project reaches production and does not get stuck in development. The main strategy is to release software features incrementally. This creates a tight feedback loop with users, enabling development to progress faster, and results in software that better conforms to users' needs. Because of the iterative nature of this process, every step in the chain will be executed many times. Figure 1.1 presents the DevOps cycle.

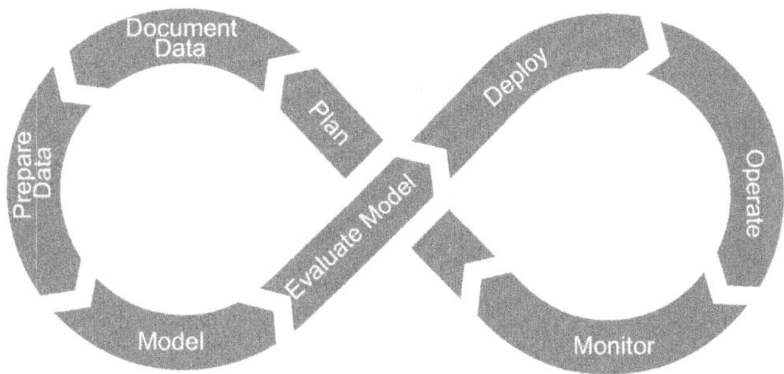

Figure 1.1: DevOps

- *Plan.* This step starts out with developing an understanding of the project's business goals, and defining when the project is successful. Next, a complete list is produced of all the tasks that need to be completed before the project can be deployed to production for the first time.

- *Document Data.* Documenting data refers to generating insight in the structure of the data by looking at relationships between tables, creating a data dictionary, running descriptives and visualizations.

- *Prepare Data.* Data preparation refers to the creation of a data set, and keeping it up to date, so that algorithms can learn and produce models.

- *Model.* Modeling entails choosing an algorithm, fitting a model to data, and monitoring the model's convergence from a statistical point of view.

- *Evaluate Model.* Before the model can be deployed, it needs to be tested against a set of business requirements. For example, if we are developing a price recommendation algorithm, in the modeling step we might have concluded that a model has accurately learned to recommend an optimal price. In this step we might test whether the recommended price is in a valid range approved by executives.

- *Deploy.* Deployment refers to making the software available in production so that it is accessible to users or downstream systems, often through an API. This includes integrating the solution into the existing business/IT environment.

- *Operate.* Once a model is in production (i.e., operational) people or systems will start consuming it, and feedback will start flowing to the development team.

- *Monitor.* The results of model consumption need to be monitored. For example, if the model recommends improved prices, do product sales satisfy the desired pattern?

The above process is iterative in nature. After having monitored the model in production, the next iteration of the planning step occurs, and a new list of tasks is produced taking into account feedback from users. In our experience a total of 20 cycles is normal. In this book, we denote **Data Engineering** to be the **combination of Documenting Data and Preparing Data**.

1.2 Documenting Data

The data understanding stage consists in exploring the data at the table and variable level. At the table level we need an entity relationship diagram (ERD) that explains how the different tables are related. At the variable level we need a data dictionary. Only proper understanding of the data can result in a high quality analysis and therefore this stage should not be taken lightly. It will speed up any subsequent stages considerably. To generate this proper understanding we may need to create variables, change object types, subset the data, read in the data, run descriptives, and impute missing values. We will also need to look at manual pages, install and load packages and monitor and manage memory usage.

1.2.1 Entity relationship diagram

Figure 1.2 provides an example of an entity relationship diagram (ERD) for three tables. There are many different designs of diagrams and the choice of a specific design is driven by preference. We prefer a basic design as displayed in Figure 1.2. Every ERD should display the cardinality (one-to-many, many-to-many, or one-to-one), the variable that is used as the key to merge two datasets and the names of the tables. For example, if we focus on the relationship between the Subscriptions and Customers table in Figure 1.2 we see that every customer can have one-to-many subscriptions and that every subscription can have exactly one customer. The two tables can be merged by the variable CustomerID. As to the Subscription-Product relationship we see that each subscription can have only one product and that every product can have one-to-many subscriptions. The key to merge on is ProductID.

1.2.2 Data dictionary

There are different degrees of detail that we can use to compile a data dictionary. As a minimum, we use a table of three columns: variable name, definition, and update time of the record per variable. The latter can be different per variable, and this information is often difficult to obtain. As will become clear later in the book, the next best piece of information is then when any variable in the record was last updated. This information is available much more often, in the form of an 'updated on' variable. In addition to these columns, we also recommend to have a column in the data dictionary (not shown in Table 1.1) with summary information. This

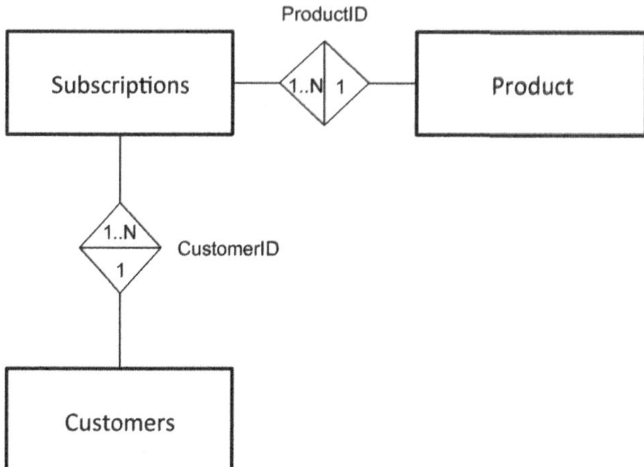

Figure 1.2: Example of an ERD for three tables

may be statistics about the variable such as whether there are any missing values or nulls in the variable and how many, what are the most frequent categories, what is the minimum, mean, standard deviation, median, and maximum. It helps to have this information readily accessible, as opposed to having to recompute it every time one needs it. Table 1.1 provides an example of a transactions table.

Table 1.1: Example of a data description for a transactions table

Variable	Definition	Last Updated
transID	The transaction ID	updatedon
custID	The customer ID	updatedon
price	Price paid for the product	updatedon
prodID	The product ID	updatedon
purchDt	The date of the purchase	updatedon
createdon	When the record was created	updatedon
updatedon	When the record was last updated	updatedon

1.3 Preparing data

The data preparation stage consists in computing variables and aggregating and merging tables. The final objective of this phase is to create a basetable. A basetable contains information from multiple tables and is ready to apply algorithms to. In general, the more variables we have computed, the higher the likelihood that the model is of high predictive performance. In complex projects, or in projects that are executed by teams, it is always a good idea to create a code flowchart. This also forces us to think about all the tasks that need to be completed to compute a basetable. A code flowchart can form the basis for creating a task division among team members. In addition it is very handy for code maintenance.

This section will provide code examples of several important tasks that we will need to perform when preparing our basetable for analysis: creating dummy variables, summarizing (aggregating) data, merging (joining) data, applying functions to data frames, working with dates, creating functions, conditional processing, creating loops, and timing code.

A code flowchart summarizes all the steps that lead to the basetable. Try to fit everything on one page and put actions in more blocks when necessary. Provide as much detail as possible but keep it comprehensible. Figure 1.3 contains an example for a single table.

1.4 Why R, Python, PostgreSQL?

In this book we use R, Python, and PostgreSQL because of the following reasons:

- **Functionality**. At the time of this writing, all three languages (R, Python, and PostgreSQL) have mature and stable functionality and can be extended with additional modules with very little effort.

- **Transparency**. They are open- source: one can easily see all functions. Hence, one is not limited to documentation and can go and look at the code if something is not clear.

- **Availability**. They are available on almost all operating systems including Microsoft Windows, macOS, and Linux.

- **Ease of install**. Precompiled binaries are available for the aforementioned operating systems.

- **Cost.** They are free.

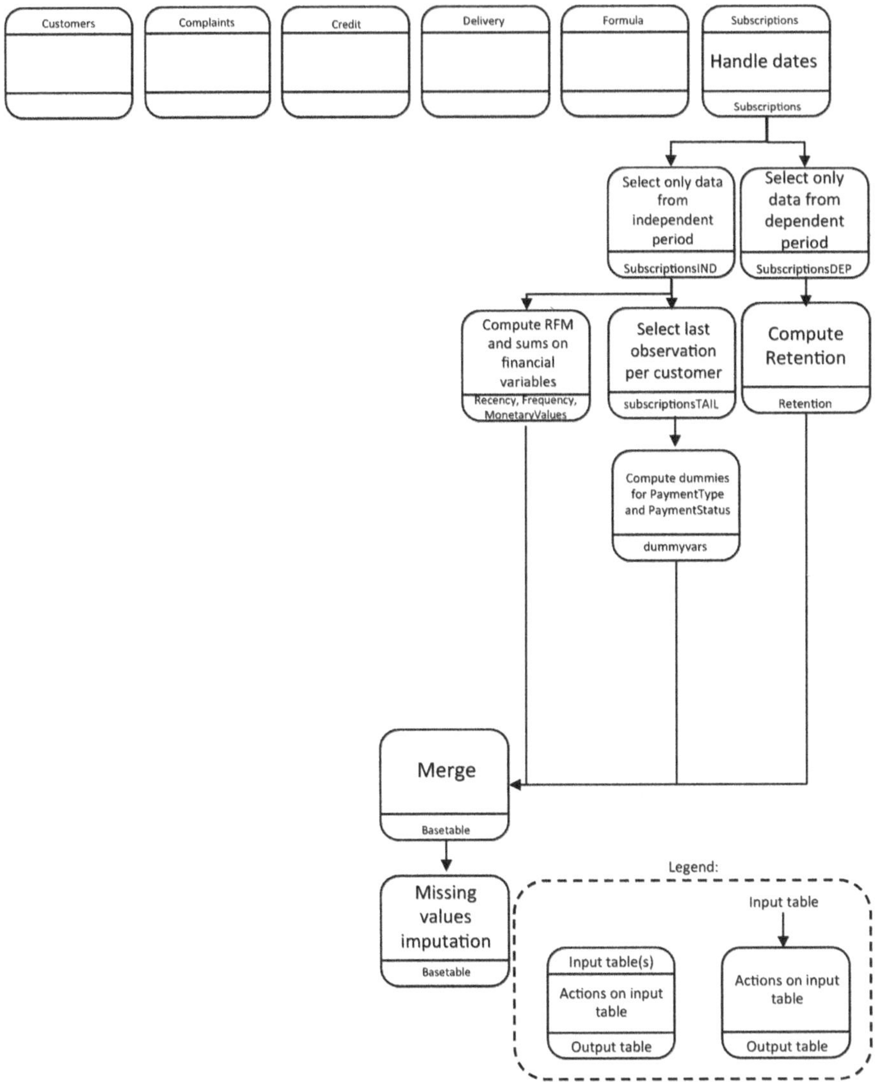

Figure 1.3: Example of a code flowchart

1.5 When to use R, Python, and PostgreSQL

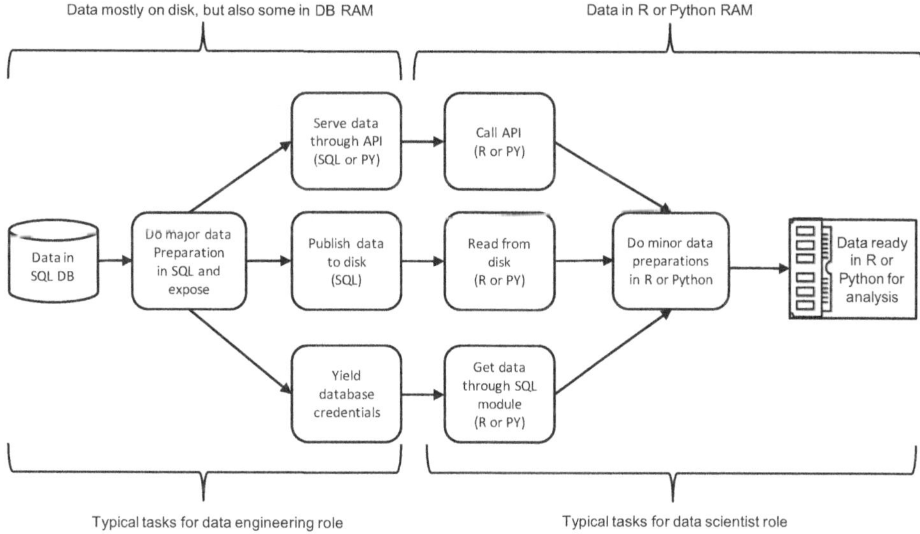

Figure 1.4: Most common workflow

1.6 Evolution of R, Python and PostgreSQL

R. John Chambers, Rick Becker and Allan Wilks designed a statistical computing language when they were at Bell Laboraties in 1976. They didn't know how to name the project so they looked at other languages for inspiration. There was the C programming language, also developed at Bell Labs - a one letter name. This inspired them to choose S, presumably meaning Statistics. S was available under a commercial license and was further developed until 1998. In 1992 Ross Ihaka and Robert Gentleman at the University of Auckland set out to produce a free implementation of something resembling version 3 of the S language. They called this implementation R, as a play on the name S, and partly after their first names. In 1993 Ihaka famously sent an email to the S-news list subscribers announcing R, and in all caps wrote *'This is not an official release. Please don't bug us about it. We are fully occupied with teaching and administrative work at present. When the source code is stable, we will make it available through Statlib.'*. In 1993 the first binaries were published at Statlib. In 1997 three major milestones were the creation of the R core group, the formation of the Comprehensive R Archive Network (CRAN) by Kurt Jornik and Fritz Leisch, and the launch of R alpha version 0.16 with base functionality (no packages). In 1999 `r-project.org` was founded and in 2000, R 1.0.0 was released. Version 2, first released in 2004, comprised support for a new compiler function to convert functions to byte-code, with significant speed gains as a result, mandatory namespaces for packages, and a new parallel package. From 2013 onwards, version 3 included support for numeric index values beyond 2^{32} on 64 bit systems, default just-in-time compilation of loops and functions, default byte-compilation of external packages, and a new serialization format to support compact internal representations. In 2015, R version 3.2.3 had 7,754 available packages. The latest release at the time of this writing is version 4.4.2, and has 21,738 available packages.

Python. Python was created in the National Institute for Mathematics and Computer Science, Amsterdam, by Guido van Rossum in 1989, who derived the name from the British comedy group Monty Python. Van Rossum lead the Python project until 2018 and famously introduced the term 'Benevolent dictator for life (BDFL)', a title now typically given to project founders who retain the final say in disputes within the community. The first release, in 1991, was version 0.9.0 and included core datatypes. Version 1.0 was released in 1994 with major new features such as lambda functions, map, reduce, and filter. From 2000 onwards, version 2.0 introduced list comprehensions and unified Python's types and classes. Python 3.0 was released in 2008 and fixed several fundamental design flaws, which broke full backwards compatibility. Version 3.13 is the latest version at the time of this writing.

PostgreSQL. In the 1970s two scientists at the University of California, Berkeley raised funding to create a geographic database system, which they called Ingres (INteractive Graphics REtrieval System). They decided to fund a relational database system instead and developed it for over a decade. In the mid 1980s one of the two scientists who created Ingres, launched Postgres, meaning Post Ingres, to solve many of the problems inherent to Ingres. Version 1 of Postgres was released in 1989, and it used a language called Postquel. By the early 1990s the project was released under an MIT-style license so other developers could become involved in developing the many features that were requested by Postgres users. In the second half of the 1990s PostQuel was replaced by SQL, and Postgres was announced with a more liberal open source license to attract more users. In 1996 the project was subsequently renamed to PostgreSQL to reflect the change to SQL. The first PostgreSQL release was version 6.0 in 1997. In 1998, a major feature upgrade was made with PL/pgSQL. Version 7 marked many SQL language expansions, and optimizations, hardening the system. Version 8 features included table partitioning and windowing functions. Version 9 brought a major breakthrough with parallel query support, foreign tables (allowing data stored outside the database to be used as native PostgreSQL data) and extensions to simplify packaging of additions. Version 10 and 11 brought many features, especially improved support of parallel queries. Version 17 is the latest version at the time of this writing. Postgres as a service is offered on Amazon Web Services.

Spark. Spark was started by Matei Zaharia at UC Berkeley in 2009 and open sourced a year later. In 2014 it became a top level Apache Software Foundation project. Zaharia went on to found Databricks focused on web-platform for working with Spark and training, and organizing the annual Spark Summit. Spark is one of the most active Apache projects

MongoDB. MongoDB was initially developed by a company called 10gen, which was established in 2007 and renamed to MongoDB, Inc in 2013 after realizing the potential of the MongoDB project. Since October 2018 MongoDB is released under the Server Side Public License as the MongoDB Cummunity Server. This license is nearly identical to the GNU GPL 3 licence, but requires those who make the software available as a service to also release the entire source code.

Chapter 2

Installing and Using Software

2.1 Essentials of the Command Line Interface

When using the software covered in this book, one will, sooner or later, arrive at the point where the command-line interface (cli) is unavoidable. The command-line interface, or 'shell', that we use in this book is 'bash', short for 'Bourne-again shell'. Bash is an open-source version of the popular Bourne shell, develped by Stephen Bourne at Bell Labs in the seventies. If you are running Linux or macOS (Unix) then you already have bash installed. If you have Windows, then you can install Git Bash (available at `https://gitforwindows.org/`). In this section we cover a small number of basic commands, such as navigating the file system, finding and opening files, copying and moving files, reading files, and making simple edits.

2.1.1 Opening the shell

To open your shell under macOS, open the `Terminal.app`. In Windows, right click Git Bash and 'Run as administrator'.

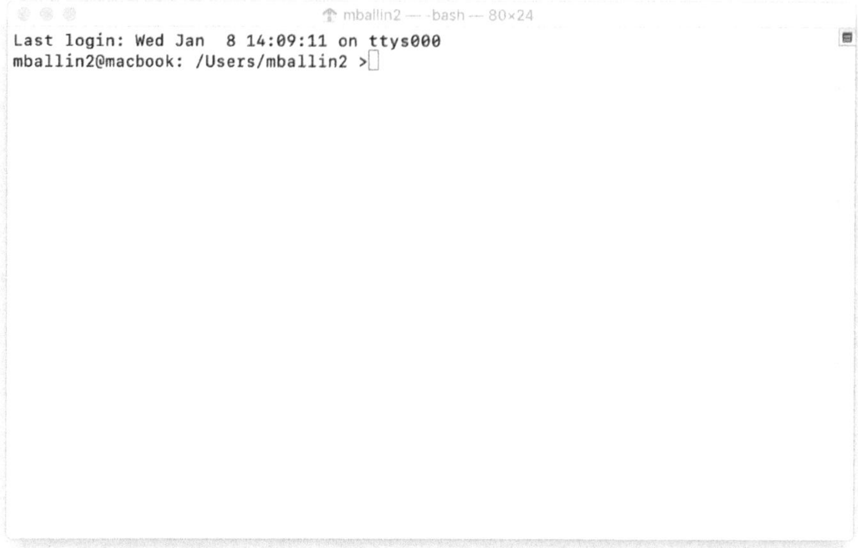

Figure 2.1: A blank shell on macOS

2.1.2 Navigating the file system

What directory are we currently in (i.e., our working directory)? Input `pwd` , short for 'print working directory' as follows

```
pwd
```

and hit enter. We get `Users/mballin2` , where `mballin2` is our username. This may be slightly different on Windows. To list the contents of our working directory use

```
ls
```

We can modify the output by using 'flags'. To list the contents in long format use flag `-l` , with Bytes, Kilobyes, . . . , Gigabytes as opposed to bits use flag `-h` , and to also show the hidden files use flag `-a` as follows:

```
ls - lha
```

To get all the available flags, one can request the manual page as follows (in Windows this may be `help help`):

```
man ls
```

To quit the manual page use the command

```
q
```

To only see files with the `.py` use the wildcard operator `*` as follows:

```
ls * .py
```

To navigate to another directory inside your current directory (i.e., moving down the tree structure), say the desktop directory, use the change directory command

```
cd desktop
```

To move one level up the tree structure use

```
cd ..
```

To go back to your home directory (the directory you are in when you first open a new shell) use tilde:

```
cd ~
```

If you ever see a single dot, it means the current directory. The following, albeit useless command, means change directory to the current directory:

```
cd .
```

The dot can be used to copy from another folder to the current directory, for example. Trick: To see previous commands, hit up. To see more recent commands, hit down.

2.1.3 Viewing, copying, and renaming files

To use your computer's standard program to open a file, use the `open` on macOS or the `explorer` command on Windows. First let's download this file to our desktop `http://hde.onl/subscriptions.txt` (after going to the url, right click the page and save to desktop). Then to open 'subscriptions.txt' use

```
cd desktop
open subscriptions.txt
```

on a Mac, or `explorer subscriptions.txt` on Windows. To view 'subscriptions.txt' in the shell use the `cat` command - short for concatenate and print files:

```
cat subscriptions.txt
```

To view the first 10 lines:

```
head subscriptions.txt
```

To view the last 10 lines:

```
tail subscriptions.txt
```

To move (or simply rename) a file we use `mv sourcefile targetfile` . For example, to rename 'subscriptions.txt' to 'subs.txt' use:

```
mv subscriptions.txt subs.txt
```

To verify, we can list the file, if it is there:

```
ls subs.txt
ls subscriptions.txt
```

To move the file to another directory, say one directory up, use:

```
mv subs.txt ../subs.txt
```

Let's verify if that was successful:

```
ls subs.txt
cd ..
ls subs.txt
```

Finally, to copy a file, we use the `cp` command:

```
cp subs.txt subs_backup.txt
ls subs*.txt
```

2.1.4 Creating, editing, and deleting files

Our favorite editor is 'nano'. To create a file with nano called 'myfile.txt' type:

```
nano myfile.txt
```

Figure 2.2: An empty file viewed with the nano editor on macOS

At this point, we can type something, say 'Hello World' and save the file. At the bottom of the editor we see that we need to type control-o to start the 'Write'. We confirm the file name by entering. To close the file we use control-x. To re-open the file we use the same command as the one we used to create the file.
To remove 'myfile.txt' use:

```
rm myfile.txt
ls myfile.txt
```

To create a directory we use the make directory command:

```
mkdir mydirectory
ls
```

and put an empty new file (using `touch`) in it:

```
cd mydirectory
touch newfile.txt
```

To remove the directory use the `rm` command with the option recursive flag.

```
cd ..
rm -r mydirectory
```

Tricks:

- To avoid issues, avoid spaces in names.
- To clear the screen use control-l.
- To go to the start of the line use control-a, and to go to the end of the line use control-e.
- A hashtag makes a command a comment.

2.2 Installation and Administration of Software

2.2.1 R

The R Project for Statistical Computing website is `https://www.r-project.org/`. R can be downloaded from `http://cran.rstudio.com`. Pre-compiled binary point-and-click installers are available. This will give you a bare bones interface. Refer to Section 2.2.4 for installation instructions of better interfaces.

2.2.2 Python

Python's website is https://www.python.org/. To install Python go here: https://www.python.org/downloads/. Pre-compiled binary point-and-click installers are available. Then try the following command in your terminal:

```
python3 - -version
```

If you receive an error stating the `python3` command is not recognized try `python -version` instead. If it is still not recognized then you need to add the path to your Python executable to your PATH environment variable.

2.2.3 PostgreSQL

PostgreSQL's homepage is https://www.postgresql.org. Pre-built binary Postgres distributions are available for all major operating systems at https://www.postgresql.org/download/, or
https://www.enterprisedb.com/downloads/postgres-postgresql-downloads. For Windows and MacOS point and click install interfaces are available along with installation instructions:
https://www.enterprisedb.com/postgres-tutorials/installation-postgresql-mac-os.

When asked to select components, we recommend to deselect pgAdmin4 and Stack Builder. Specify a password and write it down somewhere. As you will see later, our password is 'book'. It is best to leave the port to the default 5432. Copy the settings and store them somewhere. Ours look like this:

```
Installation Directory: /Library/PostgreSQL/17
Server Installation Directory: /Library/PostgreSQL/17
Data Directory: /Library/PostgreSQL/17/data
Database Port: 5432
Database Superuser: postgres
Operating System Account: postgres
Database Service: postgresql-17
Command Line Tools Installation Directory: /Library/PostgreSQL/17
```

If our installation was successful, we can connect to PostgreSQL with the `psql` command in the terminal. First, we need to determine if the `psql` command can be found by our computer using `which psql`. In our case this returns

`/Library/PostgreSQL/17/bin/psql` . This means that our computer knows where to look for the executable when we issue the `psql` command. However, if nothing is returned we need to tell the computer where to look for the executable, as decribed here:

- First, we need to find the Installation Directory via the settings that we stored earlier. In our case that was `/Library/PostgreSQL/17` . Next we add `/bin` to that path: `/Library/PostgreSQL/17/bin` .
- Second, we need to add the path from the previous step to our environment variables. This process is different if we are on a Mac or a Windows computer.
  - On a Mac, open your bash and type `sudo nano /etc/paths` . It will ask for your computer's password. Then, add the path from the previous step to that file. Type control-o to save, hit enter to confirm the file name, and control-x to close the file. Then open a new bash and type `which psql` . If it returns the path with `/psql` appended then you are done.
  - On a Windows machine, type 'environment variables' in the taskbar's search box. Click the 'edit environment variables' menu that appears. Click the environment variables box in the resulting menu (bottom right). Then, click the user's `path` variable and click edit. Add the path from step one. Then, reboot the computer. After restarting the computer open a new bash and type `which psql` . If it returns the path with `/psql` appended then you are done.

Now that we have located `psql` go to Section 2.3.3 to connect to Postgres using the terminal utility and Section 2.4.3 to connect through an Interactive Development Environment.

Note that Postgres will automatically start up when we reboot our computer. We can turn off postgres. To verify if postgres is running, we first need to log into the postgres user (using our computer's password), then query the status, as below. The final command in the code chunk below returns the manual page of the `pg_ctl` command, which will tell us that we can shut down postgres using `pg_ctl stop -D /Library/PostgreSQL/17/data` .

```
mballin2@macbook: /Users/mballin2 >sudo -iu postgres

Michels-MacBook-Pro:~ postgres$ pg_ctl -D /Library/PostgreSQL/17/data status
pg_ctl: server is running (PID: 143)
/Library/PostgreSQL/17/bin/postgres "-D/Library/PostgreSQL/17/data"

pg_ctl --help
```

If for whatever reason you wish to uninstall PostgreSQL, please refer to the instructions at `https://www.enterprisedb.com/docs/supported-open-source/postgresql/installer/05_uninstalling_postgresql/`. On a Mac this might still leave files on your disk. To remove those files do the following in terminal:

- `sudo rm /etc/postgres-reg.ini`
- Press return
- `sudo rm -rf /Library/PostgreSQL`
- Press return

Finally, to remove the PostgreSQL user account from your Mac do the following:

- Click the Apple Menu and choose System Preferences
- Choose Users and Groups
- Click the padlock and type in your admin username and password
- Select the PostgreSQL user
- CLick the '-' at the bottom of the window
- Quit System Preferences

PostgreSQL will now be completely uninstalled.

2.2.4 Interactive Development Environment (IDE)

2.2.4.1 R

R, Python and PostgreSQL will come with a bare bones interface. To be productive we need an Interactive Developent Environment (IDE). Our preference goes to IDEs that can run code locally on one's laptop and on a remote server. Two such IDEs are RStudio (R and Python only) and Visual Studio Code (R, Python, and PostgreSQL). Because Visual Studio Code (VSCode) can run many software languages we recommend it over RStudio. RStudio can be downloaded here: `http://rstudio.com/products/RStudio/#Desktop`.

2.2.4.2 Python

VSCode can be downloaded from `https://code.visualstudio.com/download` (see Figure 2.3).

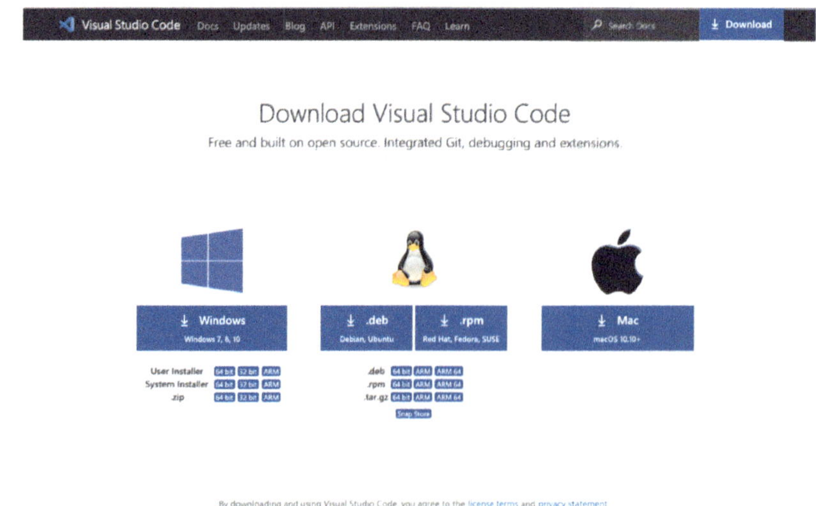

Figure 2.3: Downloading VSCode

After downloading the file, double click it and follow the instructions. Upon opening VSCode, we see Figure 2.4.

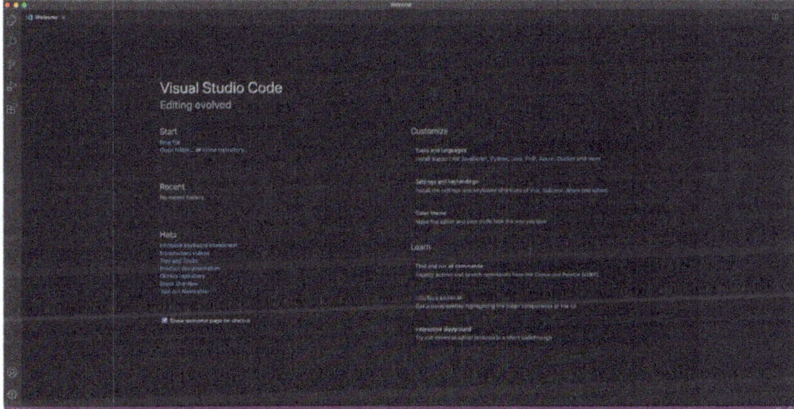

Figure 2.4: Opening VSCode the first time

Next, we need to install the Python extension, as displayed in Figures 2.5, 2.6, and 2.7.

Figure 2.5: Extension tab

Install Python extension

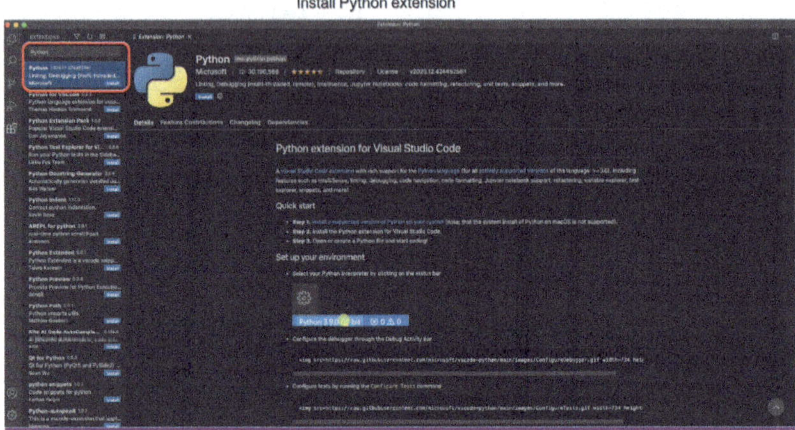

Figure 2.6: Search for Python extension

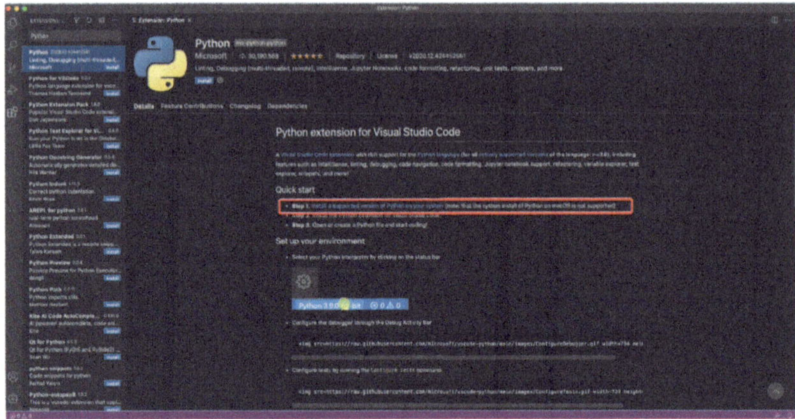

Figure 2.7: Install supported version of Python

Clicking the link in Figure 2.7 will lead to the webpage in Figure 2.8. If you are using a Mac and Homebrew is not installed, get it at `https://brew.sh/`. Also note the requirements for installing Homebrew.

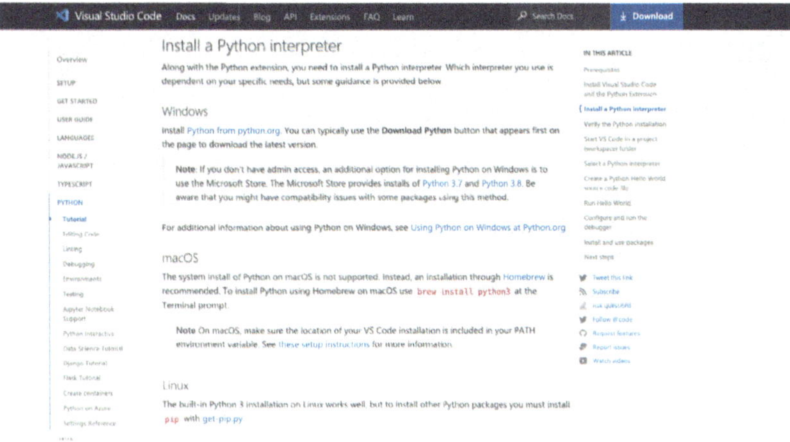

Figure 2.8: Pythone interpreter installation instructions

To finalize installing the Python extension, click the install button per Figure 2.9.

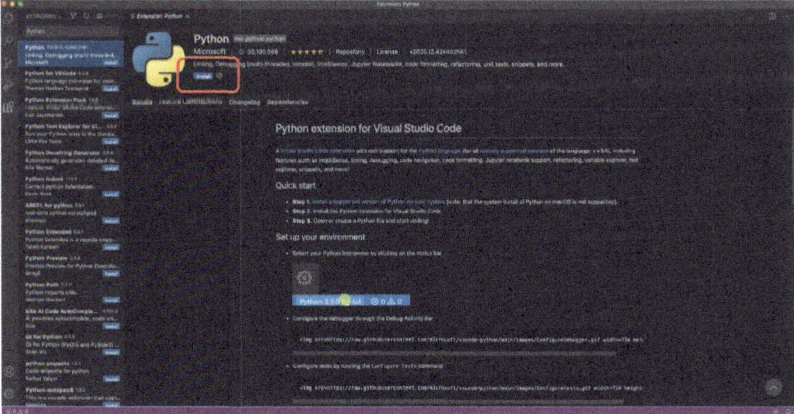

Figure 2.9: Install the Python extension

What remains is to select the Python Interpreter, per Figures 2.10, 2.11, 2.12.

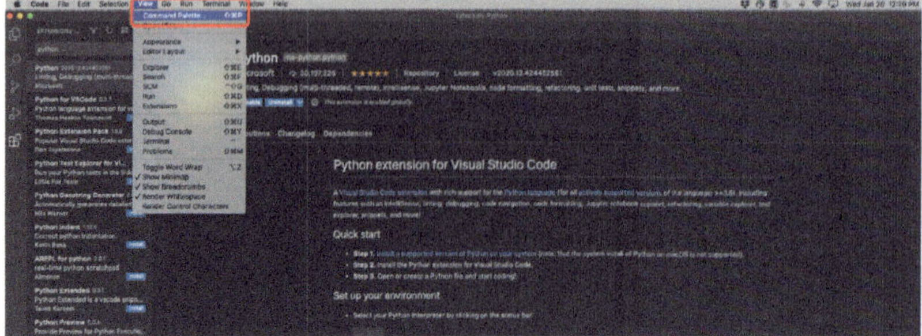

Figure 2.10: Opening the Command Palette

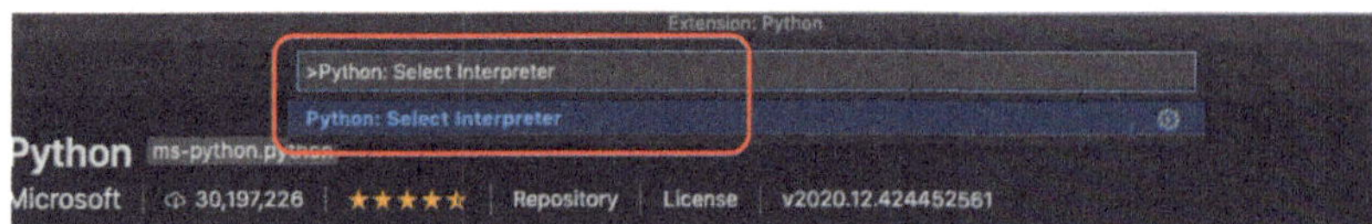

Figure 2.11: Using the Command Palette

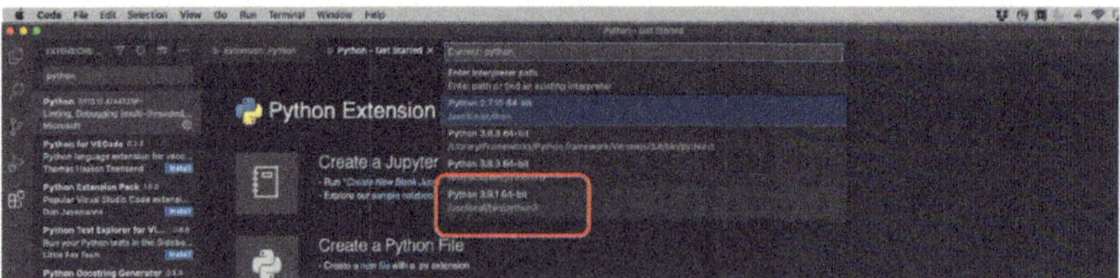

Figure 2.12: Selecting the Python Interpreter

2.2.4.3 PostgreSQL

To run PostgreSQL from VSCode we need to install the SQLTools extension. We provide screenshots below to guide you through this process.

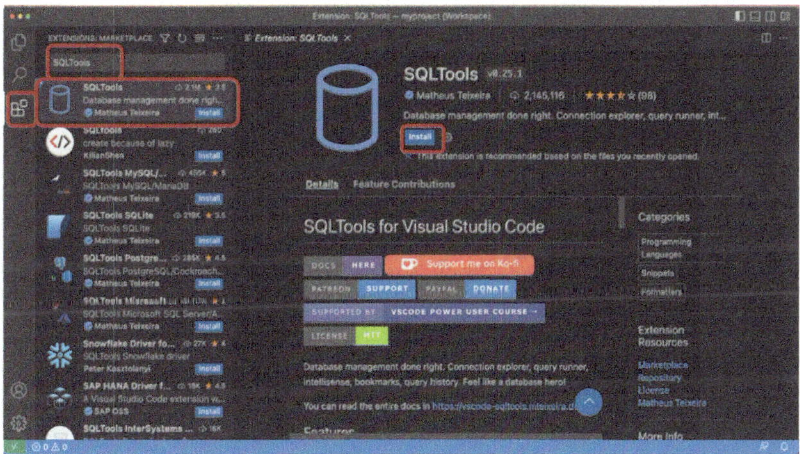

Figure 2.13: Installing SQLTools

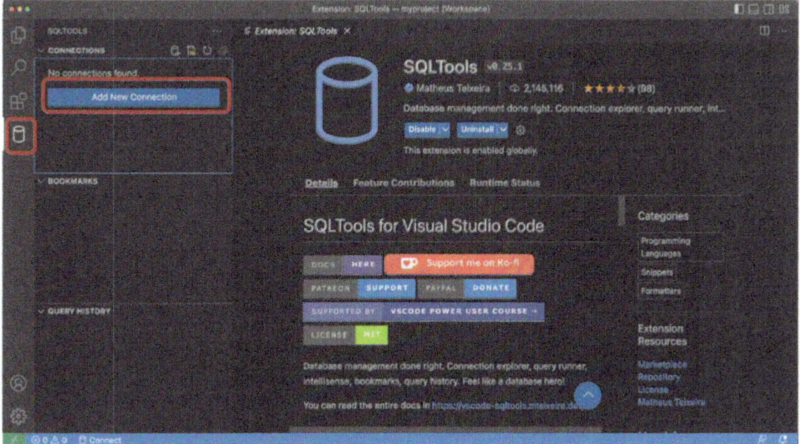

Figure 2.14: Adding a new connection

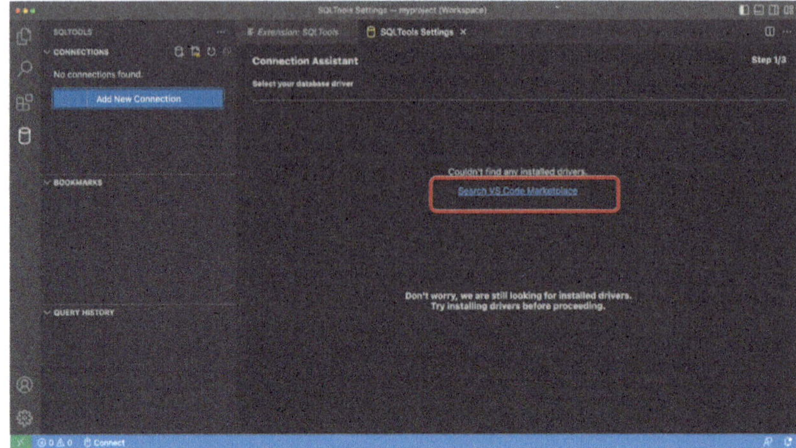

Figure 2.15: Searching for the Postgres driver

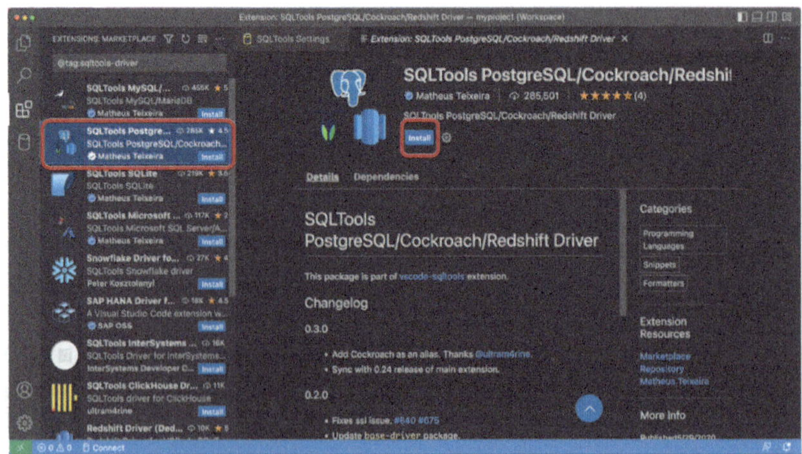

Figure 2.16: Installing the SQLTools PostgreSQL driver

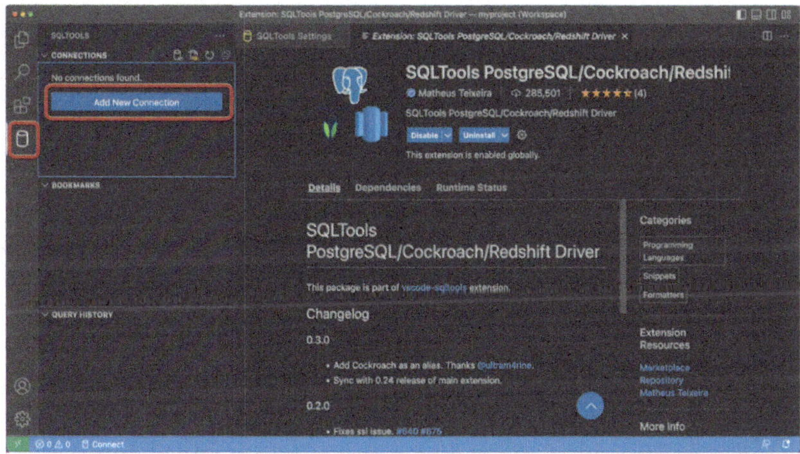

Figure 2.17: Adding a new connection

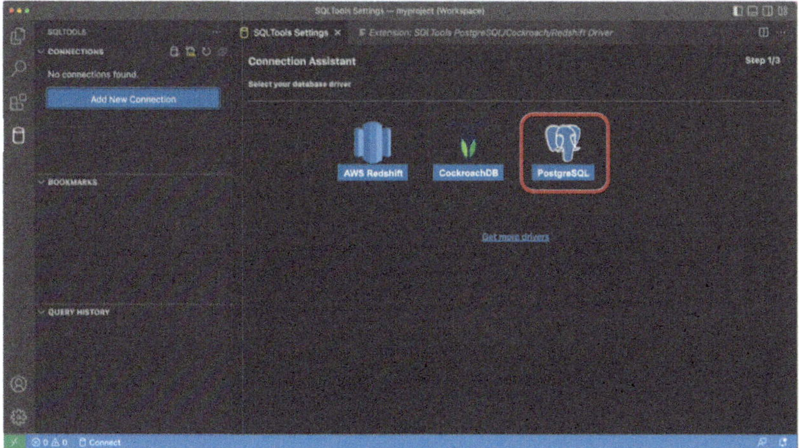

Figure 2.18: Selecting the PostgreSQL driver

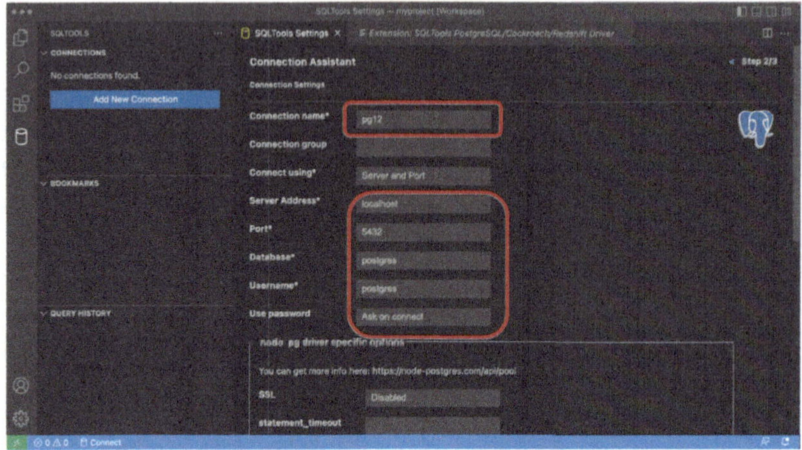

Figure 2.19: Completing the connecting settings

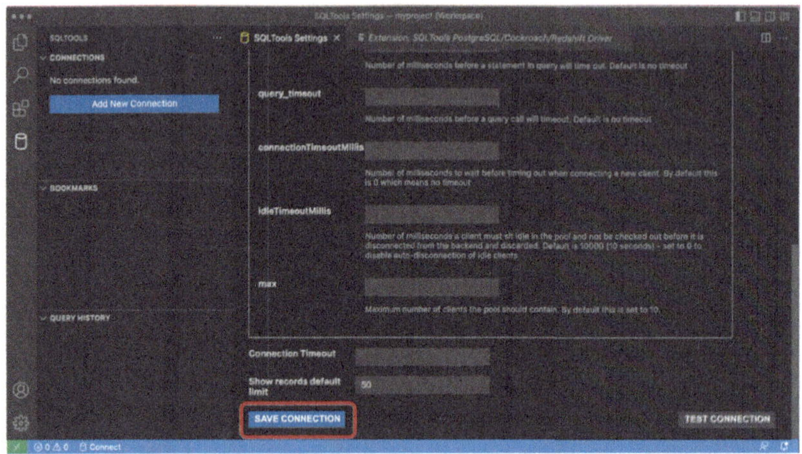

Figure 2.20: Saving the connection

We now have a stored connection profile that we can use to run SQL logic (see Section 2.4.3).

2.3 Command Line Interfaces to R, Python and PostgreSQL

2.3.1 R

Executing `R` in the terminal will return:

```
mballin2@macbook: /Users/mballin2 >R

R version 3.6.2 (2019-12-12) -- "Dark and Stormy Night"
Copyright (C) 2019 The R Foundation for Statistical Computing
Platform: x86_64-apple-darwin15.6.0 (64-bit)

R is free software and comes with ABSOLUTELY NO WARRANTY.
You are welcome to redistribute it under certain conditions.
Type 'license()' or 'licence()' for distribution details.

  Natural language support but running in an English locale

R is a collaborative project with many contributors.
Type 'contributors()' for more information and
'citation()' on how to cite R or R packages in publications.

Type 'demo()' for some demos, 'help()' for on-line help, or
'help.start()' for an HTML browser interface to help.
Type 'q()' to quit R.

[Previously saved workspace restored]

> 1+1
[1] 2
> quit()
Save workspace image? [y/n/c]: y
mballin2@macbook: /Users/mballin2 >
```

To exit the R software enter `quit()` .

2.3.2 Python

The CLI to Python is sometimes called REPL (read-eval-print loop, but this can be said of the R and pg CLI too):

- Read the user input (Python commands).

- Evaluate the code.
- Print any results.
- Loop back to step one.

```
mballin2@macbook: /Users/mballin2 >python3
Python 3.9.0 (v3.9.0:9cf6752276, Oct  5 2020, 11:29:23)
[Clang 6.0 (clang-600.0.57)] on darwin
Type "help", "copyright", "credits" or "license" for more information.
>>> 1+1
2
>>> exit()
mballin2@macbook: /Users/mballin2 >
```

On a Windows machine, type `python3 -i` , where $-i$ stands for interactive mode. If an error message appears when trying to enter the Python interpreter stating that it cannot find the command, it means that the computer does not know where to look for the executable. This can be solved by adding the path to the executable in the PATH environment variable and rebooting the computer. On a Windows machine one can open the Python app, and the path will be displayed at the top of the app.

Some users report that the command hangs up the terminal. When this happens, try `winpty` . For more information see https://stackoverflow.com/questions/48199794/winpty-and-git-bash.

2.3.3 Postgres

We can connect to Postgres by issuing `psql -d postgres -U postgres` in the terminal. This means that we are connecting to database (`-d`) postgres, with user `-U` postgres. You will be asked for the password that you created during the installation. You will then see the following:

```
mballin2@macbook: /Users/mballin2 >psql -d postgres -U postgres
Password for user postgres:
psql (17.0)
Type "help" for help.

postgres=#
```

Postgres is now ready to accept queries. Let's exit from Postgres by typing `\q` for quit.

```
mballin2@macbook: /Users/mballin2 >psql -d postgres -U postgres
Password for user postgres:
psql (17.0)
Type "help" for help.

postgres=# \q
mballin2@macbook: /Users/mballin2 >
```

2.4 Accessing R, Python and Postgres through an IDE

2.4.1 R

RStudio can be launched through an icon that is placed on your computer when you first install it. Figure 2.21 is a screen shot of the RStudio environment. We like to have the code development pane (called Source) in the top left, the output of our code in the top right (called Console), the help and plotting areas in the bottom right, and the environment area in the bottom left. This can be modified in Tools > Global Options > Pane Layout. In the beginning new R users will benefit mostly from syntax highlighting which is not available in plain R. Once the user becomes more advanced there are lots of other productivity-increasing features. We refer to `rstudio.com` for more information.

```
1 #This is where we develop our code
2 #The result will appear in the top
3 #pane to the right, called Console
4 #For example:
5 1+1
6
```

```
> 1+1
[1] 2
>
```

Environment is empty

Figure 2.21: RStudio

2.4.2 Python

To open VSCode, we click the icon that was placed on our computer during installation. Figure 2.22 is a screenshot of what we will see upon opening the application and clicking the documents icon.

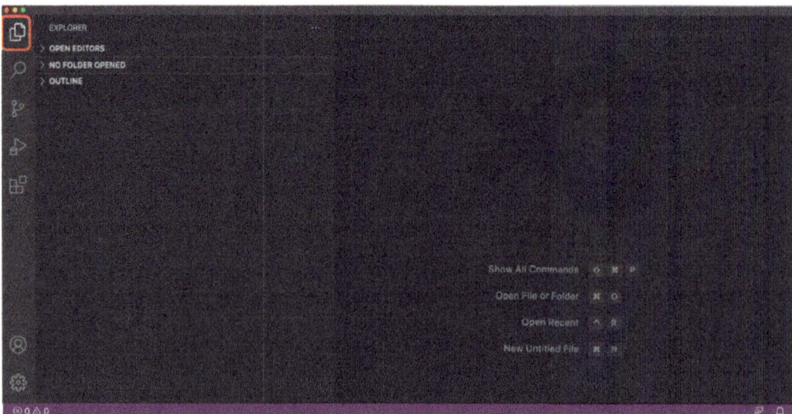

Figure 2.22: VSCode opening screen

The first thing we'll do is click the 'Open Folder' button per Figure 2.23. This will allow us to select an existing folder on disk or create a new one. In our case we created a new folder called *project_folder_1*.

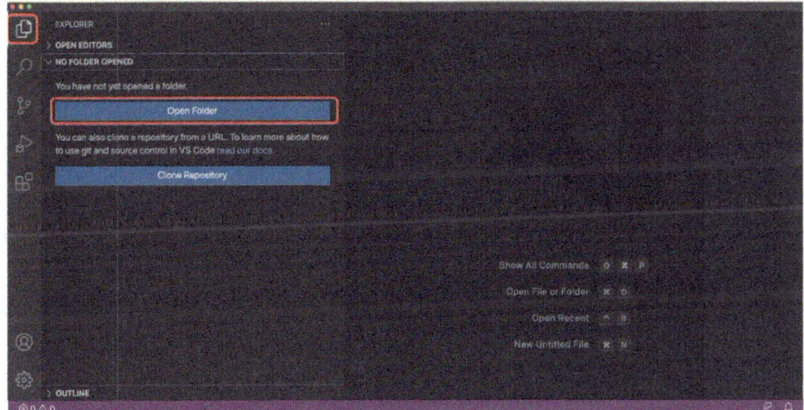

Figure 2.23: Opening a folder in VSCode

VSCode is now scoped to that folder and this is indicated in the sidebar (see Figure 2.24).

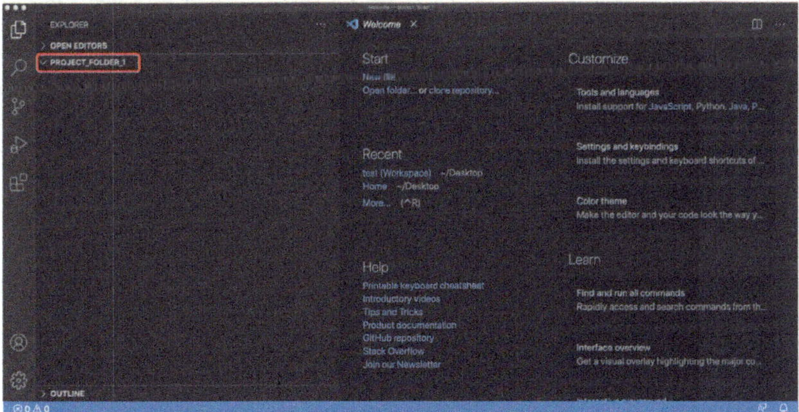

Figure 2.24: Sidebar indicates the scoped folder

Once we are in our folder we can create a new file or subfolder using the icons indicated in Figure 2.25.

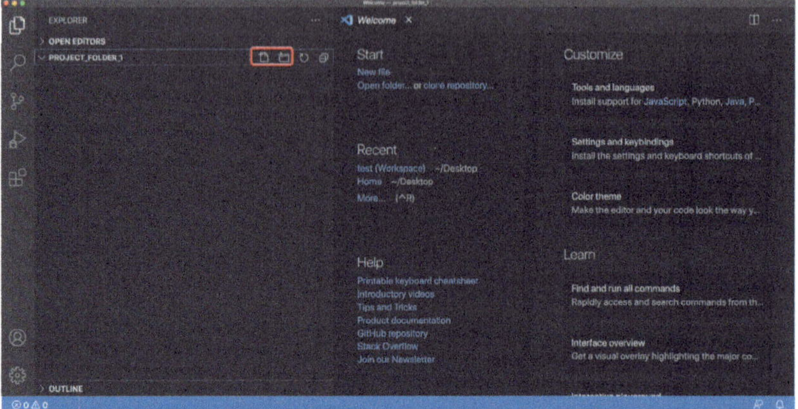

Figure 2.25: New file and subfolder buttons

In Figure 2.26 we clicked the *create new file* button and typed the filename *helloworld.py*. When we specify the *py* extension, a small Python icon appears in front of the filename.

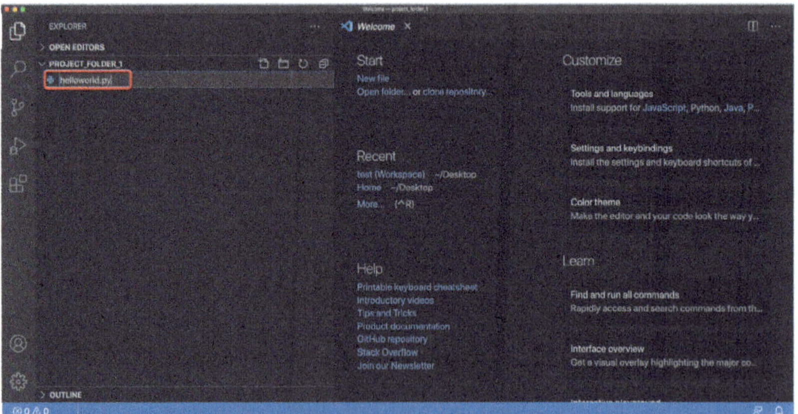

Figure 2.26: Naming the file

After hitting enter upon writing the filename, the file opens and we write our Hello World code (see Figure 2.27).

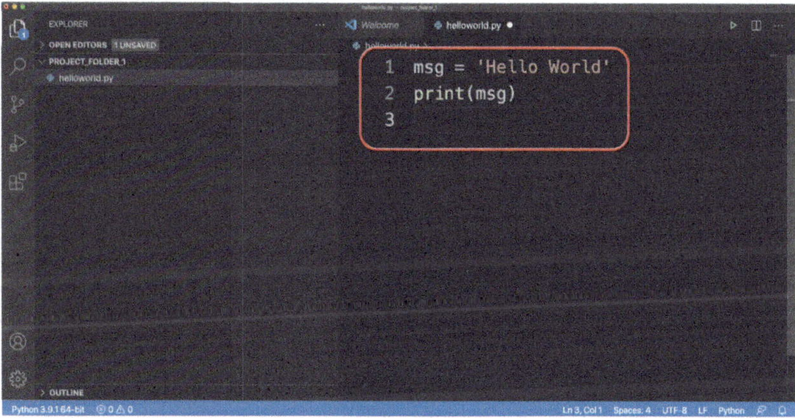

Figure 2.27: Coding the Hello World example

Figure 2.28 shows how to execute the code. We first select the code that we want to run and then right-click that selection. This brings out a menu. We click 'Run Selection/Line in Python Terminal'. Note the shortcut.

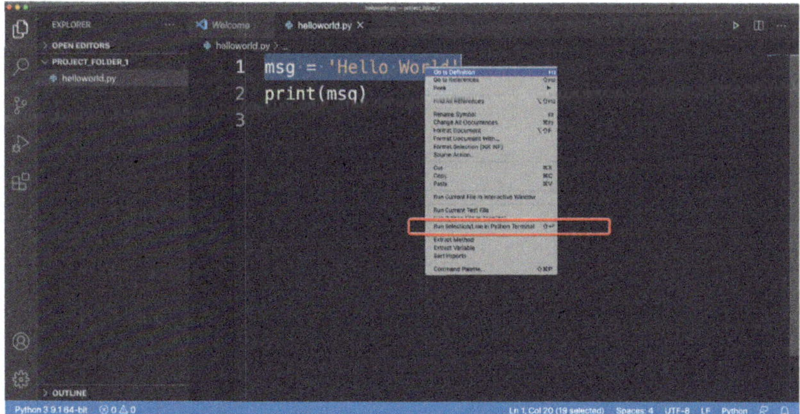

Figure 2.28: Running selected code

Upon running the selection VSCode opens a terminal, opens a Python Interpreter, and runs the selection (see Figures 2.29, 2.30, 2.31).

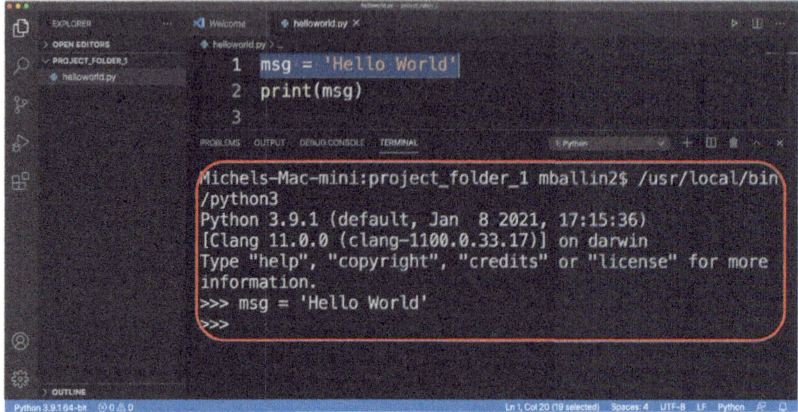

Figure 2.29: Running selected code

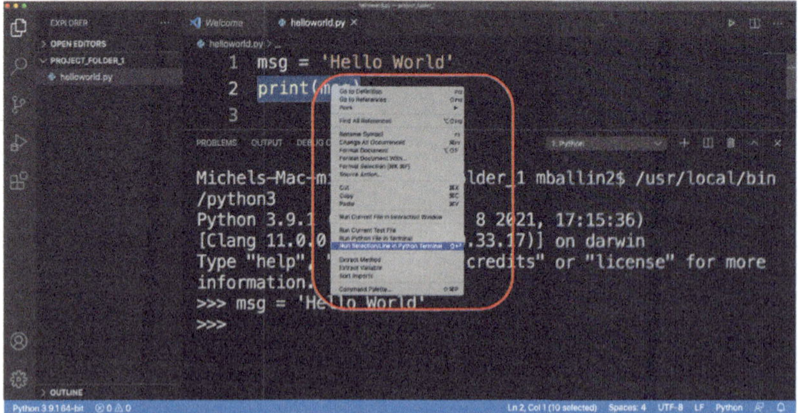

Figure 2.30: Running selected code

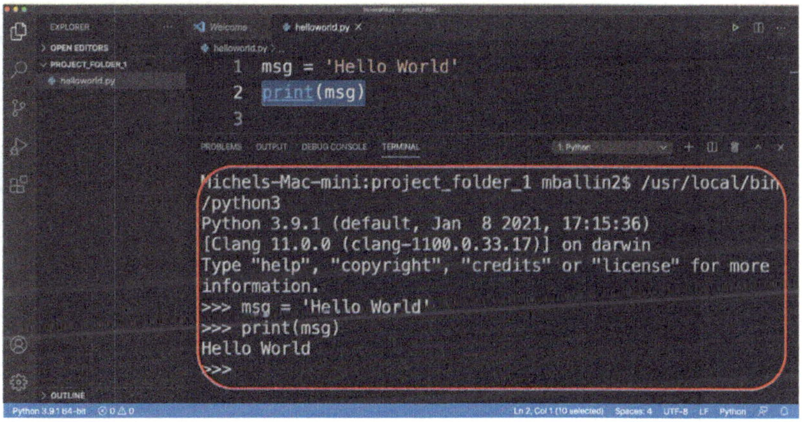

Figure 2.31: Running selected code

Figure 2.32 shows the *outline* section, which contains the objects that we have created so far.

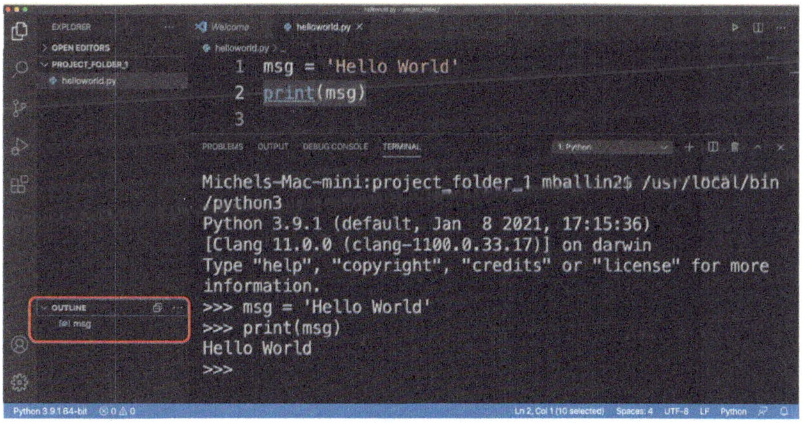

Figure 2.32: Outline

Next, suppose we want to see another folder in the sidebar, but it is stored in another location on our computer. This often happens when we are collaborating on a project and need to bring in other people's code. Alternatively, this may be a cross-project folder with functions. To open another folder, right-click the sidebar and click 'Add Folder to Workspace' (see Figure 2.33).

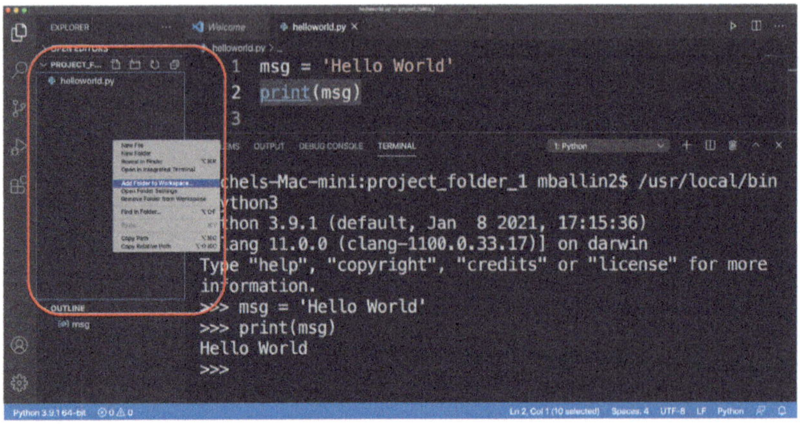

Figure 2.33: Adding a folder to our project

In our case the added folder was called *project_folder_2*. In Figure 2.34 we now see that the header that was previously called *project_folder_1* is renamed to *untitled (workspace)*, and the *project_folder_1* folder is now inside that workspace in addition to the *project_folder_2* folder.

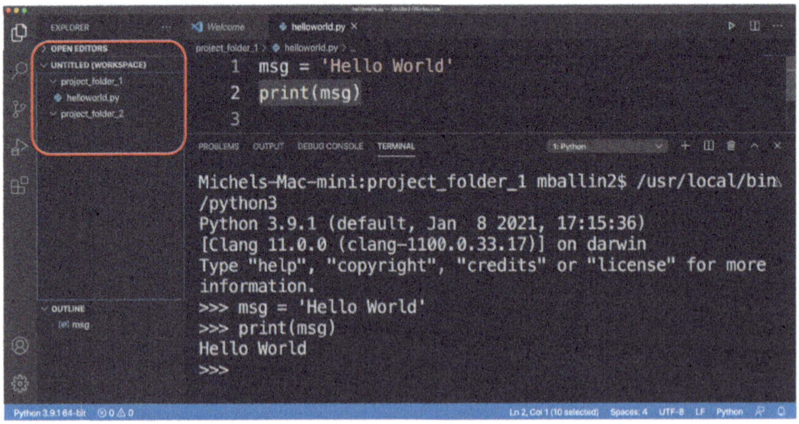

Figure 2.34: Multi-root workspace

Figure 2.35 shows how to save and name the workspace.

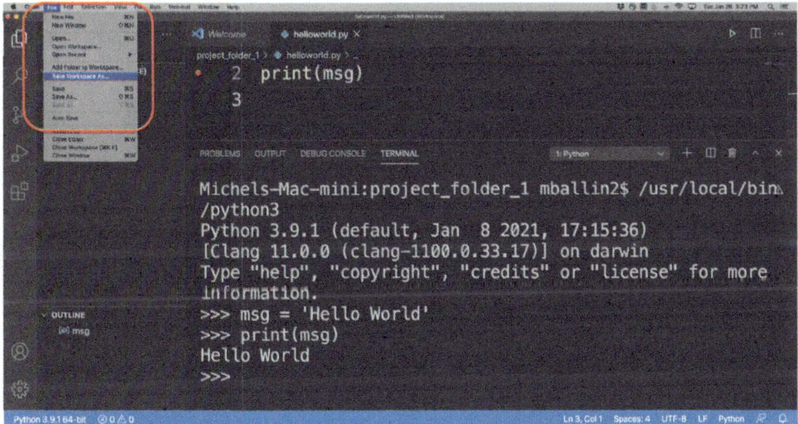

Figure 2.35: Storing the workspace

Here, we called the file *myproject.code-workspace* (see Figure 2.36). We can store this file anywhere; it does not have to be in the *project_folder_1* or *project_folder_2* folders. In this example we stored it in *project_folder_1*.

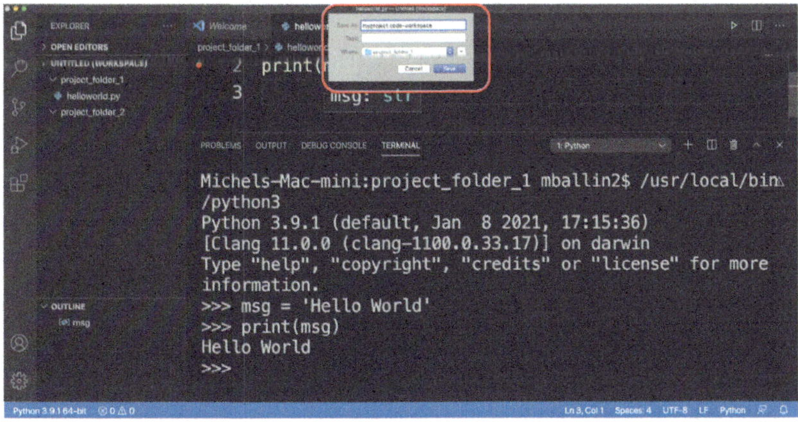

Figure 2.36: Storing the workspace

In Figure 2.37 we see that the workspace has been renamed to *myproject*.

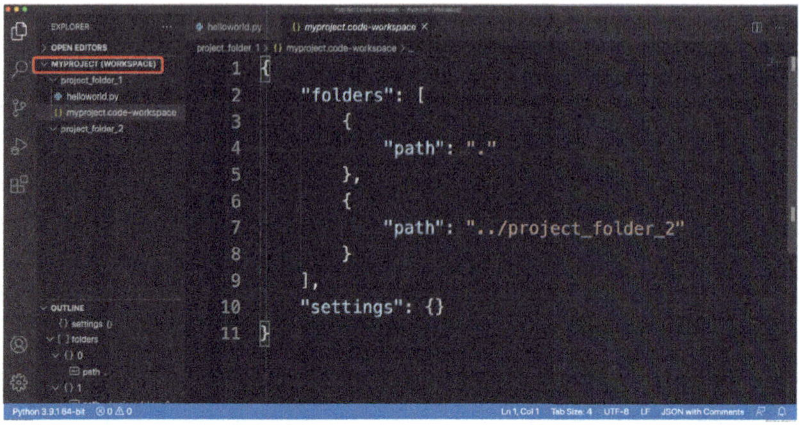

Figure 2.37: Renamed workspace

At this given juncture, we might wonder what a workspace is. A workspace is a project and its main utility is to group multiple independent folders that compound a project. This is a very useful feature when projects grow in complexity. For example:

```
-MYPROJECT --> This is the workspace name
--project_folder_1 --> This is a folder with files (e.g., /user/documents/
--project_folder_2 --> This is another folder (e.g, /user/home/)
```

What is contained in the *.code-workspace* file? We can see the contents by clicking on the file (see Figure 2.38). It stores the paths to our folders, and workspace-specific settings. When we double-click this file in our operating system's file browser VSCode will open to this workspace.

```
{
    "folders": [
        {
            "path": "."
        },
        {
            "path": "../project_folder_2"
        }
    ],
    "settings": {}
}
```

Figure 2.38: Workspace file

Moving on to the next tab, Figure 2.39 shows the search dialog; this is self-explanatory and we won't discuss this futher.

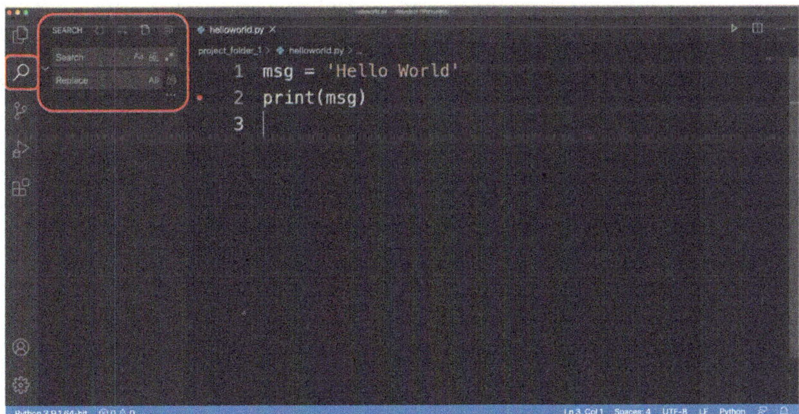

Figure 2.39: Search dialog

Figure 2.40 shows what happens when we right-click the vertical bar containing the icons: it allows us to select which icons should be shown. We remove the checkmark from 'Source Control' and 'Run'. These functionalities are very convenient but out-of-scope for this book.

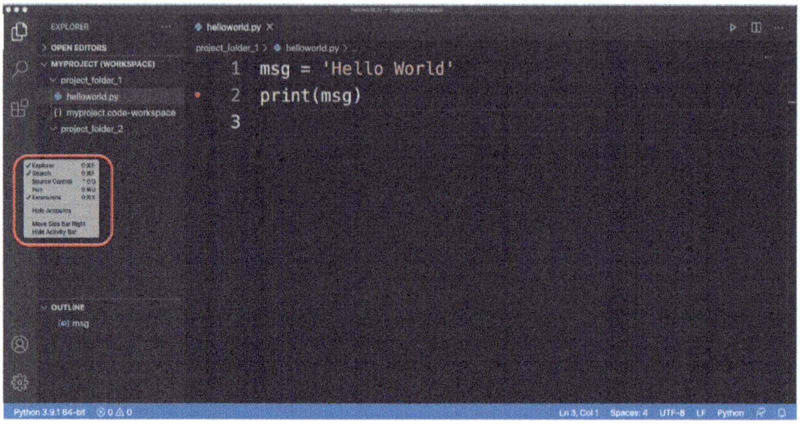

Figure 2.40: Selecting icons

Figure 2.41 shows the extension manager. We haved used this in the installation process and we won't mention it any further here.

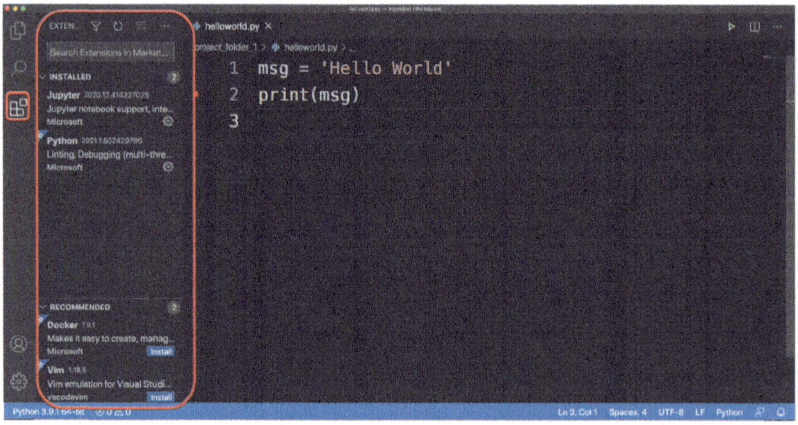

Figure 2.41: Extension manager

In the bottom-left of the screen, Figure 2.42 shows the account and settings icons. In the bottom strip of the screen the selected interpreter will be displayed (this may have moved to the bottom right in more recent versions of VSCode) and the presence of any code-problems are indicated.

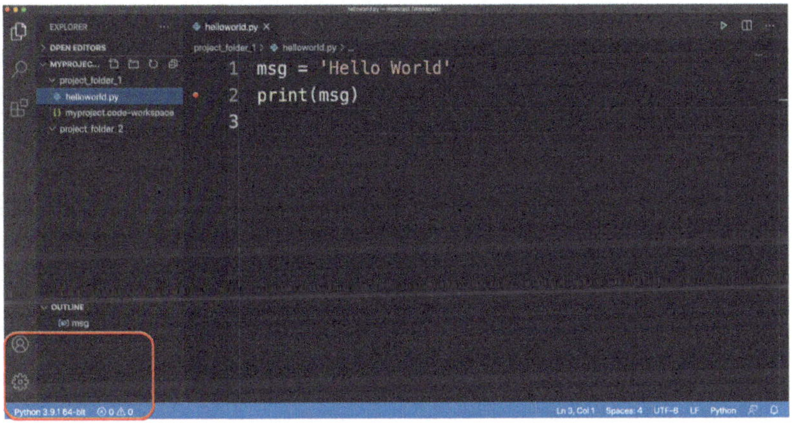

Figure 2.42: Bottom-left of the screen

In the bottom-right of the screen, Figure 2.43 displays the position of our cursor in the code file, amongs other details.

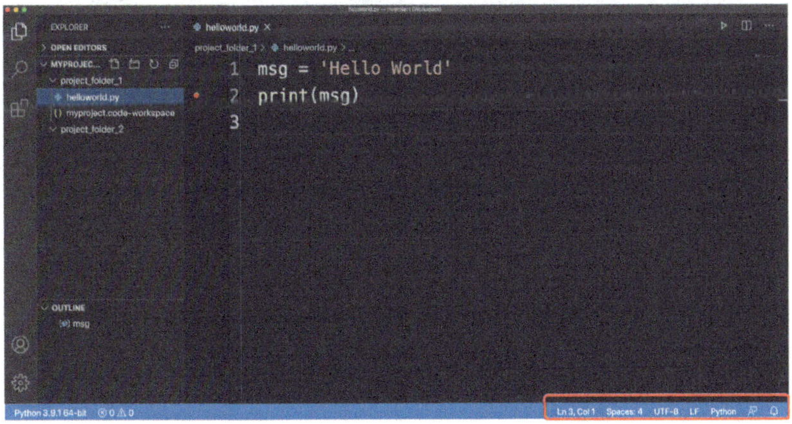

Figure 2.43: Bottom-right of the screen

Figure 2.44 displays the terminal. To close the terminal, click the little garbage-can symbol.

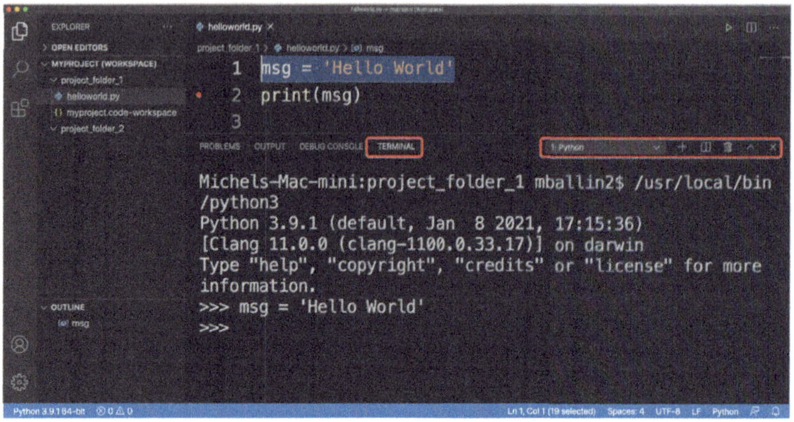

Figure 2.44: Terminal

Figure 2.45 shows the *run* button that we can use if we want to execute entire files, and the split screen button.

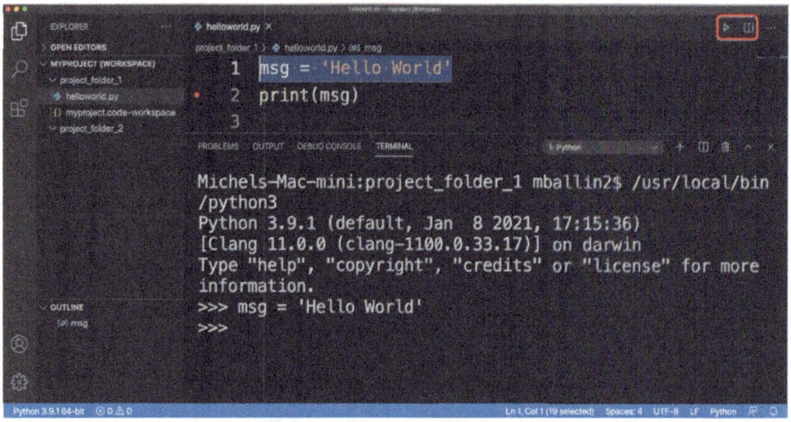

Figure 2.45: Run and split screen buttons

The split screen button is very convenient when we have long files and want to have a view on two different locations that cannot be displayed simultaneously (see Figures 2.46 and 2.47).

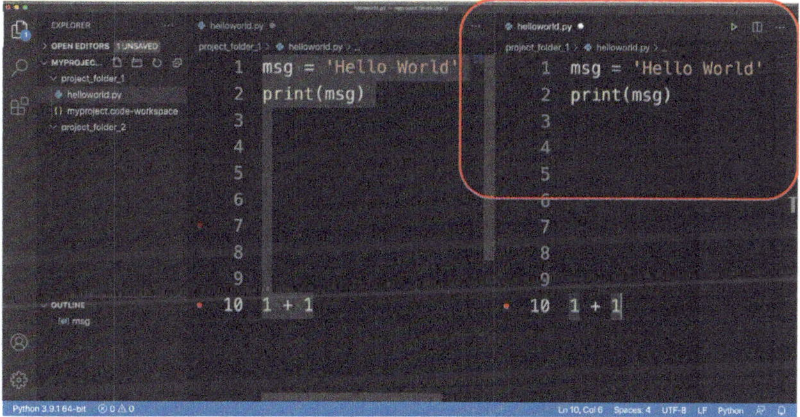

Figure 2.46: Split screen functionality

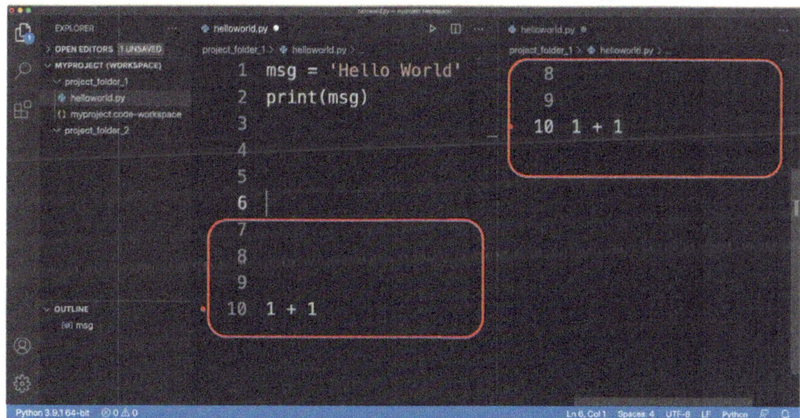

Figure 2.47: Split screen functionality

VSCode has many other interesting features, and we encourage you to explore menu items and settings for increased coding productivity.

2.4.3 PostgreSQL

In this section we will be using the workspace set up in section 2.4.2. We recommend that you review it for important details on workspaces, file structures, and a tour of

VSCode. Information on Python in that section can be ignored for the purposes of this section. The print screens below show how to run SQL logic.

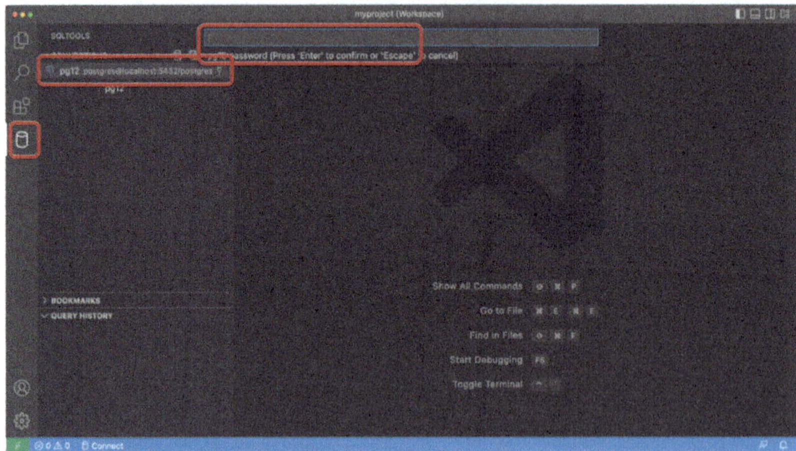

Figure 2.48: Connecting to Postgres

After establishing the connection VSCode will automatically open a file. You can use this file and rename it later (Figure 2.49). We choose to close the file and create a new file with a name of our choice (Figure 2.50).

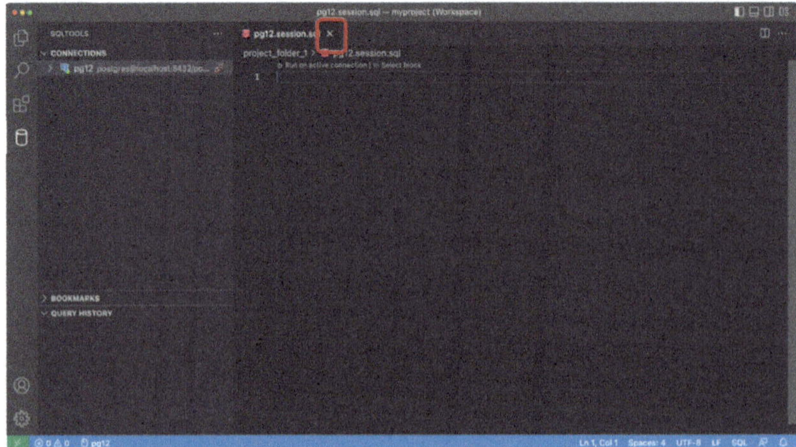

Figure 2.49: Closing the file that opened upon connecting

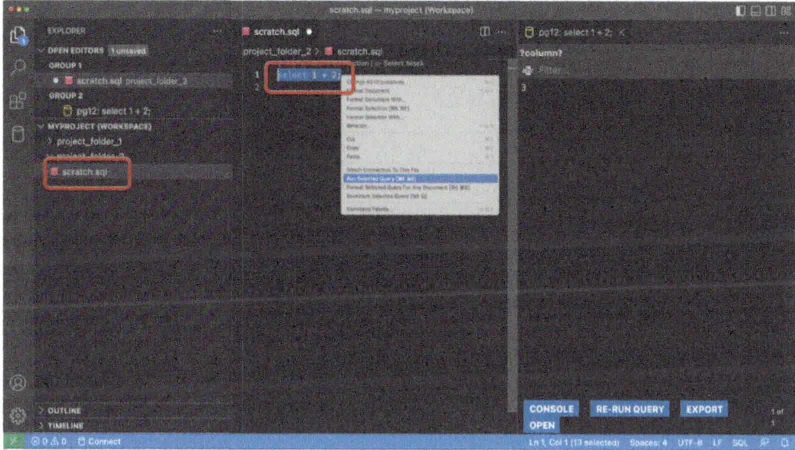

Figure 2.50: Running SQL logic

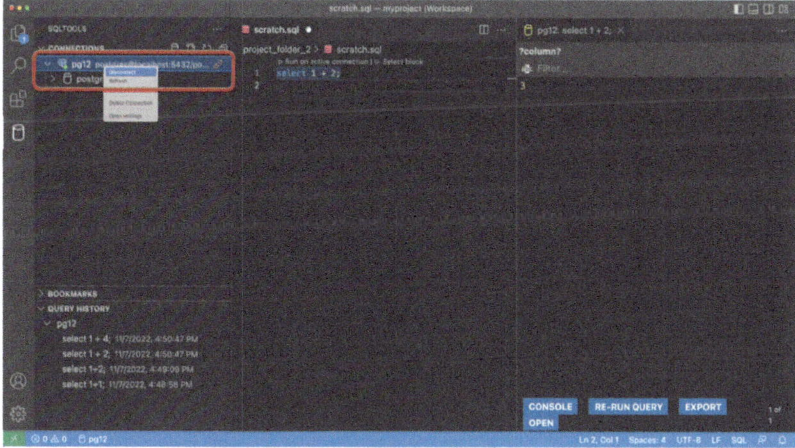

Figure 2.51: Closing the connection

2.5 Scheduling jobs

Data pipelines should be fully automated. To accomplish this goal we sometimes need to tell our server or computer to run a script at a given time. For example, we may need to call an API or a run SQL script every day at 1am.

We will first see how to do this in Linux, as this task is likely to be completed on a server, and most servers run Linux. At the end of this section we will explain how to do this on Mac and Windows.

Let's first create a Python script. Since we want to verify if our script runs at the set times, we are going to create a script that creates a file if it does not exist yet, and then appends the current time. This way we can easily see if the script is working. This script is of course a placeholder for whatever code you want to run.

Create a file called `testcron.py` with the following contents, making sure to adapt the path to the sample file with the path on you computer where you want to store the file:

```
import datetime as dt
file_object = open('/Users/mballin2/documents/sample.txt', 'a')
file_object.write('Executed on ' + str(dt.datetime.now()) + '\n')
file_object.close()
```

Next, type `which python3` in bash. This returns `/usr/local/bin/python3` in our case. We need this path to our executable in the next step (unfortunately we cannot simpy use the `python3` alias, so let's copy this output to our clipboard.

Then in our bash type `EDITOR=nano crontab -e` . The `EDITOR=nano` part is there to ensure that we are using `nano` and not some other editor. We now have opened what is called a `crontab` file. In this file we specify what is called `cron` jobs. Each line in a crontab file represents a job and looks like Figure 2.52.

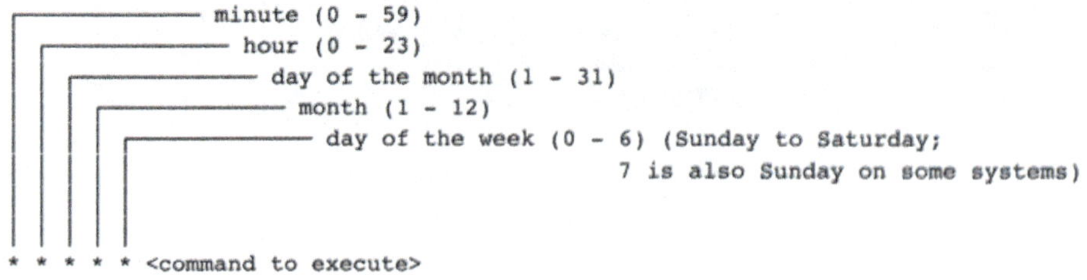

```
┌───────────── minute (0 - 59)
│ ┌───────────── hour (0 - 23)
│ │ ┌───────────── day of the month (1 - 31)
│ │ │ ┌───────────── month (1 - 12)
│ │ │ │ ┌───────────── day of the week (0 - 6) (Sunday to Saturday;
│ │ │ │ │                                   7 is also Sunday on some systems)
│ │ │ │ │
│ │ │ │ │
* * * * * <command to execute>
```

Figure 2.52: Structure of cron jobs

Then, add the following line to the empty file that

```
* * * * * /usr/local/bin/python3 /Users/mballin2/Desktop/testcron.py
```

Use the `https://crontab.guru/` website to help you specify a schedule. Next, navigate to the `sample.txt` file. There will be an update to the file every minute. Look at the contents of the file as follows:

```
cat/Users/mballin2/documents/sample.txt
```

Mac users are lucky in that all this works the same on their system. If the file never gets created, run `EDITOR=nano crontab -e` again and close the file. There will then be a message saying there is mail for you. Simply use `cat` followed by the printed path to print the message. If you receive the `Operation not permitted error` , take the following steps:

- In the Apple menu, choose `System Preferences` > `Privacy and Security`
- Go to `Full Disk Access` on the left-hand side of the panel
- Click the lock to make changes
- Click on the Plus (`+`) sign
- Go to `Applications` > `Utilities` > `Terminal.app`
- Click on the (`+`) sign again;
- Press `Command + Shift + G` and move to `/usr/sbin/cron`
- Restart the Computer

Windows users can use a point and click system. See the following link for a step-by-step guide with print screens:
`https://www.jcchouinard.com/python-automation-using-task-scheduler/`. Note: the 'Start in (optional)' field does not support quotes (`https://superuser.com/questions/885550/task-scheduler-returns-directory-name-invalid-for-valid-path`) and should not end in a slash.

Chapter 3

The Very Basics: Creating, Storing and Inspecting Objects

3.1 R

```
# create object and store the value 1
a <- 1
a

#-# [1] 1

# Whenever you see a function name you don't
# know, just run ?functionname to get more
# information about it. This also works for
# operators such as '<-'. Operators need to be
# quoted when using ?, whereas functions do
# not.For example:
`?`("<-")

# look at its contents
a

#-# [1] 1

# create, store and look simultaneously
(a <- 2)

#-# [1] 2
```

```
# If you want to prevent R from running a line of
# code, put a # in front of it This is called
# commenting (a <- 3)
a

#-# [1] 2

# a is still 2, meaning that #(a <- 3) did not
# run

# To remove a from the environment use the rm
# function
rm(a)
# Check to see if a still exists: a It does not
# exist anymore.
```

3.2 Python

```
#create object and store the value 1
a = 1

#look at its contents
a
#-# 1

#or
print(a)

#-# 1

#Whenever you see a function name you don't know,
#just run help(functionname) to get more information about it. This does not work for all
#operators. For example "=" is not found. Operators need
#to be quoted when using help, whereas functions
#do not.For example:
#help('+')
#help(print)

#If you want to prevent Python from running a line of code, put a # in front of it
#This is called commenting
#a = 3
a
```

```
#-# 1

#a is still 1, meaning that #(a = 3) did not run

# To remove a from the environment use the del keyword
del a
#Check to see if a still exists:
#a
#It does not exist anymore.
```

3.3 PostgreSQL

```
--create an empty table called a with three columns
create table a (
    col_a integer,
    col_b integer,
    col_c integer);


--insert some data
insert into a (col_a, col_b, col_c)
values (1, 2, 3),
       (4, 5, 6),
       (7, 8, 9),
       (10, 11, 12);


--look at the contents of a
select * from a;
#-#   col_a col_b col_c
#-# 1     1     2     3
#-# 2     4     5     6
#-# 3     7     8     9
#-# 4    10    11    12


--if for some reason, we would want to add a constant, say 1000, or 'something' :
select 1000, 'something', * from a;
```

```
#-#   ?column?  ?column? col_a col_b col_c
#-# 1     1000 something     1     2     3
#-# 2     1000 something     4     5     6
#-# 3     1000 something     7     8     9
#-# 4     1000 something    10    11    12
```

```
--we can give arbitrary names, say integer_constant and text_constant, to columns as follows:
select 1000 as integer_constant, 'something' as text_constant, * from a;
```

```
#-#   integer_constant text_constant col_a col_b col_c
#-# 1             1000     something     1     2     3
#-# 2             1000     something     4     5     6
#-# 3             1000     something     7     8     9
#-# 4             1000     something    10    11    12
```

```
--Note that Postgres knows when a query ends through the semi-colon.
--That means queries can span multiple lines:
select *
from a;
```

```
#-#   col_a col_b col_c
#-# 1     1     2     3
#-# 2     4     5     6
#-# 3     7     8     9
#-# 4    10    11    12
```

```
--Comments start with a double dash.
--Multi-line comments are accomplished with /* */
--Example
/*
select *
from a;
*/
```

PostgreSQL also has a procedural extension, called PL/pgSQL, which is short for Procedural Language PostgreSQL. Its structure begins with `DO $$`, ends with `END $$;` and is called an anonymous block. More about the `$$` soon. If variables are used in the block, they will need to be defined in a `DECLARE` section. The action happens in the `BEGIN` section. For example here we are defining and summing `var_a` and `var_b` and storing the result in `var_c`. We then print the result. Printing is accomplished with the `RAISE NOTICE` statement. Its syntax is `RAISE NOTICE 'format', expressions`. A %-sign in the format denotes a placeholder for the expression and is matched with expressions by position.

```
DO $$
DECLARE
  var_a  integer;
  var_b  integer;
  var_c  integer;
BEGIN
  var_a = 1;
  var_b = 1;
  var_c = var_a + var_b;

  RAISE NOTICE 'var_a:%, var_b:%',var_a,var_b;
  RAISE NOTICE 'var_c:%',var_c;
END $$;

#-# NOTICE:  var_a:1, var_b:1
#-# NOTICE:  var_c:2
```

The `$$` are a substition for a single quote ('). When defining an anonymous block we need to pass its body in the form of a literal string. Below is the same example but with the alternative notation. This requires us to escape single quotes in the body, and syntax highlighting marks the whole block as a string making it harder for us to develop our code. The use of `$$` avoids the double quoting and highlighting issues and is therefore recommended.

```
DO '
DECLARE
  var_a  integer;
  var_b  integer;
  var_c  integer;
BEGIN
  var_a = 1;
  var_b = 1;
  var_c = var_a + var_b;

  RAISE NOTICE ''var_a:%, var_b:%'',var_a,var_b;
```

```
    RAISE NOTICE ''var_c:%'',var_c;
END ';

#-# NOTICE:  var_a:1, var_b:1
#-# NOTICE:  var_c:2
```

We can also select from, define, insert into, and update tables in an anonymous block. We provide an example below on how to select from a table and store the result in a variable.

```
DO $$
DECLARE
    variable_a int;
BEGIN
    select col_a from a into variable_a;
    RAISE NOTICE 'variable_a: %', variable_a;
END $$;

#-# NOTICE:  variable_a: 1
```

Note that 'select into' only selects a single row, and it is not guaranteed which row will be taken. 'Select into' is therefore only useful for queries that return a single record, such as queries that aggregate data. Alternatively we can use a cursor, to return multiple rows. This is covered in Section 15.3.

```
--To remove all records from a table:
truncate a;
--If we would have two tables to truncate, say a and b, we can use TRUNCATE a,b;
--Alternatively we could have used: delete from a;
--The delete statement has the advantage that it can have a where clause whereas the truncate
statement cannot.


--To confirm
select * from a;

#-# [1] col_a col_b col_c
#-# <0 rows> (or 0-length row.names)
```

```
--To see all tables
select *
from pg_catalog.pg_tables
where schemaname != 'pg_catalog' and
      schemaname != 'information_schema';

#-#   schemaname tablename tableowner tablespace hasindexes
#-# 1     public         a   postgres       <NA>      FALSE
#-#   hasrules hastriggers rowsecurity
#-# 1    FALSE       FALSE        FALS


--To remove a table entirely:
drop table a;
```

Chapter 4

Getting Help

4.1 R

If we don't know how to do something Google is where we should look first. If we know the name of the function but need more information on how to use it, or its parameters we use R's built-in help system as follows: `help(function)` or `?function`. If no help is provided we can also use `help.search("function")` or `??function` to dig deeper.

4.2 Python

Google is definitely a good source if we do not not know the name of the function. If we do know the name, we can get help by using `help(function)` (e.g., `help(pd.DataFrame)`). This will pull up the help file. To exit the help file, hit `q` in the terminal.

4.3 PostgreSQL

Postgres does not have have a built-in help function. The definite source of information is `https://www.postgresql.org/docs/current/index.html`. In the documentation brackets ([and]) are used to indicate optional parts of the command. Braces ({ and }) and vertical liness (|) are used to indicate that one alternative must be chosen. Three dots (...) mean that preceding elements can be repeated.

For example, the documentation for the `insert` command at `https://www.postgresql.org/docs/current/sql-insert.html` states that we are not required to specifcy column names as denoted by the brackets, but are allowed to specify multiple ones (denoted by the three dots). Additionally, we are required to specify either `default values` , `values` , or a `query` as denoted by the braces.

Chapter 5

Installing and Loading Packages

5.1 R

```
# repos='https://cran.rstudio.com/') To check the
# version of R we can do:
getRversion()

#-# [1] '4.4.1'

# Installing packages can be done using
# 'install.packages'.  For example if we want to
# install package 'randomForest' we would use:

install.packages("randomForest", repos = "https://cran.rstudio.com/",
    quiet = TRUE)

# The repos and quiet parameters are optional.

# To check the version of the package:
packageVersion("randomForest")

#-# [1] '4.7.1.2'

# To obtain a description:
# packageDescription('randomForest')

# Loading the package (making it active) goes as
# follows:
library(randomForest)
```

```
#-# randomForest 4.7-1.2
#-# Type rfNews() to see new features/changes/bug fixes.

# To get more information while loading the
# package use the help parameter:
library(help = randomForest)

# If we try to load an uninstalled package we get
# an error:
library(azYYmihza)

#-# Error in library(azYYmihza): there is no package called 'azYYmihza'

# If we want to store in a variable if we loaded
# the package successfully we can do (note the
# parameter logical.return):
loaded <- library(randomForest, logical.return = TRUE)
loaded

#-# [1] TRUE

# Note that the error is replaced by a warning.

# If we try to load an uninstalled package
# (azAoef) we get FALSE:
loaded_lib <- library(azAoef, logical.return = TRUE)

#-# Warning in library(azAoef, logical.return = TRUE): there is no package called 'azAoef'

loaded_lib

#-# [1] FALSE

# require() is equivalent to library with
# logical.return=TRUE
loaded_req <- require(azAoef)

#-# Loading required package: azAoef
#-# Warning in library(package, lib.loc = lib.loc, character.only = TRUE, logical.return =
TRUE, : there is no package called 'azAoef'

loaded_req

#-# [1] FALSE
```

```
# Unloading a package goes as follows. You might
# want to do this to avoid conflicts:
unloadNamespace("randomForest")

# Get a list of all the loaded packages:
search()

#-#  [1] ".GlobalEnv"        "package:RPostgres"
#-#  [3] "package:DBI"       "package:knitr"
#-#  [5] "package:stats"     "package:graphics"
#-#  [7] "package:grDevices" "package:utils"
#-#  [9] "package:datasets"  "package:methods"
#-# [11] "Autoloads"         "package:base"

# It is always a good idea to first check if a
# package is already installed to avoid losing
# time reinstalling it.  The function 'require'
# loads the package.  In addition it returns
# FALSE if the package is not installed,
# otherwise it returns TRUE. An exclamation point
# negates the value.  It means NOT. For example:
!FALSE

#-# [1] TRUE

# An 'if' statement is only executed if its value
# is TRUE. Hence, if the package 'randomForest'
# is not installed, we will get a FALSE, which is
# tranformed into a TRUE, which in turn will
# trigger the execution of the statements in the
# 'if' statement: install and load the package.
# If the package is installed, it will simply be
# loaded by the first require. That first require
# will also return a TRUE, which is transformed
# into a FALSE, which in turn does not trigger
# the statements in the 'if' statement.

if (!require("randomForest")) {
    install.packages("randomForest", repos = "https://cran.rstudio.com/",
        quiet = TRUE)
    require("randomForest")
}
```

```
#-# Loading required package: randomForest
#-# randomForest 4.7-1.2
#-# Type rfNews() to see new features/changes/bug fixes.

# Name clashes can happen when installing
# packages If two packages have a function with
# the same function name the function of the
# package that was loaded last will be accessible
# on the search path. While loading the package a
# warning will be printed to say that a function
# is masked. Note that we need to set quiet=FALSE
# in install.packages.

# This can lead to surprising error messages. One
# time the function works, and then it stops
# working. This is because after loading a new
# package that masks our function, we are now
# using another function (with the same name).

# Let's load a package called AUC and use the
# function auc.

if (!require("AUC")) {
    install.packages("AUC", repos = "https://cran.rstudio.com/",
        quiet = FALSE)
    require("AUC")
}

#-# Loading required package: AUC
#-# AUC 0.3.2
#-# Type AUCNews() to see the change log and ?AUC to get an overview.

data(churn)
auc(roc(churn$predictions, churn$labels))

#-# [1] 0.8439201

# If we would now load a package that also has
# the auc function there will be message stating
# our auc function is masked.

# We can either unload the second package or
# simply put 'packagename::' in front of the
# function.  This will tell R that we need the
```

```
# function of that specific package.  In our case
# that works out as follows:

AUC::auc(roc(churn$predictions, churn$labels))

#-# [1] 0.8439201

# From time to time it is a good idea to make
# sure you are running the latest versions of all
# packages We can do that with the following
# function: update.packages(ask=FALSE,
# repos='https://cran.rstudio.com/')
```

5.2 Python

```
#Installing and loading modules:


##############in Terminal##################

#To install a module (say pandas) use the following:
#-m stands for module
# python3 -m pip install pandas

#To upgrade a module that is already installed:
# python3 -m pip install --upgrade  pandas

#Alternatively, use
# pip3 install pandas
#and
# pip3 install --upgrade pandas

#Importing installed modules
# When we import a module, we make it available to us in
# our current program as a separate namespace (this is really a space with names). Therefore,
we need to refer to it as [module].[function]

# Next, to load the installed modules:
##########in Python interpreter#############
```

```
# plain import
import pandas
#to call a pandas function (say DataFrame) use
pandas.DataFrame([1,2,3])
#-#    0
#-# 0  1
#-# 1  2
#-# 2  3

#using an alias
import pandas as pd
pd.DataFrame([1,2,3])

#-#    0
#-# 0  1
#-# 1  2
#-# 2  3

#if we would not want to type the pd, we can do:
from pandas import DataFrame
DataFrame([1,2,3])

#-#    0
#-# 0  1
#-# 1  2
#-# 2  3


#Note:
# What happens when we install a module? If there is no compiled code, it merely downloads
a [module].py file.
#When we do import [module] it simply runs that file.
#We can create our own file. For example:

# If we create hello.py file with contents...
# def world():
#     print('Hello World')
# ...and store it on disk...
# ...we can then, in another file, do...
# import hello
# hello.world()
# ...and
# 'Hello World' will be printed.
```

```
#If this complains about not being able to find the module,
#then you can use the following:

#Check you working directory:
# import os
# os.getcwd()

#To change your working directory
# os.chdir(path)

#Instead of changing your working directory, you can add
#the path to the file as follows:
# import sys
# sys.path.append("/path/to/my/modules/")
```

5.3 PostgreSQL

Contributed extensions are found in the `contrib` directory of a PostgreSQL distribution. Let's install an external module called `pg_stat_statements` that allows us to gather statistics about our queries.

Because modules can require additional shared memory they need to be loaded by adding the module name to `shared_preload_libraries` in `postgresql.conf`. First, let's verify if `pg_stat_statements` is loaded:

```
show shared_preload_libraries;

#-# shared_preload_libraries
```

This means that we have to add `pg_stat_statements` to the configuration file, and restart PostgreSQL for the settings to take effect. We can locate the configuration file as follows:

```
show config_file;

#-# config_file
#-# /Library/PostgreSQL/12/data/postgresql.conf
```

Next, we use our favorite shell text editor, say `nano` to open the configuration file and start editing. If you are a Linux or Unix/Mac user, in the shell you would first have to switch to the `postgres` user as follows. If you are a Windows user, do not run the code chunk immediately below, but instead right-click your shell program and click 'run as administor'.

```
sudo -iu postgres
```

Then, in the shell we would type:

```
nano /Library/PostgreSQL/12/data/postgresql.conf
```

Once `nano` has opened the file, we search for shared_preload_libraries (control w). This will bring us to a section in the configuration file that looks like this:

```
# - Shared Library Preloading -

#shared_preload_libraries = ''  # (change requires restart)
```

We then edit that part by removing the # and adding pg_stat_statements:

```
# - Shared Library Preloading -

shared_preload_libraries = 'pg_stat_statements'  # (change requires restart)
```

After saving the file (control o) and exiting nano (control x) we can then restart Postgres.

```
show data_directory;
#-# /Library/PostgreSQL/12/data
pg_ctl restart -D /Library/PostgreSQL/12/data
```

To verify if Postgres is running, we use the following query. In the event that it is not running, we need to make sure we did not make a typographical error when editing the configuration file.

```
pg_ctl status -D /Library/PostgreSQL/12/data
#-# pg_ctl: server is running (PID: 28137)
#-# /Library/PostgreSQL/12/bin/postgres "-D/Library/PostgreSQL/12/data"
```

Next, we need to create the extension in our sql file:

```
create extension pg_stat_statements;
```

Finally we can check whether `pg_stat_statements` is loaded:

```
show shared_preload_libraries;
#-# shared_preload_libraries
#-#       pg_stat_statements
```

Now that the module is installed and loaded, we can start to use it. Suppose we would run `select * from a` and then look at `pg_stat_statements` , we would get:

```
select query,
       calls,
       min_time,
       mean_time,
       stddev_time,
       max_time,
       rows
from pg_stat_statements;

#-#                          query calls min_time mean_time stddev_time max_time rows
#-# select * from pg_stat_statements     1    0.135     0.135           0    0.135    2
#-#                  select * from a     1     0.02      0.02           0     0.02    6
```

This section is not about the `pg_stat_statements` module, but rather how to install modules, so full coverage about this module here is not intended. For more information about this module, go to https://www.postgresql.org/docs/current/pgstatstatements.html.

Chapter 6

Data Objects

There are many ways to categorize data object types. In this document we provide the main ones. The first grouping is **atomic vs compound**. Atomic objects are not subscriptable; they are the smallest possible element that cannot be broken down in smaller pieces. A compound object is a collection of atomic objects. The second dimension is **ordered vs unordered**. In an ordered object the element position or order of insertion is recorded. In an unordered object, order of insertion or element position is not guaranteed. The order may change at any given point and depends on internal optimizations. Ordering is important when subsetting objects. The third grouping is **unique vs non-unique** and refers to whether the elements in the object are unique; no two elements in that object can be the same. The fourth grouping is **single vs multi-type**. For example, is the entire object made up of integers, or can it be made up of integers and characters? The fifth categorization is **mutable vs immutable** and refers to whether an element in an object can be changed. This is important for integrity guarantees and efficiency. The sixth grouping is **shared vs separate** objects. An object can only be shared if it is mutable. This is explained immediately below.

R, Python, and PostgreSQL each can be conceived of as being comprised of systems with three components: names (also called variables), references, and objects. In Figure 6.1 there is a name called a that references an object containing three numbers (3, 2, 5). Objects are allocated memory, names are labels attached to these objects (one can think of labels as physical tags), and references are pointers from names to objects (one can think of references as little cords that attach tags to the objects).

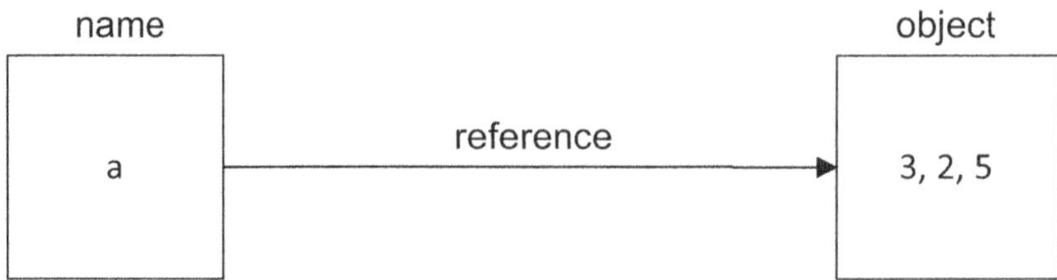

Figure 6.1: Names, references, and objects

Now, let's consider what happens in the following situation. We would execute the four lines of code below in order of appearance. Do you know what will be printed to the screen in the fourth line of code?

```
First, set name a equal to object 3, 2, 5
Second, set name b equal to name a
Third, change the first element of name a to object 100
Fourth, print the contents of name b
```

There are two possible answers, and it depends on whether the object is shared or separate. Figure 6.2 depicts the two possible situations that can occur after running the four lines of code above. If the object is shared (left pane in Figure 6.2) then line four will print 100, 2, 5. If the object is separate, the fourth line will print 3, 2, 5.

In the shared object scenario it is important to note that the names *a* and *b* are never linked to eachother directly. Because both names point to the same object, the change that happened through *a* will also be reflected when looking at the object through *b*. In the separate object scenario the second line of code will make a copy of the object (i.e., allocate new memory), and so the third line will not impact the object that *b* references[1].

Both scenarios can happen in each of R, Python and PostgreSQL, and it is important to be aware of the scenario under which we are operating. So why are there two scenarios? Each scenario has its strenghts and weaknesses. The shared

[1]To be more accurate, at the cost of adding some confusion, the copy is often only made when the third line is run. This is a way for the system to be more efficient. The copy is only made, when an element of *a* is changed. This is of little importance.

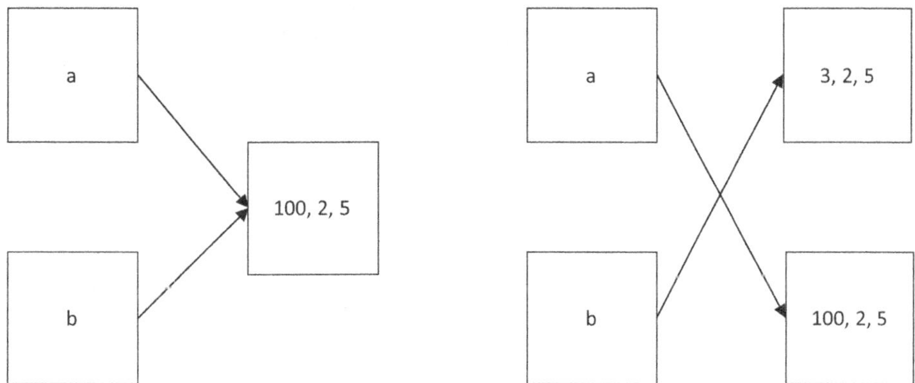

Figure 6.2: Shared (left) vs separate (right) objects

object scenario is more efficient, but can be confusing. The separate object scenario is less confusing, but can be slow. It is slow because in the second line of code, the entire object needs to be copied. Depending on the situation we may prefer one scenario or the other, and we will be exploring both scenarios in this book.

6.1 R

Table 6.1 contains an overview of the different data types in R. It appears the aforementioned dimensions are not the best differentiators for this platform. All are compound, ordered, non-unique, mutable and separate. The only differentiating dimension is contained in the single- vs multi-type column. Data frames and lists can contains multiple types whereas all the other objects are single type. Date and time types are covered in Section 20.

There are a few specific differences not captured in the table that we need to know about. First, matrices and data frames have two dimensions, whereas everything else have a single dimension. Second, a matrix is closer to a vector than to a data frame, even though matrices and data frames have two dimensions and vectors only one dimension. The reason is that a matrix is in essence a vector that was just given an additional dimension. Data frames (and lists) are different in that they are truly collection of different vectors (objects). Third, the vectors comprising a data frame have to be of the same length. This is not the case for lists. In fact, lists can comprise anything, including data frames, matrices, and lists.

Table 6.1: Data objects in R

Note	class()	atomic vs compound	ordered vs un-ordered	unique vs non-unique	single-vs multi-type	mutable vs im-mutable	shared vs sepa-rate
Numeric vector	numeric	compound	ordered	non-unique	single	mutable	separate
Integer vector	integer	compound	ordered	non-unique	single	mutable	separate
Logical vector	logical	compound	ordered	non-unique	single	mutable	separate
Character vector	character	compound	ordered	non-unique	single	mutable	separate
Factor vector	factor	compound	ordered	non-unique	single	mutable	separate
Matrix	matrix	compound	ordered	non-unique	single	mutable	separate
Data frame	data.frame	compound	ordered	non-unique	multiple	mutable	separate
List	list	compound	ordered	non-unique	multiple	mutable	separate

```
# Examples

# --numeric vector: decimal numbers Let's create
# a numeric sequence of 26 numbers
(num_vector <- as.numeric(seq(from = 1, to = 3.5, by = 0.1)))  #?seq

#-#  [1] 1.0 1.1 1.2 1.3 1.4 1.5 1.6 1.7 1.8 1.9 2.0 2.1 2.2 2.3
#-# [15] 2.4 2.5 2.6 2.7 2.8 2.9 3.0 3.1 3.2 3.3 3.4 3.5

# --character vector: strings
(char_vector <- as.character(c("a", "b", "c", "d",
    "e", "f", "g", "h", "i", "j")))

#-#  [1] "a" "b" "c" "d" "e" "f" "g" "h" "i" "j"

# OR (char_vector <- letters[seq( from = 1, to =
# 10 )])

# --integer vector: integer numbers
(int_vector <- as.integer(1:10))  #help(':')

#-#  [1]  1  2  3  4  5  6  7  8  9 10
```

```
# --factor vector: integer but with labels
(fact_vector <- as.factor(c("a", "b", "c", "d", "e",
    "f", "g", "h", "i", "j")))

#-#  [1] a b c d e f g h i j
#-# Levels: a b c d e f g h i j

# help(c)
str(fact_vector)

#-#  Factor w/ 10 levels "a","b","c","d",..: 1 2 3 4 5 6 7 8 9 10

str(char_vector)

#-#  chr [1:10] "a" "b" "c" "d" "e" "f" "g" "h" "i" "j"

# --logical vector
(log_vector <- c(TRUE, FALSE, TRUE, FALSE))

#-# [1]  TRUE FALSE  TRUE FALSE

str(log_vector)

#-#  logi [1:4] TRUE FALSE TRUE FALSE

# --matrix: vectors of same type and length
help(matrix)
(mat <- matrix(data = 1:25, nrow = 5, ncol = 5))

#-#      [,1] [,2] [,3] [,4] [,5]
#-# [1,]    1    6   11   16   21
#-# [2,]    2    7   12   17   22
#-# [3,]    3    8   13   18   23
#-# [4,]    4    9   14   19   24
#-# [5,]    5   10   15   20   25

# --data.frame (what we work with most often):
# vectors can be of different type but same
# length
(df <- data.frame(int_vector, fact_vector))
```

```
#-#    int_vector fact_vector
#-# 1           1           a
#-# 2           2           b
#-# 3           3           c
#-# 4           4           d
#-# 5           5           e
#-# 6           6           f
#-# 7           7           g
#-# 8           8           h
#-# 9           9           i
#-# 10         10           j

# --list can contain anything
(l <- list(df, mat, int_vector))

#-# [[1]]
#-#    int_vector fact_vector
#-# 1           1           a
#-# 2           2           b
#-# 3           3           c
#-# 4           4           d
#-# 5           5           e
#-# 6           6           f
#-# 7           7           g
#-# 8           8           h
#-# 9           9           i
#-# 10         10           j
#-#
#-# [[2]]
#-#      [,1] [,2] [,3] [,4] [,5]
#-# [1,]    1    6   11   16   21
#-# [2,]    2    7   12   17   22
#-# [3,]    3    8   13   18   23
#-# [4,]    4    9   14   19   24
#-# [5,]    5   10   15   20   25
#-#
#-# [[3]]
#-#  [1]  1  2  3  4  5  6  7  8  9 10

# It is useful to understand how we determined
# the values of the table above.

# Compound: To test whether an object is compound
```

```
# we try to subset it.  If it is subsetable it
# means it is compound For example
a <- 1
a[1]

#-# [1] 1

# results in 1, does not produce an error and is
# therefore subsetable

# Ordered All objects support integer
# subscripting, and therefore must be ordered
# (i.e., it is guaranteed that order is preserved
# otherwise integer subsetting would be sensible.

# Non-unique.
a <- c(1, 1)
a

#-# [1] 1 1

# results in 1 1, is not reduced to 1, and can
# therefore contain non-unique values

# mutable. We can go inside the object (not
# recreate it) and change a value
a[1] <- 10
a

#-# [1] 10  1

# the statement above changed the first value to
# 10 without error, and it is therefore mutable

# separate. If we first create an original object
# (a <- 1), then assign that object to a new
# object (b <- a), then change that new object (b
# <- 2), and view the original object (a), we
# have a separate system if the original object
# (a) is unchanged from its original value (1),
# and shared system if it it would have the value
# of the new object (2)
a <- 1
b <- a
```

```
b <- 2
a

#-# [1] 1
```

There is a difference between `as.numeric()` and `numeric()` , `as.character()` and `character()` , and `integer()` and `as.integer()` . The short versions only have one argument (i.e., `length`) and are used to initialize a vector. The long versions have the argument `x` which is the object to be coerced.

In the case of factors this is a little bit different. Both `as.factor()` and `factor()` have the argument `x` , but the latter one has more arguments and is rather used to initialize the vector.

6.2 Python

Table 6.2: Data Objects in Python

Note	type()[2]	atomic vs compound	ordered vs unordered	unique vs non-unique	single- vs multi type	mutable vs immutable	shared vs separate
Boolean (true or false)	bool, np.bool_	atomic	/	/	single	immutable	/
8 bit integer (-128 to 127)	np.int8	atomic	/	/	single	immutable	/
16 bit integer (-32768 to 32767)	np.int16	atomic	/	/	single	immutable	/
32 bit integer (-2147483648 to 2147483647)	np.int32	atomic	/	/	single	immutable	/
64 bit integer (-9,223,372,036, 854,775,808 to 9,223,372,036, 854,775,807)	np.int64	atomic	/	/	single	immutable	/
Arbitrary precision integer	int	atomic	/	/	single	immutable	/

[2]np stands for numpy and pd stands for pandas

8 bit unsigned integer (0 to 255)	np.uint8	atomic	/	/	single	immutable	/
16 bit unsigned integer (0 to 65535)	np.uint16	atomic	/	/	single	immutable	/
32 bit unsigned integer (0 to 4294967295)	np.uint32	atomic	/	/	single	immutable	/
64 bit unsigned integer (0 to 18,446,744,073, 709,551,615)	np.uint64	atomic	/	/	single	immutable	/
16 bit (half precision) float	np.float16	atomic	/	/	single	immutable	/
32 bit (single precision) float	np.float32	atomic	/	/	single	immutable	/
64 bit (double precision) float	float, np.float64	atomic	/	/	single	immutable	/
String	str, np.str_	compound	ordered	non-unique	single	immutable	/
List: can contain different length, different type objects. Can be arbitrarily nested. Can dynamically grow and shrink.	list	compound	ordered	non-unique	multiple	mutable	shared
Tuple: can contain different length, different type objects. Can be arbitrarily nested.	tuple	compound	ordered	non-unique	multiple	immutable	/

Dictionary: keys with values that can contain different length, different type objects. Keys are unique. Can be arbitrarily nested. Can dynamically grow and shrink.	dict	compound	ordered	unique and non-unique	multiple	mutable	shared
Set: keys without values. Keys are unique. Can contain different object types but they have to be immutable (e.g., not a list as element). Can dynamically grow and shrink.	set	compound	unordered	unique	multiple	mutable	shared
Frozen Set: Same as set but immutable.	frozenset	compound	unordered	unique	multiple	immutable	/
N- dimensional array: supports different length, different type objects	np.ndarray	compound	ordered	non-unique	single[3]	mutable	shared

[3]Arrays can be of type *Object*. This means that the data are references to Python objects, not objects themselves. In that sense arrays can behave more like, for example, lists, in that their contents can be of different types. Note that if an item of such an array is accessed the actual item will be returned.

Data frame: supports same length, different type vectors	pd.core.frame.DataFrame	compound	ordered	non-unique	multiple	mutable	shared

Date and time types are covered in Section 20.

```
#This code chunk presents several tests for all data objects:

#1. Compound: A data object is compound if it can be subset, is mutable or iterable

#2. Ordered: If an object can be subset with an integer, then it is ordered.
#If it can only be subset with a key then it is unordered.

#3. Uniqueness is tested by adding an additional, already existing element.
# Note that uniqueness violations usually do not throw errors.

#4. Single vs multi-type: try to make an object with different types

#5. Mutability is tested by assignment tests.
#Note that recreating objects is different from mutating objects.

#6. Shared vs separate, test as explained in the introduction of this section

#!pip3 install numpy
import numpy as np


#######################################
#boolean
a = True
type(a)

#-# <class 'bool'>

a = np.bool_(True)
type(a)

#-# <class 'numpy.bool_'>
```

```
#1. Compound?

#a[0]

#no

#2. Ordered?

#No. Can only contain one element.

#3. Unique?

#No. Can only contain one element.

#4. Multi?

#No. Can only contain one element.

#5. Mutable?

#No. Cannot be subset (and thus not changed) according to test 1.

#6. Shared?

#the following is not the correct test for whether the object is shared,
#because it is destroyed and recreated.
#The third line should be a mutation.
#An object can only be shared if it supports mutation.
a

#-# True

a2 = a
a = False #a is destroyed and recreated here
a2

#-# True

a

#-# False

#No. Because does not support mutation.
```

```
########################################
#8 bit integer
b = np.int8(1)
type(b)

#-# <class 'numpy.int8'>

#1. Compound?

#b[0]

#no

#2. Ordered?

#No. Can only contain one element.

#3. Unique?

#No. Can only contain one element.

#4. Multi?

#No. Can only contain one element.

#5. Mutable?

#No. Cannot be subset (and thus not changed) according to test 1.

#6. Shared?

#No. Because does not support mutation.

########################################
#16 bit integer
c = np.int16(1)
type(c)

#-# <class 'numpy.int16'>

#1. Compound?

#c[0]
```

```
#no

#2. Ordered?

#No. Can only contain one element.

#3. Unique?

#No. Can only contain one element.

#4. Multi?

#No. Can only contain one element.

#5. Mutable?

#No. Cannot be subset (and thus not changed) according to test 1.

#6. Shared?

#No. Because does not support mutation.

######################################
#32 bit integer
d = np.int32(1)
type(d)

#-# <class 'numpy.int32'>

#1. Compound?

#d[0]

#no

#2. Ordered?

#No. Can only contain one element.

#3. Unique?

#No. Can only contain one element.
```

```
#4. Multi?

#No. Can only contain one element.

#5. Mutable?

#No. Cannot be subset (and thus not changed) according to test 1.

#6. Shared?

#No. Because does not support mutation.

########################################
#64 bit integer
e = np.int64(1)
type(e)

#-# <class 'numpy.int64'>

#1. Compound?

#e[0]

#no

#2. Ordered?

#No. Can only contain one element.

#3. Unique?

#No. Can only contain one element.

#4. Multi?

#No. Can only contain one element.

#5. Mutable?

#No. Cannot be subset (and thus not changed) according to test 1.

#6. Shared?
```

```
#No. Because does not support mutation.

######################################
#arbitrary precision integer
f = 1
type(f)

#-# <class 'int'>

f = int(1)
type(f)

#-# <class 'int'>

#1. Compound?

#f[0]

#no

#2. Ordered?

#No. Can only contain one element.

#3. Unique?

#No. Can only contain one element.

#4. Multi?

#No. Can only contain one element.

#5. Mutable?

#No. Cannot be subset (and thus not changed) according to test 1.

#6. Shared?

#No. Because does not support mutation.

######################################
#8 bit unsigned integer
g = np.uint8(1)
type(g)
```

```
#-# <class 'numpy.uint8'>

#1. Compound?

#g[0]

#no

#2. Ordered?

#No. Can only contain one element.

#3. Unique?

#No. Can only contain one element.

#4. Multi?

#No. Can only contain one element.

#5. Mutable?

#No. Cannot be subset (and thus not changed) according to test 1.

#6. Shared?

#No. Because does not support mutation.

######################################
#16 bit unsigned integer
h = np.uint16(1)
type(h)

#-# <class 'numpy.uint16'>

#1. Compound?

#h[0]

#no

#2. Ordered?

#No. Can only contain one element.
```

```
#3. Unique?

#No. Can only contain one element.

#4. Multi?

#No. Can only contain one element.

#5. Mutable?

#No. Cannot be subset (and thus not changed) according to test 1.

#6. Shared?

#No. Because does not support mutation.

#####################################
#32 bit unsigned integer
i = np.uint32(1)
type(i)

#-# <class 'numpy.uint32'>

#1. Compound?

#i[0]

#no

#2. Ordered?

#No. Can only contain one element.

#3. Unique?

#No. Can only contain one element.

#4. Multi?

#No. Can only contain one element.

#5. Mutable?
```

```
#No. Cannot be subset (and thus not changed) according to test 1.

#6. Shared?

#No. Because does not support mutation.

########################################
#64 bit unsigned integer
j = np.uint64(1)
type(j)

#-# <class 'numpy.uint64'>

#1. Compound?

#j[0]

#no

#2. Ordered?

#No. Can only contain one element.

#3. Unique?

#No. Can only contain one element.

#4. Multi?

#No. Can only contain one element.

#5. Mutable?

#No. Cannot be subset (and thus not changed) according to test 1.

#6. Shared?

#No. Because does not support mutation.

########################################
#16 bit float
k = np.float16(1.1)
type(k)
```

```
#-# <class 'numpy.float16'>

#1. Compound?

#k[0]

#no


#2. Ordered?

#No. Can only contain one element.

#3. Unique?

#No. Can only contain one element.

#4. Multi?

#No. Can only contain one element.

#5. Mutable?

#No. Cannot be subset (and thus not changed) according to test 1.

#6. Shared?

#No. Because does not support mutation.

#####################################
#32 bit float
l = np.float32(1.1)
type(l)

#-# <class 'numpy.float32'>

#1. Compound?

#l[0]

#no

#2. Ordered?
```

```
#No. Can only contain one element.

#3. Unique?

#No. Can only contain one element.

#4. Multi?

#No. Can only contain one element.

#5. Mutable?

#No. Cannot be subset (and thus not changed) according to test 1.

#6. Shared?

#No. Because does not support mutation.

######################################
#64 bit float
m = np.float64(1.1)
type(m)

#-# <class 'numpy.float64'>

m = 1.1
type(m)

#-# <class 'float'>

m = float(1.1)
type(m)

#-# <class 'float'>

#1. Compound?

#m[0]

#no

#2. Ordered?

#No. Can only contain one element.
```

```
#3. Unique?

#No. Can only contain one element.

#4. Multi?

#No. Can only contain one element.

#5. Mutable?

#No. Cannot be subset (and thus not changed) according to test 1.

#6. Shared?

#No. Because does not support mutation.


########################################
#string

p = 'word'
type(p)

#-# <class 'str'>

p = str('word')
type(p)

#-# <class 'str'>

p = np.unicode_('word')
type(p)

#-# <class 'numpy.str_'>

#1. Compound?

p[0]

#-# 'w'

#yes

#2. Ordered?
```

```
#yes because can be subset with integers

#3. Unique?

p = 'ww'
p

#-# 'ww'

#no

#4. Multi?

p = '1a'
p[0]

#-# '1'

#no '1' is a string


#5. Mutable?

#p[0] = 'W'

#no because cannot change a letter

#6. Shared?

#No. Because does not support mutation.

########################################
#list
q = [1,'word',1.1, np.array([[3,4],[4,5],[6,6]]) ]
type(q)

#-# <class 'list'>

q = list([1,'word',1.1, np.array([[3,4],[4,5],[6,6]]) ]) #these functions are only useful
when transforming from another type
type(q)

#-# <class 'list'>
```

```
#1. Compound?

q[0]

#-# 1

#yes

#2. Ordered?

#yes because can be subset with integers

#3. Unique?

[1,1]

#-# [1, 1]

#no uniqueness constraint

#4. Multi?

#yes, per the example

#5. Mutable?

q[0] = 999999
q

#-# [999999, 'word', 1.1, array([[3, 4],
#-#        [4, 5],
#-#        [6, 6]])]

#yes

#6. Shared?
q

#-# [999999, 'word', 1.1, array([[3, 4],
#-#        [4, 5],
#-#        [6, 6]])]

q2 = q
q[0] = 10
q2
```

```
#-# [10, 'word', 1.1, array([[3, 4],
#-#         [4, 5],
#-#         [6, 6]])]

q

#-# [10, 'word', 1.1, array([[3, 4],
#-#         [4, 5],
#-#         [6, 6]])]

#yes

#######################################
#tuple (see the section on Immutable vs Mutable objects on how a tuple is different from a
list)
r = (1,'word',1.1, np.array([[3,4],[4,5],[6,6]]))
type(r)

#-# <class 'tuple'>

r = tuple((1,'word',1.1, np.array([[3,4],[4,5],[6,6]])))
type(r)

#-# <class 'tuple'>

#1. Compound?

r[0]

#-# 1

#yes

#2. Ordered?

#Yes because supports integer-based subsetting

#3. Unique?

(1,1)

#-# (1, 1)

#no uniqueness constraint

#4. Multi?
```

```
#yes per the example

#5. Mutable?

#r[0] = 9999

#no

#6. Shared?

#No. Because does not support mutation.


######################################
#dictionary (keys : values)
s = {'name': 'John', 'age': 25, 'info': np.array([[3,4],[4,5],[6,6]]) }
type(s)

#-# <class 'dict'>

s = dict({'name': 'John', 'age': 25, 'info': np.array([[3,4],[4,5],[6,6]]) })
type(s)

#-# <class 'dict'>

#1. Compound?

s['name']

#-# 'John'

#yes, because supports subsetting

#2. Ordered?

#s[0]

#no because does not support integer based subsetting
#This recently changed. Order is now insertion-preserved since Python 3.7

#3. Unique?

{'a':1,'a':2,'b':2}

#-# {'a': 2, 'b': 2}
```

```
#uniques constraint for keys, not for values

#4. Multi?

{'a':1,10:'b'}

#-# {'a': 1, 10: 'b'}

#yes, even for keys


#5. Mutable?

#values
s

#-# {'name': 'John', 'age': 25, 'info': array([[3, 4],
#-#         [4, 5],
#-#         [6, 6]])}

s['name'] = 'Doe' #mutating a dictionary's values

#yes

#keys
s.pop('name') #mutating a dictionary's keys

#-# 'Doe'

s['lastname'] = 'Doe' #mutating a dictionary's keys
s

#-# {'age': 25, 'info': array([[3, 4],
#-#         [4, 5],
#-#         [6, 6]]), 'lastname': 'Doe'}

#yes. entire object does not need to be recreated


#6. Shared?

#values
s = {'name': 'John', 'age': 25, 'info': np.array([[3,4],[4,5],[6,6]]) }
s2 = s
```

```
s['name'] = 'Doe' #mutating a dictionary's values
s

#-# {'name': 'Doe', 'age': 25, 'info': array([[3, 4],
#-#        [4, 5],
#-#        [6, 6]])}

s2

#-# {'name': 'Doe', 'age': 25, 'info': array([[3, 4],
#-#        [4, 5],
#-#        [6, 6]])}

#yes

#keys
s = {'name': 'John', 'age': 25, 'info': np.array([[3,4],[4,5],[6,6]]) }
s2 = s
s.pop('name') #mutating a dictionary's keys

#-# 'John'

s['lastname'] = 'Doe' #mutating a dictionary's keys
s

#-# {'age': 25, 'info': array([[3, 4],
#-#        [4, 5],
#-#        [6, 6]]), 'lastname': 'Doe'}

s2

#-# {'age': 25, 'info': array([[3, 4],
#-#        [4, 5],
#-#        [6, 6]]), 'lastname': 'Doe'}

#yes

#####################################
#set (keys without values)
t = {'name', 'age', 'info', 1, 2}
type(t)

#-# <class 'set'>

t = set({'name', 'age', 'info', 1, 2})
type(t)
```

```
#-# <class 'set'>

#1. Compound?

#t['name']

#cannot be subset, but below we show how to mutate it.
#So yes, it is compound.

#2. Ordered?

#t[0]

#no

#3. Unique?
{1,1}

#-# {1}

#yes

#4. Multi?
# yes per the example

#5. Mutable?

t.discard('name')
t.add('firstname')
t

#-# {'firstname', 1, 'info', 2, 'age'}

#yes, entire object does not need to be recreated

#6. Shared?

#set (keys without values)
t = {'name', 'age', 'info', 1, 2}
t2 = t
t.discard('name')
t.add('firstname')
t

#-# {'firstname', 1, 'info', 2, 'age'}
```

```
t2

#-# {'firstname', 1, 'info', 2, 'age'}

#yes, because t2 is also changed


########################################
#frozenset (Sames as set, but immutable after creation)
u = frozenset(t)
type(u)

#-# <class 'frozenset'>

#1. Compound?

#u['age']

#no

#2. Ordered?
#u[0]

#no

#3. Unique?

frozenset({1,1})

#-# frozenset({1})

#yes

#4. Multi?

u

#-# frozenset({'firstname', 1, 'info', 2, 'age'})

#yes per the example


#5. Mutable?

u
```

```
#-# frozenset({'firstname', 1, 'info', 2, 'age'})

#u.discard('info')

#no

#6. Shared?

#no because not mutable

########################################
# N dimensional array
#(N = 1)
v = np.array([1,2,3,4,5])
type(v)

#-# <class 'numpy.ndarray'>

#(N = 3)

v = np.array([[1,1.1,2],[3,4],{'a'}], dtype = object)
type(v)

#-# <class 'numpy.ndarray'>

#Note: data type can be specified as follows: np.array([1,2,3,4,5], dtype='unicode')



#1. Compound?

v[0]

#-# [1, 1.1, 2]

#yes

#2. Ordered?
#yes because supports integer-based subsetting

#3. Unique?

np.array([1,1])

#-# array([1, 1])
```

```
#no

#4. Multi?
np.array([1,'a'])

#-# array(['1', 'a'], dtype='<U21')

#no

#note: if multiple objects (say lists) are contained in an
#array, then the object type is 'object',
#which is a reference to the individual objects
#(not the actual objects)


#5. Mutable?
v = np.array([1,2,3,4,5])
v[0] = 100
v

#-# array([100,   2,   3,   4,   5])

#yes

#6. Shared?

# 1- dimensional array

v = np.array([1,2,3,4,5])
v2 = v
v[0] = 20
v

#-# array([20,  2,  3,  4,  5])

v2

#-# array([20,  2,  3,  4,  5])

#yes

######################################
#pandas.DataFrame
import pandas as pd
w = pd.DataFrame([[1,2,3],[4,5,6]])
type(w)
```

```
#-# <class 'pandas.core.frame.DataFrame'>

w

#-#    0  1  2
#-# 0  1  2  3
#-# 1  4  5  6

#1. Compound?

w[0]

#-# 0    1
#-# 1    4
#-# Name: 0, dtype: int64

#yes

#2. Ordered?
w.iloc[:,0] #more about this later

#-# 0    1
#-# 1    4
#-# Name: 0, dtype: int64

#yes because supports integer-based subsetting

#3. Unique?
#no, per the example

#4. Multi?
w = pd.DataFrame()
w['x1'] = [1,2,3]
w['x2'] = [1.1,2.2,3.3]
w['x1']

#-# 0    1
#-# 1    2
#-# 2    3
#-# Name: x1, dtype: int64

w['x2']

#-# 0    1.1
#-# 1    2.2
#-# 2    3.3
#-# Name: x2, dtype: float64
```

```
#yes

#5. Mutable?

w.iloc[0,0] = 100
w

#-#      x1   x2
#-# 0   100  1.1
#-# 1     2  2.2
#-# 2     3  3.3

#yes

#6. Shared?

w = pd.DataFrame([[1,2,3],[4,5,6]])
w2 = w
w[0] = 100
w

#-#        0  1  2
#-# 0    100  2  3
#-# 1    100  5  6

w2

#-#        0  1  2
#-# 0    100  2  3
#-# 1    100  5  6


#yes
```

6.3 PostgreSQL

The main data objects in PostgreSQL (pgSQL) and Procedural Language PostgreSQL (PL/pgSQL) are listed in Table 6.3. There are two main categories of objects. Variables (used in PL/pgSQL) and columnar structures (tables, foreign tables, views, and materialized views). Columns in columnar structures can take on any data type that is listed for the variables.

Table 6.3: Selected Data Objects in PostgreSQL

Note	type	atomic vs compound	ordered vs unordered	unique vs non-unique	single-vs multi type	mutable vs immutable	shared vs separate
Small-range integer variable (2 bytes), +-32768	smallint variable	atomic	/	/	single	immutable	separate
Typical-range integer variable (4 bytes), +-2147483648	int variable	atomic	/	/	single	immutable	separate
Large-range integer variable (8 bytes), +-9223×10^{14}	bigint variable	atomic	/	/	single	immutable	separate
Exact arbitrary precision variable, up to 131072 digits before decimal point and 16383 after	numeric or decimal variable	atomic	/	/	single	immutable	separate
Single precision floating-point (4 bytes) (i.e.,exact), 6 decimal digits precision	real variable	atomic	/	/	single	immutable	separate
Double precision floating-point (8 bytes) (i.e.,exact), 15 decimal digits precision	double precision variable	atomic	/	/	single	immutable	separate
Variable-length character with limit	varchar(n) variable	atomic	/	/	single	immutable	separate
Fixed-length character, blank padded	char(n) variable	atomic	/	/	single	immutable	separate

Variable unlimited length character	text variable	atomic	/	/	single	immutable	separate
Boolean (1 byte), true or false	boolean variable	atomic	/	/	single	immutable	separate
Arrays of any of the types specfied above	array variable	compound	ordered	non-unique	single	mutable	separate
Composite types are created with the 'create type' statement and can contain any combination of single types.	variable	compound	ordered	non-unique	multiple	mutable	separate
A regular table contains actual data	table	compound	unordered	non-unique	multiple	mutable	separate
A foreign table stores pointers to actual data that is stored in another database (e.g., Oracle). It looks like a normal table, but needs to fetch data from another database, potentially over a network.	foreign table	compound	unordered	non-unique	multiple	mutable	shared

A view stores pointers to actual data that is stored in one or more other tables in the same database. It represents data through a 'select' statement. The 'select' statement is executed every time the view is accessed. The advantages are that users can query the view with a simple statement without having to form a potentially complex query, and that no storage is required.	view	compound	unordered	non-unique	multiple	mutable	shared

A materialized view is a disk-stored view that can be refreshed. The underlying 'select' is not executed every time the view is accessed. This is faster than a view, but it also means the data is out-of-date. A materialized view lies in between regular tables and views.	materialized view	compound	unordered	non-unique	multiple	mutable	shared

One notable special-purpose data type is ranges. Ranges can be replicated with two columns (a start and end), and it may not be worth taking the time to study their specific syntax. We do want to mention them here because they can speed up certain lookup operations considerably. Date and time types are covered in Section 20. Foreign tables behave very similarly to views and setting them up is out of the scope of this book. We therefore do not mention them further.

Below we show how to create each of these objects. Variables can only be defined in PL/pgSQL, but their types can be used to define columns in columnar structures such as tables. We will show both ways immediately below and follow up with the columnar structures.

Variables:

```
--First create a composite type of int and text:
create type composite_example as (
    m int,
```

```
   n text
);


--Demonstrate all variable types
DO $$
DECLARE
   a    smallint;
   b    int;
   c    bigint;
   d    numeric;
   e    real;
   f    double precision;
   g    varchar(50); --limit to 50 characters
   h    char(50); --blank pad to 50 characters
   i    text;
   j    boolean;
   k    integer array; --can be any type
   l    composite_example;
BEGIN
   a = 2; --smallint
   RAISE NOTICE 'a:%', a; --print to the screen, RAISE NOTICE 'format' [, expressions]

   b = 2222222; --int
   RAISE NOTICE 'b:%',b;

   c = 2222222222222; --bigint
   RAISE NOTICE 'c:%',c;

   d = 2.2; --numeric
   RAISE NOTICE 'd:%',d;

   e = 2.2; --real
   RAISE NOTICE 'e:%',e;

   f = 222.2; --double precision
   RAISE NOTICE 'f:%',f;

   g = 'hello'; --varchar
   RAISE NOTICE 'g:%',g;

   h = 'hello'; --char
   RAISE NOTICE 'h:%',h;
```

```
    i = 'hello'; --text
    RAISE NOTICE 'i:%',i;

    j = TRUE; --boolean
    RAISE NOTICE 'j:%',j;

    k = '{1,2,3,4,5,6,7}'; --integer array (the input routine requires quotes)
    k = array[1,2,3,4,5,6,7]; --alternative syntax
    RAISE NOTICE 'k:%',k;

    l = (2,'hello'); --composite_example
    RAISE NOTICE 'l:%',l;
END $$;

#-# NOTICE:  a:2
#-# NOTICE:  b:2222222
#-# NOTICE:  c:2222222222222
#-# NOTICE:  d:2.2
#-# NOTICE:  e:2.2
#-# NOTICE:  f:222.2
#-# NOTICE:  g:hello
#-# NOTICE:  h:hello
#-# NOTICE:  i:hello
#-# NOTICE:  j:t
#-# NOTICE:  k:{1,2,3,4,5,6,7}
#-# NOTICE:  l:(2,hello)
```

Regular tables:

```
--using types in a table:
create table mytable  (
    a     smallint,
    b     int,
    c     bigint,
    d     numeric,
    e     real,
    f     double precision,
    g     varchar(50),
    h     char(50),
    i     text,
    j     boolean,
    k     integer array,
```

```
  l     composite_example
);


--inserting the data
insert into mytable
values (2,2222222,2222222222222,2.2,2.2,222.2,
       'hello','hello','hello',true,'{1,2,3,4,5,6,7}',(2,'hello'))



--querying the data
select * from mytable;

#-#   a       b              c   d   e     f     g
#-# 1 2 2222222 2222222222222 2.2 2.2 222.2 hello
#-#                                                 h     i
#-# 1 hello                                           hello
#-#       j               k        l
#-# 1 TRUE {1,2,3,4,5,6,7} (2,hello)


--There is one object type, record, that we have not mentioned up until now.
--The reason for not bringing it up earlier is because it is not
--a true object type, only a placeholder.
--It does not have a predefined structure, and takes the row structure
--of the row that is assigned during a select into or for command.

--To select columns from the record, use the dot notation per the example below.

--Example:

DO $$
DECLARE
  a record;
BEGIN
  select * from mytable into a;
  RAISE NOTICE 'a: %', a.a;
  RAISE NOTICE 'a: %', a.b;
  ---...
  RAISE NOTICE 'a: %', a.l;
END $$;
```

```
#-# NOTICE:  a: 2
#-# NOTICE:  a: 2222222
#-# NOTICE:  a: (2,hello)
```

Views:

```
--creating a view
--the select statement will be re-run every time we select from the view
create or replace view myview as (
    select 'hello world' as hello
);



select * from myview;

#-#         hello
#-# 1 hello world


--a more realistic example of a view:
create or replace view myview2 as (
    select * from mytable
);


select * from myview2;

#-#   a       b               c   d   e     f     g
#-# 1 2 2222222 2222222222222 2.2 2.2 222.2 hello
#-#                                                          h     i
#-# 1 hello                                                    hello
#-#       j               k         l
#-# 1 TRUE {1,2,3,4,5,6,7} (2,hello)
```

Materialized views:

```
--next create a materialized view:
create materialized view mymaterializedview as (
    select * from mytable
);
```

```
select * from mymaterializedview;

#-#   a       b             c   d   e     f     g
#-# 1 2 2222222 2222222222222 2.2 2.2 222.2 hello
#-#                                                         h     i
#-# 1 hello                                                   hello
#-#       j            k         l
#-# 1 TRUE {1,2,3,4,5,6,7} (2,hello)


--Next change the underlying table, mytable
--For example add a second record:
insert into mytable
values (3,33333,333333,3.3,3.3,333.3,
        'world','world','world',false,'{8,9,10,11,12,13,14}',(3,'world'));


--Next query myview2
select * from myview2;
--the view reflects the updated data

#-#   a       b             c   d   e     f     g
#-# 1 2 2222222 2222222222222 2.2 2.2 222.2 hello
#-# 2 3   33333        333333 3.3 3.3 333.3 world
#-#                                                         h     i
#-# 1 hello                                                   hello
#-# 2 world                                                   world
#-#         j                    k         l
#-# 1  TRUE       {1,2,3,4,5,6,7} (2,hello)
#-# 2 FALSE {8,9,10,11,12,13,14} (3,world)


--Next query mymaterializedview
select * from mymaterializedview;
--the materialized view does not reflect the updated data

#-#   a       b             c   d   e     f     g
#-# 1 2 2222222 2222222222222 2.2 2.2 222.2 hello
#-#                                                         h     i
#-# 1 hello                                                   hello
#-#       j            k         l
#-# 1 TRUE {1,2,3,4,5,6,7} (2,hello)
```

```
--refresh the materialized view
refresh materialized view mymaterializedview;


--the updated data is now reflected in the materialized view
select * from mymaterializedview;

#-#   a       b              c   d   e     f     g
#-# 1 2 2222222 2222222222222 2.2 2.2 222.2 hello
#-# 2 3   33333        333333 3.3 3.3 333.3 world
#-#                                                       h     i
#-# 1 hello                                                 hello
#-# 2 world                                                 world
#-#       j                   k         l
#-# 1  TRUE      {1,2,3,4,5,6,7} (2,hello)
#-# 2 FALSE {8,9,10,11,12,13,14} (3,world)
```

The take-away here is that views are always up to date, but are slow if the underlying data is large. Materialized views offer an easy way to avoid that by storing the result, and offering an easy refresh mechanism, which could be used on a time interval depending on how large the lag is allowed to be. Materialized views are, however, still limited in that they refresh all the data, and that may be too expensive. If that is the case, upserts (a combination of updates and inserts) and regular tables can be used to only update the data that has changed. It is more work to implement this strategy, and in some cases it might miss some changes to the source data.

Cleaning up:

```
drop view myview2;


drop materialized view mymaterializedview;


drop table mytable;


drop view myview;
```

```
drop type composite_example;
```

Chapter 7

Subsetting

Subsetting refers to selecting part of the information stored in an object.

7.1 R

In the code chunk below we will provide examples for subsetting vectors, data frames and lists.

```
# subsetting for vectors: Use [indicator]

num_vector

#-#  [1] 1.0 1.1 1.2 1.3 1.4 1.5 1.6 1.7 1.8 1.9 2.0 2.1 2.2 2.3
#-# [15] 2.4 2.5 2.6 2.7 2.8 2.9 3.0 3.1 3.2 3.3 3.4 3.5

# select the second element
num_vector[2]

#-# [1] 1.1

# select the fist two elements
num_vector[1:2]

#-# [1] 1.0 1.1

# select element 1 and 3
num_vector[c(1, 3)]

#-# [1] 1.0 1.2
```

```
# Note that '[' is a function, whose first
# argument is the object being subset
num_vector[c(1, 3)]

#-# [1] 1.0 1.2

# subsetting for matrices and data frames:

# Use [row indicators, column indicators]
df

#-#    int_vector fact_vector
#-# 1           1           a
#-# 2           2           b
#-# 3           3           c
#-# 4           4           d
#-# 5           5           e
#-# 6           6           f
#-# 7           7           g
#-# 8           8           h
#-# 9           9           i
#-# 10         10           j

# select element on row 3, column 2
df[3, 2]

#-# [1] c
#-# Levels: a b c d e f g h i j

# select column 2
df[, 2]

#-#  [1] a b c d e f g h i j
#-# Levels: a b c d e f g h i j

df[, c(FALSE, TRUE)]

#-#  [1] a b c d e f g h i j
#-# Levels: a b c d e f g h i j

# select row 2
df[2, ]

#-#   int_vector fact_vector
#-# 2          2           b
```

```
# remove row 2
df[-2, ]

#-#    int_vector fact_vector
#-# 1           1           a
#-# 3           3           c
#-# 4           4           d
#-# 5           5           e
#-# 6           6           f
#-# 7           7           g
#-# 8           8           h
#-# 9           9           i
#-# 10         10           j

# you can also use the column names
df

#-#    int_vector fact_vector
#-# 1           1           a
#-# 2           2           b
#-# 3           3           c
#-# 4           4           d
#-# 5           5           e
#-# 6           6           f
#-# 7           7           g
#-# 8           8           h
#-# 9           9           i
#-# 10         10           j

# select column 2
df$fact_vector  #is the same as df[,2]

#-#  [1] a b c d e f g h i j
#-# Levels: a b c d e f g h i j

df[, "fact_vector"]

#-#  [1] a b c d e f g h i j
#-# Levels: a b c d e f g h i j

# drop=FALSE will ensure that the properties of
# the object are preserved. Always use this
# inside functions.
df[, 2, drop = FALSE]
```

```
#-#    fact_vector
#-# 1            a
#-# 2            b
#-# 3            c
#-# 4            d
#-# 5            e
#-# 6            f
#-# 7            g
#-# 8            h
#-# 9            i
#-# 10           j

df[, 2]

#-#  [1] a b c d e f g h i j
#-# Levels: a b c d e f g h i j

# to get similar behavior as drop=FALSE with less
# typing you can do
df[2]

#-#    fact_vector
#-# 1            a
#-# 2            b
#-# 3            c
#-# 4            d
#-# 5            e
#-# 6            f
#-# 7            g
#-# 8            h
#-# 9            i
#-# 10           j

# However, this is considered bad practice
# because it makes your code less readable and
# maintainable. If you do not have a comma in
# your brackets the reader assumes the object is
# a vector. Therefore convention is to never use
# this shortcut.

# We can also use a matrix to make our selection
# If we want the first three elements of column 1
# and the last three elements of column 2:
```

```
(mat <- matrix(c(c(rep(TRUE, 3), rep(FALSE, 7)), c(rep(FALSE,
    7), rep(TRUE, 3))), ncol = 2))

#-#        [,1]  [,2]
#-#  [1,]  TRUE FALSE
#-#  [2,]  TRUE FALSE
#-#  [3,]  TRUE FALSE
#-#  [4,] FALSE FALSE
#-#  [5,] FALSE FALSE
#-#  [6,] FALSE FALSE
#-#  [7,] FALSE FALSE
#-#  [8,] FALSE  TRUE
#-#  [9,] FALSE  TRUE
#-# [10,] FALSE  TRUE

# We can then simply use that matrix within the
# square brackets:
df[mat]

#-# [1] " 1" " 2" " 3" "h"  "i"  "j"

# subsetting for lists: Use [[]]
l

#-# [[1]]
#-#    int_vector fact_vector
#-# 1           1           a
#-# 2           2           b
#-# 3           3           c
#-# 4           4           d
#-# 5           5           e
#-# 6           6           f
#-# 7           7           g
#-# 8           8           h
#-# 9           9           i
#-# 10         10           j
#-#
#-# [[2]]
#-#      [,1] [,2] [,3] [,4] [,5]
#-# [1,]    1    6   11   16   21
#-# [2,]    2    7   12   17   22
#-# [3,]    3    8   13   18   23
#-# [4,]    4    9   14   19   24
```

```
#-# [5,]    5   10   15   20   25
#-#
#-# [[3]]
#-#  [1]  1  2  3  4  5  6  7  8  9 10

# select second element
l[[2]]

#-#      [,1] [,2] [,3] [,4] [,5]
#-# [1,]    1    6   11   16   21
#-# [2,]    2    7   12   17   22
#-# [3,]    3    8   13   18   23
#-# [4,]    4    9   14   19   24
#-# [5,]    5   10   15   20   25

# you can also use single brackets, but then the
# results will be a list with one element
l[2]

#-# [[1]]
#-#      [,1] [,2] [,3] [,4] [,5]
#-# [1,]    1    6   11   16   21
#-# [2,]    2    7   12   17   22
#-# [3,]    3    8   13   18   23
#-# [4,]    4    9   14   19   24
#-# [5,]    5   10   15   20   25

# select column two of the second element
l[[2]][, 2]

#-# [1]  6  7  8  9 10

# renaming

rownames(df)

#-#  [1] "1"  "2"  "3"  "4"  "5"  "6"  "7"  "8"  "9"  "10"

colnames(df)

#-# [1] "int_vector"  "fact_vector"
```

```
# Let's rename the second variable of df to
# 'Something'

colnames(df)[2] <- "Something"
df

#-#    int_vector Something
#-# 1           1         a
#-# 2           2         b
#-# 3           3         c
#-# 4           4         d
#-# 5           5         e
#-# 6           6         f
#-# 7           7         g
#-# 8           8         h
#-# 9           9         i
#-# 10         10         j
```

7.2 Python

```
##############################string

a = "word"

# indexing: return a single item

# positive indexing starts from the left at 0
a[0]
#-# 'w'

# negative indexing starts from the right at -1
# Example: -1 is interpreted as follows:
# Take the length of the string (len(a) in this case 4)
# and subtract 1: 4+(-1) This results in position 3 from the left,
# which should return 'd'.
a[-1]

#-# 'd'

#same as:
a[len(a)-1]
```

```
#-# 'd'

# slicing: generalized form of indexing to return a
# contiguous section of data.
# It takes the following form:
# object[lowerbound : upperbound]
# The lower bound is inclusive and the upper bound is non-inclusive
# (one higher than the position we want returned).
# The defaults are 0 and the length of the object (4 in this case).

#select all data
a[ : ] #note that this makes a copy of a (handy for mutable objects)

#-# 'word'

a[0:4]

#-# 'word'

#select second element (position 1) to third element (position 2)
a[1:3]

#-# 'or'

#select all elements after the first (i.e., exclude 0)
a[1:]

#-# 'ord'

#all but the last item
a[:-1]

#-# 'wor'

a[:len(a)-1]

#-# 'wor'

a[:4-1]

#-# 'wor'

# extended slicing takes the following form and is used for skipping:
# object[lowerbound : upperbound : step]
# This means: select all elements of
# object from lowerbound until upperbound-1 by step.
# The default step is 1
```

```
a = 'verylongword'

#start at 0 and go until the end, skipping one value
a[::2]

#-# 'vrlnwr'

#reverse
a[::-2]

#-# 'dogoye'

# note: nonconsecutive sections can be extracted by list comprehensions
# or combining multiple operations:
[ a[x] for x in [0,3] ]

#-# ['v', 'y']

[ a[0],a[3] ]

#-# ['v', 'y']

##############################list
#exactly the same as for strings

b = [1,2,3,4]

# e.g.,:
b[1:4]

#-# [2, 3, 4]

b[-2:3]

#-# [3]

# there is added complexity because lists can be nested:
# consider this matrix
b = [ [1,2,3],
      [4,5,6],
      [7,8,9]]
#get the first element
b[0]

#-# [1, 2, 3]

#get the first element of the first element
b[0][0]
```

```
#-# 1

# in addition, since lists are mutable, we can assign values:

#replace
b = [1,2,3,4]
b[1] = 200
b

#-# [1, 200, 3, 4]

#delete
b[0:2]  = []
b

#-# [3, 4]

#insert
b[1:1] = [100,200,300]
b

#-# [3, 100, 200, 300, 4]

#insert at beginning
b[:0] = [88]


#insert at end
b[len(b):] = [99]
b

#-# [88, 3, 100, 200, 300, 4, 99]

#these mutations are not very mnemonic and there are easier alternatives:

b = [1,2,3,4]

#add one item at the end
b.append(5) #same as b[len(b):] = [5] and b.insert(len(b),5)
b

#-# [1, 2, 3, 4, 5]

#add multiple items at the end
b.extend([6,7,8])
b
```

```
#-# [1, 2, 3, 4, 5, 6, 7, 8]

#insert an item somewhere
b.insert(0,100) #same b[:0] = [5]
b

#-# [100, 1, 2, 3, 4, 5, 6, 7, 8]

#remove last item
b.pop()

#-# 8

b

#-# [100, 1, 2, 3, 4, 5, 6, 7]

#remove item by position
b.pop(0)

#-# 100

b

#-# [1, 2, 3, 4, 5, 6, 7]

#remove item by value
b.remove(5)
b

#-# [1, 2, 3, 4, 6, 7]

#delete items
del b[0:3]
b

#-# [4, 6, 7]

############################ tuple

#exactly the same as for strings and lists

c = (1,2,3,4)
# e.g.,:
c[1:4]

#-# (2, 3, 4)
```

```
#remember that tuples are immutable


############################## dictionary

#Dictionaries do not support subsetting by position.
#They support subsetting by key.
#The reason is that Python (re-)orders the elements
#for speed of extraction, and that might differ by
#platform, Python version, and even session.


d = {'name' : 'John', 'age' : 30, 'info' : [1,2,3]}

d['age']

#-# 30

#does not work:
#d[0]


#Mutating a dictionary:

#replace by another value
d['age'] = 20
d

#-# {'name': 'John', 'age': 20, 'info': [1, 2, 3]}

#replace by a list
d['name'] = ['John','Doe']


#delete entry
del d['name']
d

#-# {'age': 20, 'info': [1, 2, 3]}

#add a new element
d['hobby'] = 'soccer'
d

#-# {'age': 20, 'info': [1, 2, 3], 'hobby': 'soccer'}
```

```
#subset to get the keys
d.keys()

#-# dict_keys(['age', 'info', 'hobby'])

#subset the values
d.values()

#-# dict_values([20, [1, 2, 3], 'soccer'])

#get the keys and values as tuples
d.items()

#-# dict_items([('age', 20), ('info', [1, 2, 3]), ('hobby', 'soccer')])

#avoiding errors
#d['something']


print(d.get('something'))

#-# None

#outer join
d2 = {'name' : 'Frank', 'age' : 50}
d.update(d2)
d

#-# {'age': 50, 'info': [1, 2, 3], 'hobby': 'soccer', 'name': 'Frank'}

#remove a key
d.pop('name')

#-# 'Frank'

d

#-# {'age': 50, 'info': [1, 2, 3], 'hobby': 'soccer'}

############################## set

#sets and frozensets are not subscriptable using []

e = {'name', 'age', 'info'}

#e['name']
```

```
#e[0]


#remove random element
e.pop()

#-# 'info'

e

#-# {'name', 'age'}

#remove by name
e.discard('info')
e

#-# {'name', 'age'}

#add
e.add('infoNew')
e

#-# {'name', 'age', 'infoNew'}



############################ frozen set

#sets and frozensets are not subscriptable using []

f = frozenset({'name', 'age', 'info'})

#f['name']


#f[0]


#frozensets are immutable
```

Consider the difference in indexing and slicing. In indexing one would count the positions. In slicing one would count the cuts between the positions. See Figure 7.1.

Subsetting numpy arrays and pandas data frames:

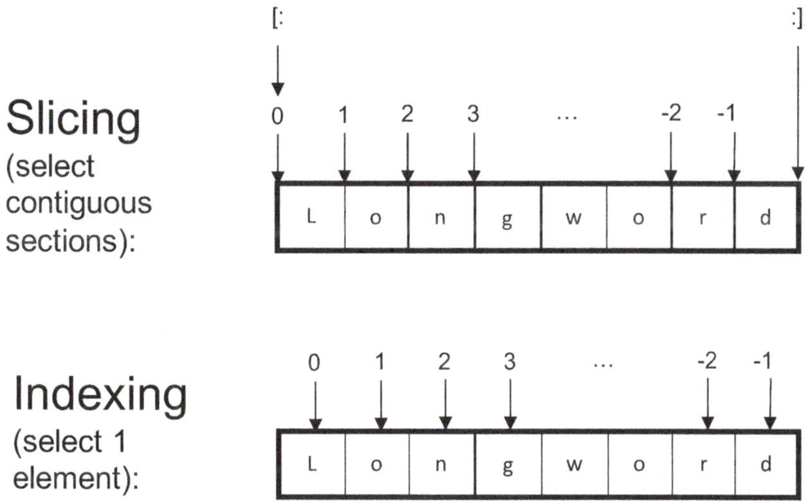

Figure 7.1: Indexing and Slicing

```
import pandas as pd
import numpy as np


#PANDAS

#create a toy DataFrame
df = pd.DataFrame(np.arange(0,40).reshape(10,4),
                  columns=['A','B','C','D'])
df


#-#     A   B   C   D
#-# 0   0   1   2   3
#-# 1   4   5   6   7
#-# 2   8   9  10  11
#-# 3  12  13  14  15
#-# 4  16  17  18  19
#-# 5  20  21  22  23
#-# 6  24  25  26  27
#-# 7  28  29  30  31
#-# 8  32  33  34  35
#-# 9  36  37  38  39
```

```
#get column and row names
list(df.columns.values)

#-# ['A', 'B', 'C', 'D']

list(df.index.values)

#-# [0, 1, 2, 3, 4, 5, 6, 7, 8, 9]

#select by name
df['A']

#-# 0     0
#-# 1     4
#-# 2     8
#-# 3    12
#-# 4    16
#-# 5    20
#-# 6    24
#-# 7    28
#-# 8    32
#-# 9    36
#-# Name: A, dtype: int64

#or
df.A

#-# 0     0
#-# 1     4
#-# 2     8
#-# 3    12
#-# 4    16
#-# 5    20
#-# 6    24
#-# 7    28
#-# 8    32
#-# 9    36
#-# Name: A, dtype: int64

#Note the difference between
type(df['A'])

#-# <class 'pandas.core.series.Series'>

#and
type(df[['A']])
```

```
#-# <class 'pandas.core.frame.DataFrame'>

#A pandas column is of type Series.
#Use double square brackets if you want a DataFrame.

#To select two or more columns, put them in a list
df[['A','B']]

#-#     A   B
#-# 0   0   1
#-# 1   4   5
#-# 2   8   9
#-# 3  12  13
#-# 4  16  17
#-# 5  20  21
#-# 6  24  25
#-# 7  28  29
#-# 8  32  33
#-# 9  36  37

#slicing rows
df[1:3]

#-#    A  B   C   D
#-# 1  4  5   6   7
#-# 2  8  9  10  11

#this does not work:
#df[:,1:3]


#slicing rows and columns:

#use loc for label based indexing.
#use iloc for integer based indexing

df.iloc[:,1:3]

#-#     B   C
#-# 0   1   2
#-# 1   5   6
#-# 2   9  10
#-# 3  13  14
#-# 4  17  18
#-# 5  21  22
```

```
#-# 6  25  26
#-# 7  29  30
#-# 8  33  34
#-# 9  37  38

df.iloc[:,[1,2]]

#-#     B   C
#-# 0   1   2
#-# 1   5   6
#-# 2   9  10
#-# 3  13  14
#-# 4  17  18
#-# 5  21  22
#-# 6  25  26
#-# 7  29  30
#-# 8  33  34
#-# 9  37  38

df.iloc[0,0:2]

#-# A    0
#-# B    1
#-# Name: 0, dtype: int64

df.iloc[0:1,0:2]

#-#    A  B
#-# 0  0  1

# In loc we can also use integers but they do not refer to the position
# They refer to the names (labels) in df.columns.values or df.index.values
#for example:
df.loc[0,]

#-# A    0
#-# B    1
#-# C    2
#-# D    3
#-# Name: 0, dtype: int64

#refers to the row with label 0
#while, this refers to the position
df.iloc[0,]
```

```
#-# A    0
#-# B    1
#-# C    2
#-# D    3
#-# Name: 0, dtype: int64

#when slicing, it is important to recognize that the stop bound
#for loc is inclusive and the stop bound for iloc is not.
df

#-#     A   B   C   D
#-# 0   0   1   2   3
#-# 1   4   5   6   7
#-# 2   8   9  10  11
#-# 3  12  13  14  15
#-# 4  16  17  18  19
#-# 5  20  21  22  23
#-# 6  24  25  26  27
#-# 7  28  29  30  31
#-# 8  32  33  34  35
#-# 9  36  37  38  39

df.iloc[0:3] #returns rows 0,1,2

#-#    A  B   C   D
#-# 0  0  1   2   3
#-# 1  4  5   6   7
#-# 2  8  9  10  11

df.loc[0:3] #returns rows  0,1,2,3

#-#     A   B   C   D
#-# 0   0   1   2   3
#-# 1   4   5   6   7
#-# 2   8   9  10  11
#-# 3  12  13  14  15

#select both rows and columns using loc
df.loc[[0,1,2],['A','B']]

#-#    A  B
#-# 0  0  1
#-# 1  4  5
#-# 2  8  9

df.loc[[0,1,2],'A':'C']
```

```
#-#    A  B   C
#-# 0  0  1   2
#-# 1  4  5   6
#-# 2  8  9  10
```

```
df.loc[df['A'] == 8,:]
```

```
#-#    A  B   C   D
#-# 2  8  9  10  11
```

```
df.loc[df['A'] == 8]
```

```
#-#    A  B   C   D
#-# 2  8  9  10  11
```

```
#Subsetting using criteria
df[df['A'] == 8]
```

```
#-#    A  B   C   D
#-# 2  8  9  10  11
```

```
df[df['A'].isin([4,8,12])]
```

```
#-#     A   B   C   D
#-# 1   4   5   6   7
#-# 2   8   9  10  11
#-# 3  12  13  14  15
```

```
#NUMPY

#1D array
a = np.arange(10)
a
```

```
#-# array([0, 1, 2, 3, 4, 5, 6, 7, 8, 9])
```

```
#2D array
b = np.arange(10).reshape(5,2)
b
```

```
#-# array([[0, 1],
#-#        [2, 3],
#-#        [4, 5],
#-#        [6, 7],
#-#        [8, 9]])
```

```
a[2]
```

```
#-# 2

a[-2]

#-# 8

b[2,1]

#-# 5

b[2][1] #this is how you would do it for a simple list

#-# 5

#see what happens when indexing a 2D array with only one dimension
b[0]

#-# array([0, 1])

a[[0,1,2]]

#-# array([0, 1, 2])

#we can also do it with a numpy array
a[np.array([0,1,2])]

#-# array([0, 1, 2])

b[np.array([0,1])]

#-# array([[0, 1],
#-#        [2, 3]])

#while we can also subset the second dimension of b with a numpy array
#it is not recommended as in general it is inconvenient
#Instead use slicing:
b[np.array([0,1]),0:2]

#-# array([[0, 1],
#-#        [2, 3]])

#or
b[0:2,0:2]

#-# array([[0, 1],
#-#        [2, 3]])

#boolean subsetting (masking arrays)
a
```

```
#-# array([0, 1, 2, 3, 4, 5, 6, 7, 8, 9])

a[a >= 5]

#-# array([5, 6, 7, 8, 9])

#if we want to prepare a list of indices with slices,
#we need to use the slice function
b

#-# array([[0, 1],
#-#        [2, 3],
#-#        [4, 5],
#-#        [6, 7],
#-#        [8, 9]])

indices = (slice(0,3),1) #same as (0:3,1), which will not work

b[indices]

#-# array([1, 3, 5])

indices = (Ellipsis,1) #same as (:,1), which will not work

b[indices]

#-# array([1, 3, 5, 7, 9])

#finally, it is important to differentiate between lists and tuples in indexing
b

#-# array([[0, 1],
#-#        [2, 3],
#-#        [4, 5],
#-#        [6, 7],
#-#        [8, 9]])

b[[0,1]] #select row 0 and row 1

#-# array([[0, 1],
#-#        [2, 3]])

b[(0,1)] #select row 0 and then column 1, same as b[0,1]

#-# 1
```

```
#in other words 0,1 is short for (0,1)


#remember that these subsets do not copy the data but produce views of the original data:
x = np.array([1, 2, 3])

y = x #usual reference

z = np.copy(x) #copy
#Note that, when we modify x, y changes, but not z:
x[0] = 10

x[0] == y[0]

#-# True

x[0] == z[0]

#-# False

#We can also copy with pandas:
s = pd.Series([1, 2], index=["a", "b"])

print(s)

#-# a    1
#-# b    2
#-# dtype: int64

s_copy = s.copy()

print(s_copy)

#-# a    1
#-# b    2
#-# dtype: int64


#For more information about the pandas copy method see
#https://pandas.pydata.org/docs/reference/api/pandas.DataFrame.copy.html
#Especially notice the complication regarding nested data
```

7.3 PostgreSQL

Creating some toy data:

```
create table a (
    id integer,
    var_1 integer,
    var_2 integer);
```

```
insert into a (id, var_1, var_2)
values (1, 2, 3),
       (2, 5, 6),
       (3, 8, 9),
       (4, 11, 12);
```

```
select * from a;

#-#   id var_1 var_2
#-# 1  1     2     3
#-# 2  2     5     6
#-# 3  3     8     9
#-# 4  4    11    12
```

Subset selection:

```
--select only data where col_a equals 2
select * from a
where id = 2;

#-#   id var_1 var_2
#-# 1  2     5     6
```

```
--using multiple conditions
select * from a
where id = 2 and var_1 = 5;

#-#   id var_1 var_2
#-# 1  2     5     6
```

Subset update:

```
--updating data at a specific location
update a set var_1 = var_1 + 100
where id = 1;
```

```
select * from a;
```

```
#-#   id var_1 var_2
#-# 1  2     5     6
#-# 2  3     8     9
#-# 3  4    11    12
#-# 4  1   102     3
```

```
update a set (var_1, var_2) = (var_1 + 100, var_2 + 200)
where id = 2;
```

```
select * from a;
```

```
#-#   id var_1 var_2
#-# 1  3     8     9
#-# 2  4    11    12
#-# 3  1   102     3
#-# 4  2   105   206
```

```
--using a select query (potentially from another table):
update a set (var_1, var_2) =
    (select var_1 + 100, var_2 + 200 from a where id = 4)
where id = 4;
```

```
select * from a;
```

```
#-#   id var_1 var_2
#-# 1  3     8     9
#-# 2  1   102     3
#-# 3  2   105   206
#-# 4  4   111   212
```

Removing subsets of data:

```
delete from a where id = 1;
```

```
select * from a;
```

```
#-#   id var_1 var_2
#-# 1  3     8     9
#-# 2  2   105   206
#-# 3  4   111   212
```

Adding and dropping variables:

```
alter table a add column var_3 integer;
```

```
select * from a;
```

```
#-#   id var_1 var_2 var_3
#-# 1  3     8     9    NA
#-# 2  2   105   206    NA
#-# 3  4   111   212    NA
```

```
update a set var_3 = var_1 + var_2;
```

```
select * from a;
```

```
#-#   id var_1 var_2 var_3
#-# 1  3     8     9    17
#-# 2  2   105   206   311
#-# 3  4   111   212   323
```

```
alter table a drop column var_3;
```

```
select * from a;
```

```
#-#   id var_1 var_2
#-# 1  3     8     9
#-# 2  2   105   206
#-# 3  4   111   212
```

Chapter 8

Memory Monitoring and Management

R and Python do everything in working memory. Another term for working memory is RAM (Random Access Memory). While this makes it fast, one might quickly run out of memory. A typical laptop computer has 16GB of RAM, and 1TB of disk space. Accessing disk space (reading and writing) is very slow compared to accessing RAM. If our computer runs out of RAM, it will try to enlist our disk space for its operations. This is called swap and should be avoided at all times. It will make our computer unresponsive. Alternatively, our software may crash. To avoid running out of RAM, it is important that we know how to monitor memory usage, and how to manage it. In this subsection we will discuss memory monitoring and management techniques.

Before moving on we need to clarify the difference between two common metric systems: binary and decimal. The binary system (IEC: International Elecrotechnical Commission) is specified using a base of 2. The decimal system (SI: Système International d'Unités; International System of Units) is specified using a base of 10. Table 8.1 shows the difference. Kibibyte stands for kilo binary and is 1024 bytes. In contrast a kilobyte is 1000 bytes.The binary system is more commonly used in relation to RAM, whereas the decimal system is more commonly used for disk storage. That is the reason why we will be seeing a lot of KiB and MiB in this section: we are looking at RAM usage.

Table 8.1: Prefixes used for bytes (B)

Decimal: SI			Binary: IEC		
Short	Long	Bytes	Short	Long	Bytes
kB	kilobyte	$10^3 = 1000$	KiB	kibibyte	$2^{10} = 1024$
MB	megabyte	$10^6 = 1000^2$	MiB	mebibyte	$2^{20} = 1024^2$
GB	gigabyte	$10^9 = 1000^3$	GiB	gibibyte	$2^{30} = 1024^3$
TB	terabyte	$10^{12} = 1000^4$	TiB	tebibyte	$2^{40} = 1024^4$
PB	petabyte	$10^{15} = 1000^5$	PiB	pebibyte	$2^{50} = 1024^5$
EB	exabyte	$10^{18} = 1000^6$	EiB	exbibyte	$2^{60} = 1024^6$
ZB	zettabyte	$10^{21} = 1000^7$	ZiB	zebibyte	$2^{70} = 1024^7$
YB	yottabyte	$10^{24} = 1000^8$	YiB	yobibyte	$2^{80} = 1024^8$

8.1 R

```
# Consider the following objects:
a <- 1
b <- 1:10

# To see all the objects that occupy the
# environment use
ls()

#-#  [1] "a"          "b"          "char_vector" "churn"
#-#  [5] "con"        "df"         "fact_vector" "int_vector"
#-#  [9] "l"          "loaded"     "loaded_lib"  "loaded_req"
#-# [13] "log_vector" "mat"        "num_vector"

# A very useful line of code is the following.
# It will remove (rm) all objects in the
# environment as listed by ls()
rm(list = ls())

# Let's check if we were successful:
ls()

#-# character(0)

# Yes, there are no more objects in the
# environment
```

```
# There are two levels at which we want to
# measure RAM consumption: micro, and macro.

# Micro level At the micro level we are concerned
# with how much RAM is consumed by individual
# objects. We use the base R function
# object.size() for this task.

# Consider a vector called a and its object size
a <- 1
object.size(a)

#-# 56 bytes

# It might be surprising that more than the usual
# 8 bytes are used to store this numeric value in
# double-precision floating-point format.  The
# underlying reason is that R uses 48 bytes to
# store meta data.  An example of meta-data is
# the length, or base type of the object.

# To see how R allocates RAM, let's grow a
# numeric vector from length 1 to length 50. The
# plot indicates that memory usage does not grow
# proportionally. For now do not lose too much
# time trying to understand the loop immediately
# below. We will cover loops in detail in
# subsequent sections.

f <- numeric()
for (i in 1:50) {
    e <- 1:i
    f[i] <- as.numeric(utils::object.size(e))
}

plot(1:50, f, type = "l", xlab = "Length", ylab = "bytes")
```

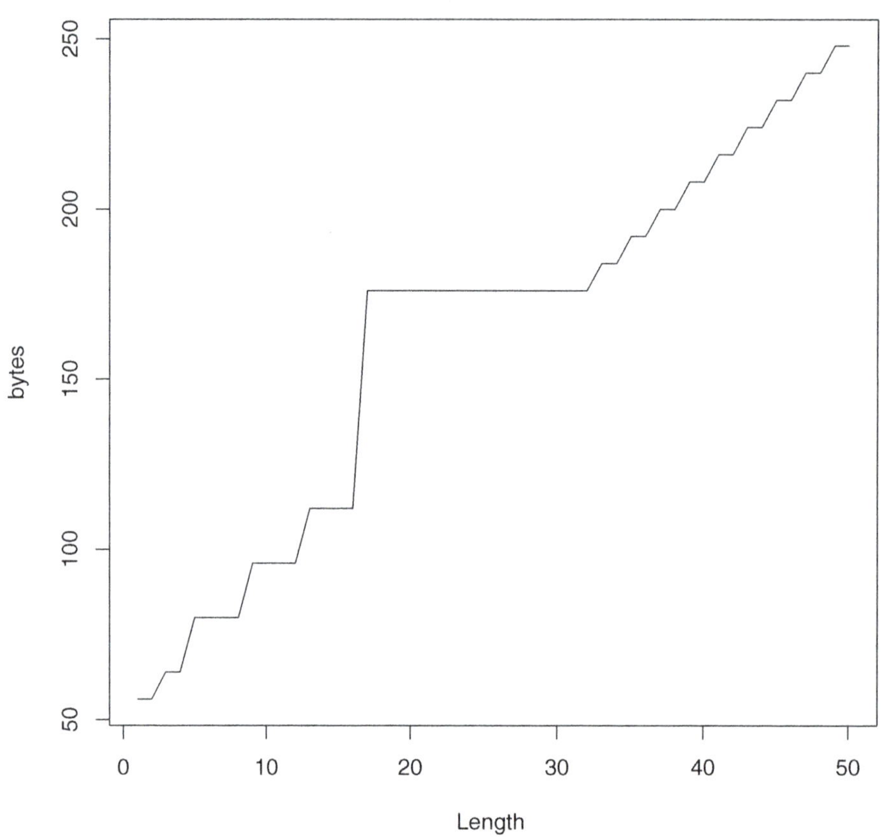


```
# Interestingly even an object of length 0 will
# consume memory to store overhead.
(e <- numeric(0))

#-# numeric(0)

object.size(e)

#-# 48 bytes

# The reason why memory usage is disproportional
# is because requesting memory from the operating
```

```
# system is expensive. If R has to ask for memory
# each time something changes it would slow down
# R. Therefore R requests more memory than it
# needs and manages that additional memory
# itself. After 128 bytes R hands over management
# of vectors to the the operating system because
# the latter is very efficient in doing that.

# Using the following function we can learn which
# objects take up the most space.  Let's first
# create some objects:
b <- matrix(runif(1000), ncol = 10)
c <- list(1:10, 1:100)
# This line of code lists all the objects in the
# working environment using the function ls(). It
# then applies the function object.size to each
# of the objects to get their size in bytes. If
# there are objects that we do not need anymore
# we can remove them. This is a very convenient
# way to free up memory.  Again, we will explain
# sapply in detail in a subsequent section.  For
# now, just use this line of code to see memory
# consumption of all the objects in memory.

(d <- sort(sapply(ls(all.names = TRUE), function(x) {
    utils::object.size(get(x))
}))) # in bytes

#-#            e           a           i           f
#-#           48          56          56         448
#-#            c .Random.seed           b
#-#          608        2552        8216

# Total memory used by R:
sum(d)

#-# [1] 11984

# Let's remove some objects from our environment
ls()

#-# [1] "a" "b" "c" "d" "e" "f" "i"
```

```
rm(a, b, c, d)
ls()

#-# [1] "e" "f" "i"

# To decrease memory usage, one has to carefully
# reflect on which type of object to use.

# Consider 1000 values, each value unique
object.size(as.integer(1:1000))

#-# 4048 bytes

object.size(as.numeric(1:1000))

#-# 8048 bytes

object.size(as.character(1:1000))

#-# 64048 bytes

object.size(as.factor(1:1000))

#-# 68432 bytes

# the last line stores 1000 integers and 1000
# labels


# Now again consider 1000 values, but there are
# only 2 unique values
object.size(as.integer(c(rep(1, 500), rep(0, 500))))

#-# 4048 bytes

object.size(as.numeric(c(rep(1, 500), rep(0, 500))))

#-# 8048 bytes

object.size(as.character(c(rep(1, 500), rep(0, 500))))

#-# 8160 bytes

object.size(as.factor(c(rep(1, 500), rep(0, 500))))
```

```
#-# 4560 bytes

# the last line stores 1k integers and 2 labels

# As a side note: Note that R has a string pool.
# This means that unique strings are stored once.
# That is the reason why the object size of the
# unique 1000 values is much larger than the 1000
# ones and zeroes.

# This is less important. What is important is
# that we know when to use a factor and when to
# use a character.  A character would be used
# when we are dealing with many unique values. If
# we are dealing with few unique values, a factor
# is recommended.

# Let's clean up our environment

# First look at what we have in the environment:
ls()

#-# [1] "e" "f" "i"

# remove everything
rm(list = ls())

# look again:
ls()

#-# character(0)

# Macro level While the micro level is concerned
# with how much RAM R uses (and objects in the
# environment), we now look at how much RAM is
# still available on our computer taking into
# account non-R processes.

# We can obtain this information from activity
# monitor on MacOS, or task manager on Windows
# (crtl-alt-del). We can also obtain this
# information in R as follows:
```

```
# Let's install the memuse package

if (!require("memuse")) {
    install.packages("memuse", repos = "https://cran.rstudio.com/",
        quiet = TRUE)
    require("memuse")
}

#-# Loading required package: memuse

Sys.meminfo()

#-# Totalram:   16.000 GiB
#-# Freeram:   669.797 MiB

# Sys.meminfo() reports our total RAM and free
# RAM. We want to make sure we have RAM available
# at all times, if not our computer will freeze
# up.  It is a good idea to always keep an eye on
# memory usage.

# Important note. Once you remove an object from
# R, by using rm(), R still hangs on to the
# memory that was used by the object, in case the
# user would need it for something else. It does
# that because returning memory to the operating
# system is expensive. If the user does not use
# it after a while, R will automatically return
# it to the operating system. It does that by
# calling the function gc(), which is short for
# garbage collection. R does this automatically
# in the background, so there is no need for you
# to call the gc() function.

# However, if you would want to see how
# Sys.meminfo() changes immediately after
# removing an object, you would run gc() so that
# R returns the RAM back to the operating system.
# Otherwise you would have to wait until R
# returns it automatically at some point in the
# future.
```

What can we conclude? Factors in R are stored as a vector of integer values with a corresponding set of labels to use when the factor is displayed. Therefore, whenever we need to choose between character and factor:

- When we have many unique values: use character
- When we have only a few unique values: use factor

We also may be tempted to store IDs as integers. We need to be careful though when working with IDs: storing them as integers will lead to incorrect imports for IDs with leading zeros:

```
as.integer("013")
```

```
#-# [1] 13
```

```
as.character("013")
```

```
#-# [1] "013"
```

8.2 Python

```
import numpy as np

a = 1.0
b = np.arange(1,10)
c = 'word'
d = 6
e = "h"

#dir()

#here we create a second version of dir() that
#only prints the variables that we can delete

def dir2():
    import __main__ #__main__ is the name of the scope in which top-level code executes
    to_exclude = "np", "var", "to_exclude", \
                 "In", "Out", "exit", "get_ipython", \
                 "quit","allvars","dir2","fl"
    allvars = []
```

```
    for var in dir(__main__):
        if var.startswith("_") == False and var not in to_exclude:
            allvars.append(var)
    return allvars

print(dir2())
#-# ['a', 'b', 'c', 'd', 'e', 'r', 'x']

#deleting objects
del(a)


dir2()

#-# ['b', 'c', 'd', 'e', 'r', 'x']

del([b,c])


dir2()

#-# ['d', 'e', 'r', 'x']

for x in dir2():
    del(vars()[x])


dir2()

#-# []

#How much ram is an object using?
import sys

#?sys.getsizeof
#return size of object in bytes

#empty array
a = np.array([],dtype=np.int8)
sys.getsizeof(a)

#-# 112

#8 bit storage
a = np.array([1,2,3,4],dtype=np.int8)
sys.getsizeof(a)
```

```
#-# 116

#100 - 96 = 4 bytes (because we have 4 elements and
#use 1 byte = 8 bits per element)

b = np.array([1,2,3,4],dtype=np.int16)
sys.getsizeof(b)

#-# 120

#104 - 96 = 8 bytes (because we have 4 elements and
#use 2 bytes = 16 bits per element)

c = np.array([1,2,3,4],dtype=np.int32)
sys.getsizeof(c)

#-# 128

#112 - 96 = 16 bytes (because we have 4 elements and use
#4 bytes = 32 bits per element)

d = np.array([1,2,3,4],dtype=np.int64)
sys.getsizeof(d)

#-# 144

#128 - 96 = 32 bytes (because we have 4 elements and use
#8 bytes=64 bits per element)

e = 1
sys.getsizeof(e)

#-# 28

f = 1.1
sys.getsizeof(f)

#-# 24

g = 'word'
sys.getsizeof(g)

#-# 53
```

```
# note: Only the memory consumption directly attributed to the object is accounted for,
# not the memory consumption of objects it refers to.
# There is lots of optimization going on in the background

for x in dir2():
    print(x,':',sys.getsizeof(vars()[x]))

#-# a : 116
#-# b : 120
#-# c : 128
#-# d : 144
#-# e : 28
#-# f : 24
#-# g : 53
#-# sys : 72

#id() function
#identity of the location of the object in memory

foo = 257
bar = foo
ham = bar

print(id(foo))

#-# 13308701904

print(id(bar))

#-# 13308701904

print(id(ham))

#-# 13308701904

#they are all the same objects

#to verify if two objects point to the same location, use
foo is bar

#-# True

#Attention
#The following creates two different objects:
foo = 257
bar = 257
foo is bar
```

```
#-# False

foo == bar

#-# True

#This is not true for values between [-5, 256]
#For efficiency reasons Python caches values between -5 and 256
#These numbers are used frequently so it is better for performance
#to already have these objects available. They are assigned during startup
#Then, each time we refer to one, we will be referring to an object that already exists.
#Python can't pre-create all possible numbers
#It can do this for small (and thus frequent numbers): [-5, 256]:
#Same each time:
foo = 256
bar = 256
foo is bar

#-# True

foo == bar

#-# True

foo = -5
bar = -5
foo is bar

#-# True

foo == bar

#-# True

foo = -6
bar = -6
foo is bar

#-# False

foo == bar

#-# True
```

```
#This means that Python preacollocates 262 * 24 =  6288 bytes (24 bytes for each number),
and thus each number between -5 and 256 is stored only once, even if created millions of
times. If, for example, the number 256 would be created a million times, it would cost 24
bytes. In constrast, if the number 257 would be created a million times, it would cost 24
million bytes.
```

8.3 PostgreSQL

PostgreSQL does not directly alter data stored in physical files (i.e., persistent files stored on disk). Instead, data is first read into local or shared random access memory, then it is changed, and then the changed data is flushed back to disk. A process first determines if the required data is already in memory (e.g., it was already requested by a process that came before it). If it is already in memory, PostgreSQL can proceed with processing immediately. Loading data from disk into memory is an expensive operation. However, in heavy data engineering tasks where R and Python would get out-of-memory errors because they load everything in memory, PostgreSQL can still do the task. This is because Postgres can be configured to only let it use a certain amount of memory. For example, if we would want to limit Postgres to only use 25% of our RAM we could do that. If we would give it more RAM, it might complete tasks faster, but if we do not, it will still finish the task. In R and Python we would have to put in the extra work to manually flush to disk by saving objects to files when executing a data processing pipeline. In addition there is no way to limit R and Python to a specific RAM limit.

From a hardware perspective, PostgreSQL can be sped up substantially by using solid state disks as opposed to mechanically spinning disks for the phyisical files, and having more RAM so that more data tables can be kept in memory. These hardware changes are not always realistic, because solid state disks and RAM can be expensive.

Figure 8.1 displays the main components of a PostgreSQL instance: local memory (allocated per process) and shared memory (allocated to all processes as a whole).
Local Memory

Temp buffers is memory that is used for storing temporary tables. Temporary tables are short-lived tables that exist for the duration of a user session. Postgres

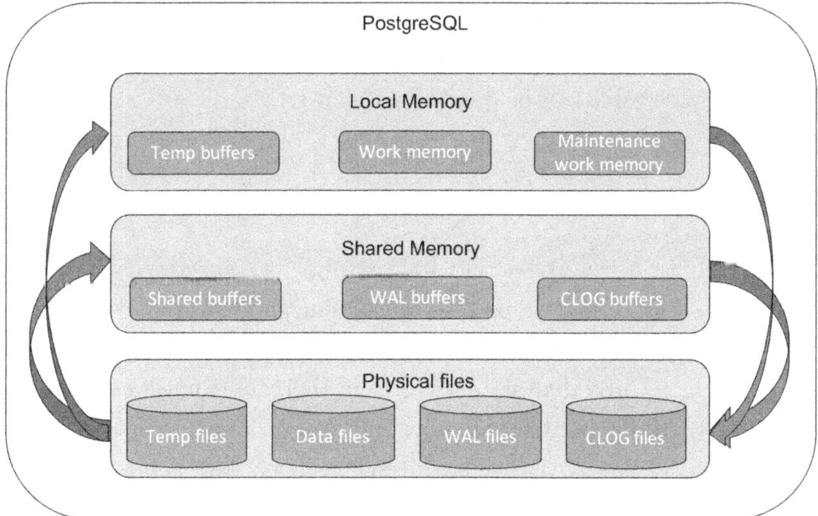

Figure 8.1: Most important PostgreSQL memory and disk components

automatically drops temporary tables at the end of a session. This allows one to avoid having to clean up after creating tables. In this book we do not use temporary tables, but they can be created with the `create temporary table` statement. The `temp_buffers` setting is per user session. If there is only one active user session, then PostgreSQL will not allocate more than the value of the buffers setting. However, if there are ten active user sessions, then one should multiply `temp_buffers` by ten to know the maximum RAM usage of temporary tables. To see the value of the temporary buffers on your system, use the following statement:

```
show temp_buffers;

#-#   temp_buffers
#-# 1          8MB
```

Work memory is used for sorting with `order by` and `distinct` operations, as well as certain join operations. The `work_mem` setting is hard to get right since this parameter is per operation. For a complex query, many operations may be running in parallel (see Section 23.3 for `max_worker_processes` and `max_parallel_workers_per_gather`) and each operation will be allowed to use as much memory as this value specifies. Also note that multiple user sessions may be active. This means that the total memory used could be many times the value of `work_mem` and it is necessary to take this into account when choosing an appropriate value. The setting's value can be queried as follows:

```
show work_mem;

#-#   work_mem
#-# 1      4MB
```

Maintenance work memory is used for vacuuming and indexing. Vacuum reclaims storage occupied by deleted or otherwise obsoleted records. Postgres does not physically remove records that are deleted from their table until a vacuum is done. Vacuuming needs to happen periodically. Indexing is a way to speed up Postgres and is covered in Section 23.3. The `maintenance_work_mem` is per operation. The risk of setting this value too high is much lower than in `work_mem` because typically there are much less maintenance operations running concurrenlty. Larger settings might improve database performance. Maintenance needs to happen periodically as to avoid critical locks on the data. Note that this setting is impacted by the `autovacuum_max_workers` parameter. To query the parameter, use:

```
show maintenance_work_mem;

#-#   maintenance_work_mem
#-# 1                 64MB
```

Shared Memory

Shared memory is allocated when the PostgreSQL server starts up and also has several components. Shared buffers are used for caching data. The more data Postgres can keep in memory the better, because then it can significantly reduce disk access which is much slower than memory access. When a user changes a record, it is modified in memory. At that point it is called dirty data. When Postgres writes the data to the physical data files the data is declared to be clean. The value of `shared_buffers` can be viewed as follows:

```
show shared_buffers;

#-#   shared_buffers
#-# 1          128MB
```

A write-ahead-log (WAL) is a mechanism to ensure that no data is lost in case of a server failure. Before data is modified, the change statements are first written to the log, which must be written to disk, before the changes are written to the database. In the event of a crash in the middle of an operation, PostgreSQL can check the WAL and compare what it was supposed to be doing when it crashed to what was actually done. It can then choose to undo what it had started, complete what it started or perform no further action. Postges writes to WAL in memory (buffers) and then these buffers are flushed to disk. The `wal_buffers` parameter is the amount of memory used for WAL data that has not yet been written to disk. Bigger values for the buffer in case of a lot of concurrent connections gives better performance. The value of WAL buffers can be queried as follows:

```
show wal_buffers;

#-#   wal_buffers
#-# 1         4MB
```

There is also a commit log (CLOG), which contains much less information than the WAL. It stores whether a given operation is in progress, commited or aborted. CLOG buffers cannot be managed by the user.

Modifying settings

Settings can be modified per session or permanently. To permanently change parameters, we have to change the configuration file with a file editor, say, `nano` . The location of the configuration file can be found as follows:

```
show config_file;

#-#                                 config_file
#-# 1 /Library/PostgreSQL/17/data/postgresql.conf
```

For the changes to have effect, we need to restart Postgres. This can be accomplished as follows:

```
pg_ctl restart -D /Library/PostgreSQL/17/data
```

To make changes that only persist for the duration of the user session, one can use the `set` statement. Valid units are kB, MB and GB. For example:

```
set temp_buffers to '10MB';
```

Chapter 9

Reading Data

9.1 R

```
# Usually we have data on our disk and we want to
# read it into R

# The first thing we do is set R to our working
# directory (where the data is stored). We use
# the setwd function. For example:
# setwd('/Users/Username/folder/'). On Windows we
# either use '\\' or '/', on Linux or Unix (Mac)
# we use '/' in the path. We can also see where
# our current working directory is with getwd()
# Once we have set our working directory we can
# download files as follows, or simply copy paste
# them into the working directory.

# Download the data:
# download.file('http://hde.onl/subscriptions.txt',
# destfile='subscriptions.txt')

# We can then simply read the subscriptions
# dataset using the read.table function
# subscriptions <-
# read.table('subscriptions.txt', header=TRUE,
# sep=';')
```

```
# We can also read directly from a URL:
URL_subs <- "http://hde.onl/subscriptions.txt"

subscriptions <- read.table(URL_subs, header = TRUE,
    sep = ";")

# Look at the structure of the data. We see that
# there are 227 observations, and 21 variables
# along with the first couple of values of each
# variable
str(subscriptions, vec.len = 0.5)

#-# 'data.frame': 227 obs. of  21 variables:
#-#  $ SubscriptionID    : int  1000024 ...
#-#  $ CustomerID        : int  1150045 ...
#-#  $ ProductID         : int  8 ...
#-#  $ Pattern           : int  1111110 ...
#-#  $ StartDate         : chr   ...
#-#  $ EndDate           : chr   ...
#-#  $ NbrNewspapers     : int  76 ...
#-#  $ NbrStart          : int  25 ...
#-#  $ RenewalDate       : chr   ...
#-#  $ PaymentType       : chr   ...
#-#  $ PaymentStatus     : chr   ...
#-#  $ PaymentDate       : chr   ...
#-#  $ FormulaID         : int  8552 ...
#-#  $ GrossFormulaPrice: num  79 ...
#-#  $ NetFormulaPrice  : num  79 ...
#-#  $ NetNewspaperPrice: num  1.04 ...
#-#  $ ProductDiscount  : int  0 ...
#-#  $ FormulaDiscount  : num  0 ...
#-#  $ TotalDiscount    : num  0 ...
#-#  $ TotalPrice       : num  79 ...
#-#  $ TotalCredit      : num  0 ...

# A special data format is JSON While there are
# several packages that can read this type of
# data we recommend the jsonlite package because
# the result is a data frame, which is usually
# what we want.

if (!require("jsonlite")) {
    install.packages("jsonlite", repos = "https://cran.rstudio.com/",
```

```
        quiet = TRUE)
    require("jsonlite")
}

#-# Loading required package: jsonlite

json_file_url <- "http://hde.onl/json_data.json"
df <- fromJSON(txt = json_file_url)
head(df)

#-#              name  group age (y) height (cm) weight (kg) score
#-# 1      Doe, John    Red      24         182        74.8    NA
#-# 2      Doe, Jane  Green      30         170        70.1   500
#-# 3   Smith, Joan Yellow      41         169        60.0    NA
#-# 4    Brown, Sam  Green      22         183        75.0   865
#-# 5 Jones, Larry  Green      31         178        83.9   221
#-# 6 Murray, Seth    Red      35         172        76.2   413

dim(df)

#-# [1] 7 6

class(df)

#-# [1] "data.frame"

# Speeding up reading in data and reducing memory
# usage:

# 1) The use of colClasses helps R read in data a
# lot faster.


# R automatically determines the column classes
# by reading in part of the data to determine the
# column classes, and then starts all over again
# to read in all the data using these classes.
# This can be slow.  If we are reading in a table
# for the first time, and we don't know the
# classes, we can use the nrow parameter in
# read.table.  We can read in just a few rows of
# the table and then create a vector of classes
# from just the few rows.
subscriptions <- read.table(URL_subs, nrow = 5, header = TRUE,
```

```
    sep = ";")
classes <- sapply(subscriptions, class)
subscriptions <- read.table(URL_subs, header = TRUE,
    sep = ";", colClasses = classes)

# In any case, having R determine the column
# class is poor form if one is reading in data as
# part of an analysis pipeline.  A single
# character vector in a numeric vector can change
# the class.  One should always set the
# colClasses manually. Example:

subscriptions <- read.table(URL_subs, header = TRUE,
    sep = ";", colClasses = c("character", "character",
        "character", "character", "character", "character",
        "integer", "integer", "character", "character",
        "factor", "character", "character", "numeric",
        "numeric", "numeric", "numeric", "numeric",
        "numeric", "numeric", "numeric"))

# Alternatively:
subscriptions <- read.table(URL_subs, header = TRUE,
    sep = ";", colClasses = c(SubscriptionID = "character",
        CustomerID = "character", ProductID = "character",
        Pattern = "character", StartDate = "character",
        EndDate = "character", NbrNewspapers = "integer",
        NbrStart = "integer", RenewalDate = "character",
        PaymentType = "character", PaymentStatus = "factor",
        PaymentDate = "character", FormulaID = "character",
        GrossFormulaPrice = "numeric", NetFormulaPrice = "numeric",
        NetNewspaperPrice = "numeric", ProductDiscount = "numeric",
        FormulaDiscount = "numeric", TotalDiscount = "numeric",
        TotalPrice = "numeric", TotalCredit = "numeric"))


# 2) Another strategy to improve the speed of
# reading in data is setting the 'nrows'
# parameter to the exact number of rows.  It can
# help a lot with memory usage. R doesn't know
# how many rows it's going to read in so it first
# makes a guess, and then when it runs out of
```

```
# room it allocates more memory. These
# allocations can take a lot of time, and if R
# overestimates the amount of memory it needs,
# our computer might run out of memory.

# Of course, we may not know how many rows our
# table has.  The easiest way to find out is to
# look at the data using a text editor. If we're
# on Unix (Mac) we can also use the 'wc' command.
# So if we run 'wc datafile.txt' in Unix, then it
# will report to you the number of lines in the
# file (the first number). We can then pass this
# number to the 'nrows' argument of
# 'read.table()'.

# If we can't use the 'wc' (wordcount) command
# for some reason, but we know that there are
# definitely less than N rows, then we can
# specify 'nrows = N' and things will still be
# okay.  A small overestimate for 'nrows' is
# better than not setting nrows.

# 3) A third strategy to improve read speed is to
# set 'comment.char' in read.table. If our file
# has no comments in it (e.g., lines starting
# with '#'), then setting comment.char = '' will
# sometimes make 'read.table()' run faster.

# 4) A fourth strategy is the data.table package,
# as explained in the dedicated data.table
# section
```

9.2 Python

```
import pandas as pd

#pd.read_table?
subscriptions = pd.read_table('http://hde.onl/subscriptions.txt',
                              delimiter=';')
```

```
subscriptions
#-#      SubscriptionID  CustomerID  ...  TotalPrice  TotalCredit
#-# 0           1000024     1150045  ...        79.0          0.0
#-# 1           1000082     1150046  ...        29.6          0.0
#-# 2            100012       89085  ...       246.8         -2.2
#-# 3            100013       89085  ...       235.0          0.0
#-# 4            100016       89087  ...       246.8         -2.2
#-# ..              ...         ...  ...         ...          ...
#-# 222          101366       89989  ...       123.0          0.0
#-# 223         1013721      159085  ...       267.0          0.0
#-# 224         1013821      449595  ...       267.0          0.0
#-# 225         1013860      659269  ...       267.0          0.0
#-# 226         1013944      760585  ...         NaN          NaN
#-#
#-# [227 rows x 21 columns]
```

```
#Setting the data type for each column
subscriptions = pd.read_table('http://hde.onl/subscriptions.txt',
                              delimiter=';',
                              dtype={'SubscriptionID':      str,
                                     'CustomerID':          str,
                                     'ProductID':           str,
                                     'Pattern':             str,
                                     'StartDate':           str,
                                     'EndDate':             str,
                                     'NbrNewspapers':       int,
                                     'NbrStart':            int,
                                     'RenewalDate':         str,
                                     'PaymentType':         str,
                                     'PaymentStatus':       str,
                                     'PaymentDate':         str,
                                     'FormulaID':           str,
                                     'GrossFormulaPrice':   float,
                                     'NetFormulaPrice':     float,
                                     'NetNewspaperPrice':   float,
                                     'ProductDiscount':     float,
                                     'FormulaDiscount':     float,
                                     'TotalDiscount':       float,
                                     'TotalPrice':          float,
                                     'TotalCredit':         float})
```

```
subscriptions.info()
```

```
#-# <class 'pandas.core.frame.DataFrame'>
#-# RangeIndex: 227 entries, 0 to 226
#-# Data columns (total 21 columns):
#-#  #   Column             Non-Null Count  Dtype
#-# ---  ------             --------------  -----
#-#  0   SubscriptionID     227 non-null    object
#-#  1   CustomerID         227 non-null    object
#-#  2   ProductID          227 non-null    object
#-#  3   Pattern            227 non-null    object
#-#  4   StartDate          227 non-null    object
#-#  5   EndDate            227 non-null    object
#-#  6   NbrNewspapers      227 non-null    int64
#-#  7   NbrStart           227 non-null    int64
#-#  8   RenewalDate        178 non-null    object
#-#  9   PaymentType        227 non-null    object
#-#  10  PaymentStatus      227 non-null    object
#-#  11  PaymentDate        215 non-null    object
#-#  12  FormulaID          227 non-null    object
#-#  13  GrossFormulaPrice  217 non-null    float64
#-#  14  NetFormulaPrice    217 non-null    float64
#-#  15  NetNewspaperPrice  217 non-null    float64
#-#  16  ProductDiscount    217 non-null    float64
#-#  17  FormulaDiscount    217 non-null    float64
#-#  18  TotalDiscount      217 non-null    float64
#-#  19  TotalPrice         217 non-null    float64
#-#  20  TotalCredit        217 non-null    float64
#-# dtypes: float64(8), int64(2), object(11)
#-# memory usage: 37.4+ KB
```

Provided that we have Postgres installed (see Section 2.2.3), we can read data from Postgres using the `psycopg2` module as follows.

```
# pip install psycopg2-binary
import psycopg2
psycopg2.__version__

#-# '2.9.10 (dt dec pq3 ext lo64)'

import pandas as pd

database = {'user': 'postgres',
            'pass': 'book',
            'name': 'postgres',
```

```
            'host': 'localhost',
            'port': '5432'}

pgConnectString = f"""host={database['host']}
                      port={database['port']}
                      dbname={database['name']}
                      user={database['user']}
                      password={database['pass']}"""

pgConnection=psycopg2.connect(pgConnectString)
query = "select * from a;"
result = pd.read_sql_query(query, pgConnection)
pgConnection.close()

print(result)

#-#    id  var_1  var_2
#-# 0   3      8      9
#-# 1   2    105    206
#-# 2   4    111    212
```

9.3 PostgreSQL

`COPY FROM` copies data from a file to a table. The file must be accessible by the postgres user, the user ID the server runs as. Postgres can read csv and text files, but reading csv files comes with more options. For example, the `header` option only works with csv files. First, we need to prepare a table with the exact same structure as the file we are reading.

```
drop table if exists subscriptions;


--Get the code here: http://hde.onl/create_subscriptions.sql
create table subscriptions (
    SubscriptionID text,
    CustomerID text,
    ProductID text,
    Pattern text,
    StartDate text,
    EndDate text,
```

```
    NbrNewspapers int,
    NbrStart int,
    RenewalDate text,
    PaymentType text,
    PaymentStatus text,
    PaymentDate text,
    FormulaID text,
    GrossFormulaPrice float,
    NetFormulaPrice float,
    NetNewspaperPrice float,
    ProductDiscount float,
    FormulaDiscount float,
    TotalDiscount float,
    TotalPrice float,
    TotalCredit float
);
```

```
select * from subscriptions;

#-#  [1] subscriptionid    customerid        productid
#-#  [4] pattern           startdate         enddate
#-#  [7] nbrnewspapers     nbrstart          renewaldate
#-# [10] paymenttype       paymentstatus     paymentdate
#-# [13] formulaid         grossformulaprice netformulaprice
#-# [16] netnewspaperprice productdiscount   formuladiscount
#-# [19] totaldiscount     totalprice        totalcredit
#-# <0 rows> (or 0-length row.names)
```

Reading from disk:

```
---------------------------------------------------------------------
--reading from disk
---------------------------------------------------------------------

--File names in a copy command are read directly by the server, and therefore
--they must be accessible to the database server machine, not the client.
--File accessibility depends on the server, not the client.

--download http://hde.onl/subscriptions.csv
--to your desktop and copy it to a folder that postgres has access to
--such as the temp folder
--Mac: cp /Users/mballin2/Desktop/subscriptions.csv /tmp
```

```
--Windows: cp c:/Users/mballin2/Desktop/subscriptions.csv c:/Temp/
--Then, run the following command:

-- On a Mac:
copy subscriptions
from '/tmp/subscriptions.csv' with (format csv, header true, delimiter ';');

--On a Windows machine:
--Use the same command as above but change the path to:
--'c:\\Temp\\subscriptions.csv'
--Alternatively: 'c:\\Users\\Public'

--select * from subscriptions;
```

Reading from a url with wget

```
truncate subscriptions;


-------------------------------------------------------------------
--reading from a url with wget
-------------------------------------------------------------------

--We can specify a PROGRAM that is to be used by postgres to run a given command,
--before reading from standard output of the program. In this case,
--we use the wget command to download a file.

--find wget in your shell with 'which wget'
--if it is not found:
--https://www.maketecheasier.com/install-wget-mac/
--http://gnuwin32.sourceforge.net/packages/wget.htm

copy subscriptions
from PROGRAM '/opt/homebrew/bin/wget -q -O - "http://hde.onl/subscriptions.csv"' with (format
csv, header true, delimiter ';');

-- The '-q' flag stands for 'quiet'
-- The '-O file' flag stands for 'output to file'
-- The '-O -' (i.e., file = - ) flag stands for 'output to standard output'


select count(*) from subscriptions;
```

```
#-#   count
#-# 1   227
```

```
select * from subscriptions limit 5;
```

```
#-#   subscriptionid customerid productid pattern  startdate
#-# 1        1000024    1150045         8 1111110 18/01/2010
#-# 2        1000082    1150046         8 1111110 14/01/2010
#-# 3         100012      89085         8 1111110 01/01/2008
#-# 4         100013      89085         8 1111110 02/01/2007
#-# 5         100016      89087         8 1111110 01/01/2008
#-#      enddate nbrnewspapers nbrstart renewaldate paymenttype
#-# 1 17/04/2010            76       25  17/03/2010          BT
#-# 2 12/03/2010            50       25  03/03/2010          BT
#-# 3 30/12/2008           304       10  21/11/2008          BT
#-# 4 31/12/2007           304       25  01/12/2007          BT
#-# 5 30/12/2008           304       10  21/11/2008          BT
#-#   paymentstatus paymentdate formulaid grossformulaprice
#-# 1          Paid  27/01/2010      8552           79.0000
#-# 2          Paid  11/02/2010     10017           51.9737
#-# 3          Paid  12/12/2007       875          249.0000
#-# 4          Paid  28/12/2006       874          235.0000
#-# 5          Paid  12/12/2007       875          249.0000
#-#   netformulaprice netnewspaperprice productdiscount
#-# 1            79.0          1.039474               0
#-# 2            29.6          0.592000               0
#-# 3           249.0          0.811842               0
#-# 4           235.0          0.773026               0
#-# 5           249.0          0.811842               0
#-#   formuladiscount totaldiscount totalprice totalcredit
#-# 1          0.0000        0.0000       79.0         0.0
#-# 2         22.3737       22.3737       29.6         0.0
#-# 3          0.0000        0.0000      246.8        -2.2
#-# 4          0.0000        0.0000      235.0         0.0
#-# 5          0.0000        0.0000      246.8        -2.2
```

Reading from a url with curl

```
truncate subscriptions;
```

```
-------------------------------------------------------------------
--reading from a url with curl
-------------------------------------------------------------------
-- curl can be installed from here if you do not have it yet:
-- Windows: https://curl.haxx.se/download.html#Win32
-- Mac: https://curl.haxx.se/download.html#MacOSX

copy subscriptions
from PROGRAM
'curl "http://hde.onl/subscriptions.csv"' with (format csv, header true, delimiter ';');


select * from subscriptions limit 5;

#-#   subscriptionid customerid productid pattern  startdate
#-# 1        1000024    1150045         8 1111110 18/01/2010
#-# 2        1000082    1150046         8 1111110 14/01/2010
#-# 3         100012      89085         8 1111110 01/01/2008
#-# 4         100013      89085         8 1111110 02/01/2007
#-# 5         100016      89087         8 1111110 01/01/2008
#-#      enddate nbrnewspapers nbrstart renewaldate paymenttype
#-# 1 17/04/2010            76       25  17/03/2010          BT
#-# 2 12/03/2010            50       25  03/03/2010          BT
#-# 3 30/12/2008           304       10  21/11/2008          BT
#-# 4 31/12/2007           304       25  01/12/2007          BT
#-# 5 30/12/2008           304       10  21/11/2008          BT
#-#   paymentstatus paymentdate formulaid grossformulaprice
#-# 1          Paid  27/01/2010      8552           79.0000
#-# 2          Paid  11/02/2010     10017           51.9737
#-# 3          Paid  12/12/2007       875          249.0000
#-# 4          Paid  28/12/2006       874          235.0000
#-# 5          Paid  12/12/2007       875          249.0000
#-#   netformulaprice netnewspaperprice productdiscount
#-# 1            79.0          1.039474               0
#-# 2            29.6          0.592000               0
#-# 3           249.0          0.811842               0
#-# 4           235.0          0.773026               0
#-# 5           249.0          0.811842               0
#-#   formuladiscount totaldiscount totalprice totalcredit
#-# 1          0.0000        0.0000       79.0         0.0
#-# 2         22.3737       22.3737       29.6         0.0
#-# 3          0.0000        0.0000      246.8        -2.2
#-# 4          0.0000        0.0000      235.0         0.0
#-# 5          0.0000        0.0000      246.8        -2.2
```

If the above options do not work for you:

```
----------------------------------------------------------------------
--If the above options do not immediately work for you, and wish to move
--on to the next section, we have prepared
--insert statements for you, that you can copy into a sql file and run as
--you would normally run statements:

--http://hde.onl/subscriptions inserts sql
----------------------------------------------------------------------
```

Chapter 10

Data Exploration

To be efficient at preparing data, it is important that we know how to determine the dimensionality of our objects, as well as computing summaries of the contents. Below we present the most common functions and methods for this purpose.

10.1 R

```
URL_subs <- "http://hde.onl/subscriptions.txt"

subscriptions <- read.table(URL_subs, header = TRUE,
    sep = ";")

# What is the class of the object?
class(subscriptions)

#-# [1] "data.frame"

# What are its dimensions? The first number is
# the number of rows, the second number is the
# number of columns.
dim(subscriptions)

#-# [1] 227  21

nrow(subscriptions)  #same as dim(subscriptions)[1]

#-# [1] 227
```

```
ncol(subscriptions)  #same as dim(subscriptions)[2]

#-# [1] 21

# Look at the structure of the object
str(subscriptions, vec.len = 0.5)

#-# 'data.frame': 227 obs. of  21 variables:
#-#  $ SubscriptionID   : int  1000024 ...
#-#  $ CustomerID       : int  1150045 ...
#-#  $ ProductID        : int  8 ...
#-#  $ Pattern          : int  1111110 ...
#-#  $ StartDate        : chr   ...
#-#  $ EndDate          : chr   ...
#-#  $ NbrNewspapers    : int  76 ...
#-#  $ NbrStart         : int  25 ...
#-#  $ RenewalDate      : chr   ...
#-#  $ PaymentType      : chr   ...
#-#  $ PaymentStatus    : chr   ...
#-#  $ PaymentDate      : chr   ...
#-#  $ FormulaID        : int  8552 ...
#-#  $ GrossFormulaPrice: num  79 ...
#-#  $ NetFormulaPrice  : num  79 ...
#-#  $ NetNewspaperPrice: num  1.04 ...
#-#  $ ProductDiscount  : int  0 ...
#-#  $ FormulaDiscount  : num  0 ...
#-#  $ TotalDiscount    : num  0 ...
#-#  $ TotalPrice       : num  79 ...
#-#  $ TotalCredit      : num  0 ...

# Display the first couple of rows
head(subscriptions)

#-#   SubscriptionID CustomerID ProductID Pattern  StartDate
#-# 1        1000024    1150045         8 1111110 18/01/2010
#-# 2        1000082    1150046         8 1111110 14/01/2010
#-# 3         100012      89085         8 1111110 01/01/2008
#-# 4         100013      89085         8 1111110 02/01/2007
#-# 5         100016      89087         8 1111110 01/01/2008
#-# 6         100017      89087         8 1111110 02/01/2007
#-#      EndDate NbrNewspapers NbrStart RenewalDate PaymentType
#-# 1 17/04/2010            76       25  17/03/2010          BT
#-# 2 12/03/2010            50       25  03/03/2010          BT
```

```
#-# 3 30/12/2008          304       10  21/11/2008            BT
#-# 4 31/12/2007          304       25  01/12/2007            BT
#-# 5 30/12/2008          304       10  21/11/2008            BT
#-# 6 31/12/2007          304       25  01/12/2007            BT
#-#   PaymentStatus PaymentDate FormulaID GrossFormulaPrice
#-# 1          Paid  27/01/2010      8552           79.0000
#-# 2          Paid  11/02/2010     10017           51.9737
#-# 3          Paid  12/12/2007       875          249.0000
#-# 4          Paid  28/12/2006       874          235.0000
#-# 5          Paid  12/12/2007       875          249.0000
#-# 6          Paid  13/12/2006       874          235.0000
#-#   NetFormulaPrice NetNewspaperPrice ProductDiscount
#-# 1            79.0          1.039474               0
#-# 2            29.6          0.592000               0
#-# 3           249.0          0.811842               0
#-# 4           235.0          0.773026               0
#-# 5           249.0          0.811842               0
#-# 6           235.0          0.773026               0
#-#   FormulaDiscount TotalDiscount TotalPrice TotalCredit
#-# 1          0.0000        0.0000       79.0         0.0
#-# 2         22.3737       22.3737       29.6         0.0
#-# 3          0.0000        0.0000      246.8        -2.2
#-# 4          0.0000        0.0000      235.0         0.0
#-# 5          0.0000        0.0000      246.8        -2.2
#-# 6          0.0000        0.0000      235.0         0.0

# Display the last couple of rows
tail(subscriptions)

#-#     SubscriptionID CustomerID ProductID Pattern  StartDate
#-# 222         101365      89989         8 1111110 14/05/2007
#-# 223         101366      89989         8 1111110 13/11/2006
#-# 224        1013721     159085         8 1111110 02/03/2010
#-# 225        1013821     449595         8 1111110 02/03/2010
#-# 226        1013860     659269         7 1111110 02/03/2010
#-# 227        1013944     760585         6 1111110 02/03/2010
#-#        EndDate NbrNewspapers NbrStart RenewalDate
#-# 222 12/11/2007           152       25  13/10/2007
#-# 223 12/05/2007           152       15
#-# 224 01/03/2011           304       10  31/01/2011
#-# 225 01/03/2011           304       10  31/01/2011
#-# 226 01/03/2011           304       10  31/01/2011
#-# 227 02/03/2010           304       10
```

```
#-#     PaymentType PaymentStatus PaymentDate FormulaID
#-# 222          BT          Paid  31/05/2007       869
#-# 223          BT          Paid  07/03/2007       153
#-# 224          BT          Paid  16/02/2010      8637
#-# 225          BT          Paid  03/03/2010      8637
#-# 226          BT          Paid  01/03/2010      8640
#-# 227          BT      Not Paid                  8896
#-#     GrossFormulaPrice NetFormulaPrice NetNewspaperPrice
#-# 222               127             127          0.026316
#-# 223               123             123          0.809211
#-# 224               267             267          0.878289
#-# 225               267             267          0.878289
#-# 226               267             267          0.878289
#-# 227                NA              NA                NA
#-#     ProductDiscount FormulaDiscount TotalDiscount
#-# 222               0               0             0
#-# 223               0               0             0
#-# 224               0               0             0
#-# 225               0               0             0
#-# 226               0               0             0
#-# 227              NA              NA            NA
#-#     TotalPrice TotalCredit
#-# 222          4        -123
#-# 223        123           0
#-# 224        267           0
#-# 225        267           0
#-# 226        267           0
#-# 227         NA          NA

# How long is a vector? This is the same as
# nrow(subscriptions)
length(subscriptions$PaymentStatus)

#-# [1] 227

# What are the column names?
colnames(subscriptions)

#-#  [1] "SubscriptionID"    "CustomerID"
#-#  [3] "ProductID"         "Pattern"
#-#  [5] "StartDate"         "EndDate"
#-#  [7] "NbrNewspapers"     "NbrStart"
#-#  [9] "RenewalDate"       "PaymentType"
```

```
#-# [11] "PaymentStatus"     "PaymentDate"
#-# [13] "FormulaID"         "GrossFormulaPrice"
#-# [15] "NetFormulaPrice"   "NetNewspaperPrice"
#-# [17] "ProductDiscount"   "FormulaDiscount"
#-# [19] "TotalDiscount"     "TotalPrice"
#-# [21] "TotalCredit"

# Look at a random subset of the data.
subscriptions[sample(1:nrow(subscriptions), 5), ]

#-#     SubscriptionID CustomerID ProductID Pattern  StartDate
#-# 170        1010293     951565         8 1111110 18/02/2010
#-# 141        1008810      71010         8 1111110 25/02/2010
#-# 115        1006710    1151631         2 1111110 26/01/2010
#-# 158         100976      89721         8 1111110 01/01/2008
#-# 1          1000024    1150045         8 1111110 18/01/2010
#-#        EndDate NbrNewspapers NbrStart RenewalDate
#-# 170 18/03/2011           329       10
#-# 141 28/05/2010            76       10  28/04/2010
#-# 115 24/04/2010            76       25  13/04/2010
#-# 158 30/06/2008           152       10  02/06/2008
#-# 1   17/04/2010            76       25  17/03/2010
#-#     PaymentType PaymentStatus PaymentDate FormulaID
#-# 170          BT          Paid  05/02/2010      9419
#-# 141          BT          Paid  05/02/2010      8801
#-# 115          BT          Paid  21/01/2010      9815
#-# 158          BT          Paid  07/01/2008       870
#-# 1            BT          Paid  27/01/2010      8552
#-#     GrossFormulaPrice NetFormulaPrice NetNewspaperPrice
#-# 170          288.9572             267          0.811550
#-# 141           79.0000              79          1.039474
#-# 115           79.0000              54          0.710526
#-# 158          138.0000             138          0.893421
#-# 1             79.0000              79          1.039474
#-#     ProductDiscount FormulaDiscount TotalDiscount
#-# 170               0        21.95724      21.95724
#-# 141               0         0.00000       0.00000
#-# 115               0        25.00000      25.00000
#-# 158               0         0.00000       0.00000
#-# 1                 0         0.00000       0.00000
#-#     TotalPrice TotalCredit
#-# 170      267.0         0.0
#-# 141       79.0         0.0
```

```
#-# 115        54.0          0.0
#-# 158       135.8         -2.2
#-# 1          79.0          0.0

# Frequencies
table(subscriptions$PaymentStatus)

#-#
#-# Not Paid     Paid
#-#       12      215

# Many functions are object-oriented: the same
# function reacts differently to different data
# types, this is called method dispatching

plot(factor(subscriptions$PaymentStatus))
```

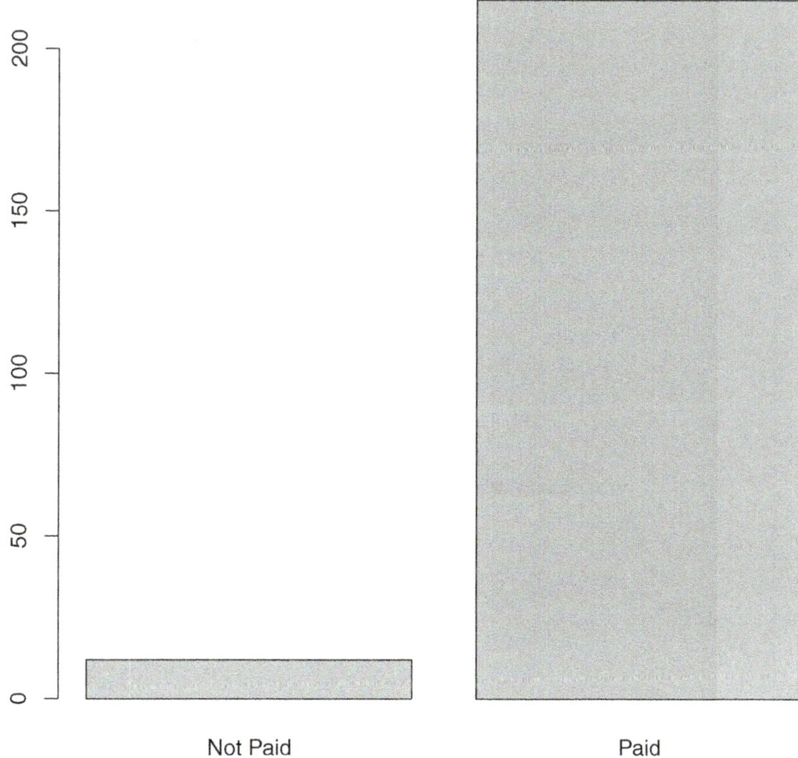


```
plot(sort(subscriptions$TotalPrice))
```

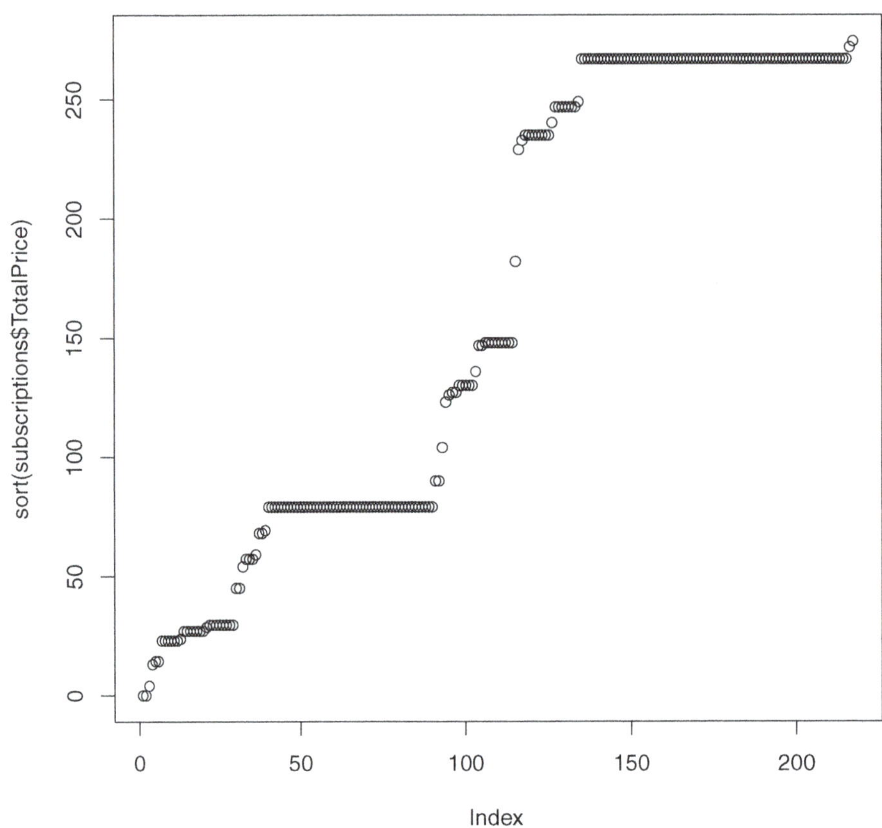


```
pairs(subscriptions[, 17:21]) # a scatterplot matrix of variables in the data
```

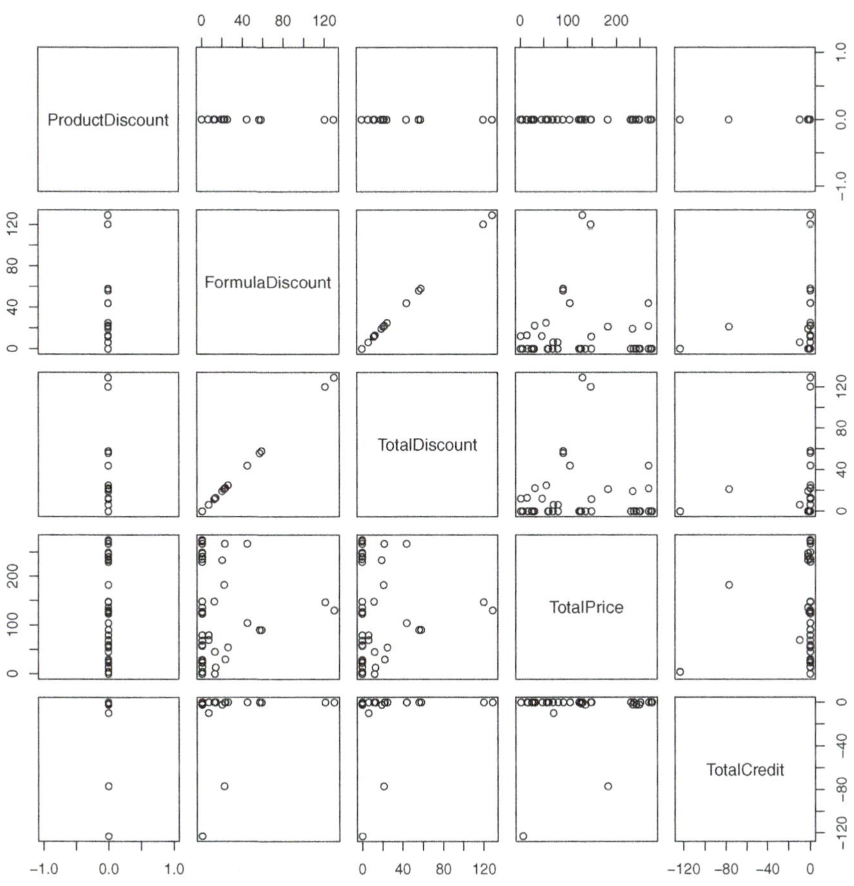


```
# summarize a factor
summary(subscriptions$PaymentStatus)

#-#    Length     Class      Mode
#-#       227 character character

# summarize a numeric variable
summary(subscriptions$TotalPrice)

#-#    Min. 1st Qu.  Median    Mean 3rd Qu.    Max.    NA's
#-#     0.0    79.0   148.0   163.1   267.0   274.4      10
```

```
# A histogram of TotalPrice
hist(subscriptions$TotalPrice)
```

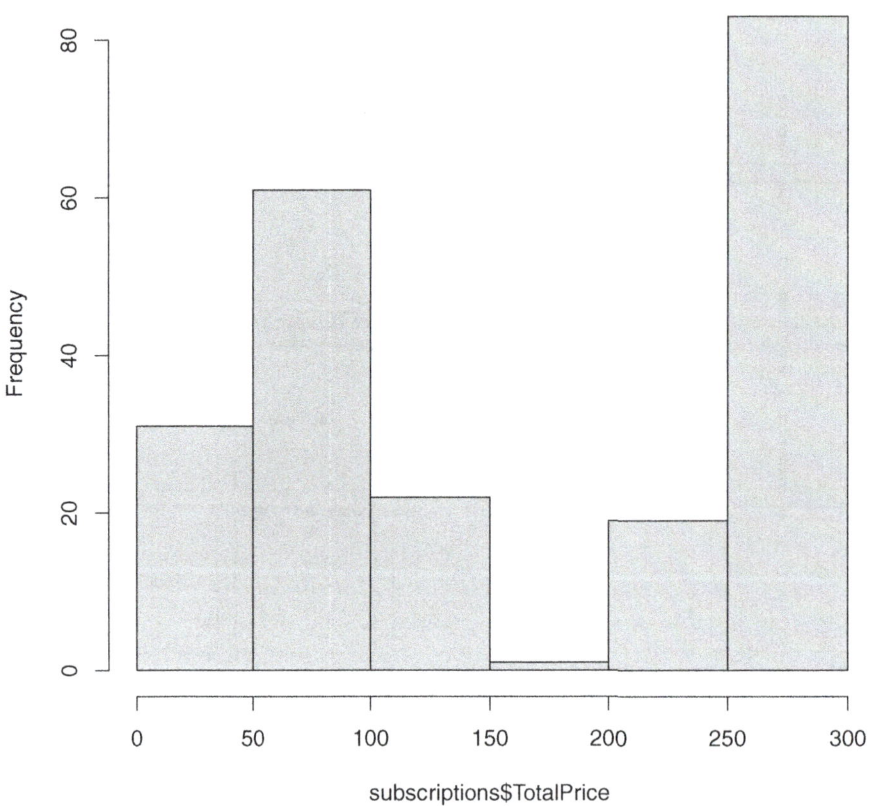


```
# Mean
mean(subscriptions$TotalPrice, na.rm = TRUE)

#-# [1] 163.0524

# Variance
var(subscriptions$TotalPrice, na.rm = TRUE)

#-# [1] 9654.953
```

```
# Standard deviation
sd(subscriptions$TotalPrice, na.rm = TRUE)

#-# [1] 98.25962

# Which values are not missing in TotalPrice?
!is.na(subscriptions$TotalPrice)

#-#   [1]  TRUE  TRUE  TRUE  TRUE  TRUE  TRUE  TRUE  TRUE  TRUE
#-#  [10] FALSE  TRUE  TRUE  TRUE  TRUE  TRUE  TRUE  TRUE  TRUE
#-#  [19]  TRUE FALSE  TRUE  TRUE  TRUE  TRUE  TRUE  TRUE  TRUE
#-#  [28]  TRUE  TRUE  TRUE  TRUE  TRUE  TRUE  TRUE  TRUE  TRUE
#-#  [37]  TRUE  TRUE  TRUE  TRUE  TRUE  TRUE  TRUE  TRUE  TRUE
#-#  [46]  TRUE  TRUE  TRUE  TRUE  TRUE  TRUE  TRUE  TRUE  TRUE
#-#  [55]  TRUE  TRUE  TRUE  TRUE  TRUE  TRUE  TRUE  TRUE  TRUE
#-#  [64]  TRUE  TRUE  TRUE FALSE  TRUE  TRUE  TRUE FALSE  TRUE
#-#  [73]  TRUE  TRUE  TRUE  TRUE  TRUE  TRUE  TRUE  TRUE  TRUE
#-#  [82]  TRUE  TRUE  TRUE  TRUE  TRUE  TRUE  TRUE  TRUE  TRUE
#-#  [91]  TRUE  TRUE  TRUE  TRUE  TRUE  TRUE  TRUE  TRUE  TRUE
#-# [100]  TRUE  TRUE  TRUE  TRUE  TRUE  TRUE  TRUE  TRUE  TRUE
#-# [109]  TRUE  TRUE  TRUE  TRUE  TRUE  TRUE  TRUE  TRUE  TRUE
#-# [118]  TRUE  TRUE  TRUE  TRUE  TRUE  TRUE  TRUE  TRUE  TRUE
#-# [127]  TRUE FALSE  TRUE  TRUE  TRUE  TRUE  TRUE  TRUE  TRUE
#-# [136] FALSE  TRUE  TRUE  TRUE  TRUE  TRUE  TRUE  TRUE  TRUE
#-# [145]  TRUE  TRUE FALSE  TRUE  TRUE  TRUE  TRUE  TRUE  TRUE
#-# [154]  TRUE  TRUE  TRUE  TRUE  TRUE  TRUE  TRUE  TRUE  TRUE
#-# [163]  TRUE  TRUE FALSE  TRUE  TRUE  TRUE  TRUE  TRUE  TRUE
#-# [172]  TRUE  TRUE  TRUE  TRUE  TRUE  TRUE  TRUE  TRUE  TRUE
#-# [181]  TRUE  TRUE  TRUE  TRUE  TRUE  TRUE  TRUE  TRUE  TRUE
#-# [190]  TRUE  TRUE  TRUE  TRUE  TRUE  TRUE  TRUE  TRUE  TRUE
#-# [199] FALSE  TRUE  TRUE  TRUE  TRUE  TRUE  TRUE  TRUE  TRUE
#-# [208]  TRUE  TRUE  TRUE  TRUE  TRUE  TRUE  TRUE  TRUE  TRUE
#-# [217]  TRUE  TRUE  TRUE  TRUE  TRUE  TRUE  TRUE  TRUE  TRUE
#-# [226]  TRUE FALSE

# Correlation between two variables
cor(subscriptions$TotalPrice[!is.na(subscriptions$TotalPrice)],
    subscriptions$NbrNewspapers[!is.na(subscriptions$TotalPrice)])

#-# [1] 0.9588973

# this is easier:
cor(subscriptions$TotalPrice, subscriptions$NbrNewspapers,
    use = "complete.obs")
```

```
#-# [1] 0.9588973

# Range of a variable
range(subscriptions$TotalPrice[!is.na(subscriptions$TotalPrice)])

#-# [1]   0.00 274.44

# Minimum
min(subscriptions$TotalPrice, na.rm = TRUE)

#-# [1] 0

# Maximum
max(subscriptions$TotalPrice, na.rm = TRUE)

#-# [1] 274.44

# Is this a numeric vector?
is.numeric(subscriptions$TotalPrice)

#-# [1] TRUE

is.numeric(subscriptions$CustomerID)

#-# [1] TRUE

# Scatterplot with regression line
plot(subscriptions$NbrNewspapers, subscriptions$TotalPrice)
abline(lm(TotalPrice ~ NbrNewspapers, subscriptions))
```

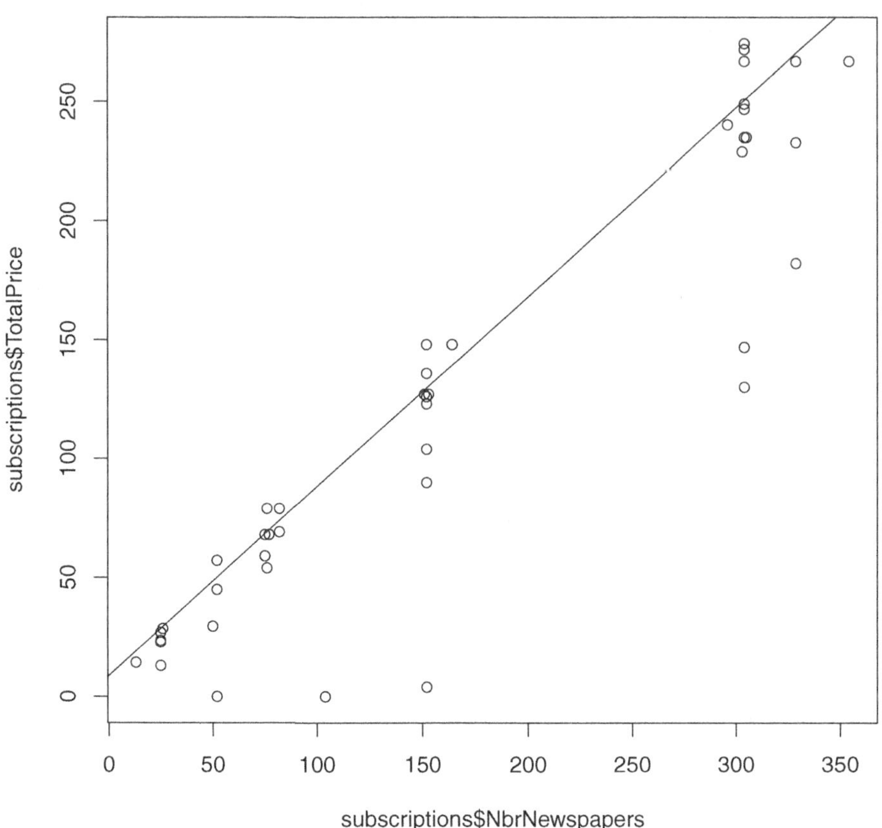


```
# a is the intercept and b is the slope
```

10.2 Python

```
#Pandas and numpy behave very similarly
#Remember that when we subset a pandas dataframe to a single
#variable we get a pandas series, unless we use double square brackets.

######PANDAS
```

```
import pandas as pd
pd.__version__
#-# '2.2.2'
```

```
import numpy as np
np.__version__
```

```
#-# '1.24.2'
```

```
subscriptions = pd.read_table('http://hde.onl/subscriptions.txt',
                              delimiter=';')
```

```
#get number of missing values:
subscriptions.isna().sum()
```

```
#-# SubscriptionID        0
#-# CustomerID            0
#-# ProductID             0
#-# Pattern               0
#-# StartDate             0
#-# EndDate               0
#-# NbrNewspapers         0
#-# NbrStart              0
#-# RenewalDate          49
#-# PaymentType           0
#-# PaymentStatus         0
#-# PaymentDate          12
#-# FormulaID             0
#-# GrossFormulaPrice    10
#-# NetFormulaPrice      10
#-# NetNewspaperPrice    10
#-# ProductDiscount      10
#-# FormulaDiscount      10
#-# TotalDiscount        10
#-# TotalPrice           10
#-# TotalCredit          10
#-# dtype: int64
```

```
#get object type
type(subscriptions)
```

```
#-# <class 'pandas.core.frame.DataFrame'>
```

```
#get the data type of each column
subscriptions.dtypes
```

```
#-# SubscriptionID          int64
#-# CustomerID              int64
#-# ProductID               int64
#-# Pattern                 int64
#-# StartDate              object
#-# EndDate                object
#-# NbrNewspapers           int64
#-# NbrStart                int64
#-# RenewalDate            object
#-# PaymentType            object
#-# PaymentStatus          object
#-# PaymentDate            object
#-# FormulaID               int64
#-# GrossFormulaPrice     float64
#-# NetFormulaPrice       float64
#-# NetNewspaperPrice     float64
#-# ProductDiscount       float64
#-# FormulaDiscount       float64
#-# TotalDiscount         float64
#-# TotalPrice            float64
#-# TotalCredit           float64
#-# dtype: object

#get dimensions of the object
subscriptions.shape

#-# (227, 21)

#Number of rows
len(subscriptions)

#-# 227

#or
subscriptions.shape[0]

#-# 227

#Number of columns
len(subscriptions.columns)

#-# 21

#or
subscriptions.shape[1]
```

```
#-# 21

#The closest equivalent to str() in R:
subscriptions.info()

#-# <class 'pandas.core.frame.DataFrame'>
#-# RangeIndex: 227 entries, 0 to 226
#-# Data columns (total 21 columns):
#-#  #   Column             Non-Null Count  Dtype
#-# ---  ------             --------------  -----
#-#  0   SubscriptionID     227 non-null    int64
#-#  1   CustomerID         227 non-null    int64
#-#  2   ProductID          227 non-null    int64
#-#  3   Pattern            227 non-null    int64
#-#  4   StartDate          227 non-null    object
#-#  5   EndDate            227 non-null    object
#-#  6   NbrNewspapers      227 non-null    int64
#-#  7   NbrStart           227 non-null    int64
#-#  8   RenewalDate        178 non-null    object
#-#  9   PaymentType        227 non-null    object
#-#  10  PaymentStatus      227 non-null    object
#-#  11  PaymentDate        215 non-null    object
#-#  12  FormulaID          227 non-null    int64
#-#  13  GrossFormulaPrice  217 non-null    float64
#-#  14  NetFormulaPrice    217 non-null    float64
#-#  15  NetNewspaperPrice  217 non-null    float64
#-#  16  ProductDiscount    217 non-null    float64
#-#  17  FormulaDiscount    217 non-null    float64
#-#  18  TotalDiscount      217 non-null    float64
#-#  19  TotalPrice         217 non-null    float64
#-#  20  TotalCredit        217 non-null    float64
#-# dtypes: float64(8), int64(7), object(6)
#-# memory usage: 37.4+ KB

#Equivalent to summary() in R:
subscriptions.describe()

#-#        SubscriptionID    CustomerID  ...  TotalPrice  TotalCredit
#-# count    2.270000e+02  2.270000e+02  ...   217.00000   217.000000
#-# mean     8.949570e+05  5.254480e+05  ...   163.05235    -1.072995
#-# std      2.985903e+05  3.820494e+05  ...    98.25962     9.849419
#-# min      1.000120e+05  4.870000e+03  ...     0.00000  -123.000000
#-# 25%      1.002182e+06  1.208705e+05  ...    79.00000     0.000000
#-# 50%      1.005625e+06  5.989740e+05  ...   148.00000     0.000000
```

```
#-# 75%      1.009744e+06  8.595450e+05  ...   267.00000    0.000000
#-# max      1.013944e+06  1.152634e+06  ...   274.44000    0.000000
#-#
#-# [8 rows x 15 columns]
```

```
#first five rows:
subscriptions.head()
```

```
#-#    SubscriptionID  CustomerID  ...  TotalPrice  TotalCredit
#-# 0         1000024     1150045  ...        79.0          0.0
#-# 1         1000082     1150046  ...        29.6          0.0
#-# 2          100012       89085  ...       246.8         -2.2
#-# 3          100013       89085  ...       235.0          0.0
#-# 4          100016       89087  ...       246.8         -2.2
#-#
#-# [5 rows x 21 columns]
```

```
#last five lines
subscriptions.tail()
```

```
#-#      SubscriptionID  CustomerID  ...  TotalPrice  TotalCredit
#-# 222          101366       89989  ...       123.0          0.0
#-# 223         1013721      159085  ...       267.0          0.0
#-# 224         1013821      449595  ...       267.0          0.0
#-# 225         1013860      659269  ...       267.0          0.0
#-# 226         1013944      760585  ...         NaN          NaN
#-#
#-# [5 rows x 21 columns]
```

```
#column names
subscriptions.columns
```

```
#-# Index(['SubscriptionID', 'CustomerID', 'ProductID', 'Pattern', 'StartDate',
#-#        'EndDate', 'NbrNewspapers', 'NbrStart', 'RenewalDate', 'PaymentType',
#-#        'PaymentStatus', 'PaymentDate', 'FormulaID', 'GrossFormulaPrice',
#-#        'NetFormulaPrice', 'NetNewspaperPrice', 'ProductDiscount',
#-#        'FormulaDiscount', 'TotalDiscount', 'TotalPrice', 'TotalCredit'],
#-#       dtype='object')
```

```
#row names
#list(subscriptions.index)


#Equivalent to table() in R:
subscriptions.PaymentType.value_counts()
```

```
#-# PaymentType
#-# BT    211
#-# DD     16
#-# Name: count, dtype: int64

#as percentages:
subscriptions.PaymentType.value_counts()/len(subscriptions.PaymentType)

#-# PaymentType
#-# BT    0.929515
#-# DD    0.070485
#-# Name: count, dtype: float64

#basic plots

import matplotlib.pyplot as plt

#histograms

#one way
# plt.hist(subscriptions['NbrNewspapers'])
# plt.suptitle('Histogram of number of newspapers') #supertitle (above all subplots)
# plt.xlabel('Newspapers')
# plt.ylabel('Frequency')
# plt.show()


#another way
subscriptions['NbrNewspapers'].plot(kind='hist', title='Histogram of number of newspapers')
plt.show()
```

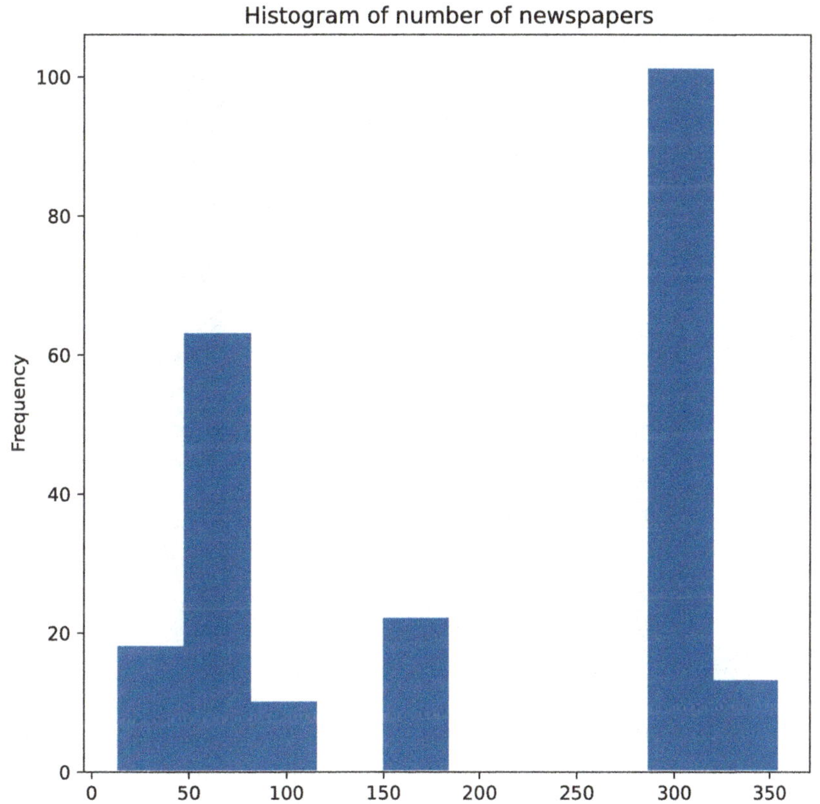


```
#yet another way
subscriptions.hist(column = 'NbrNewspapers')

#-# array([[<AxesSubplot: title={'center': 'NbrNewspapers'}>]], dtype=object)

plt.show()
```

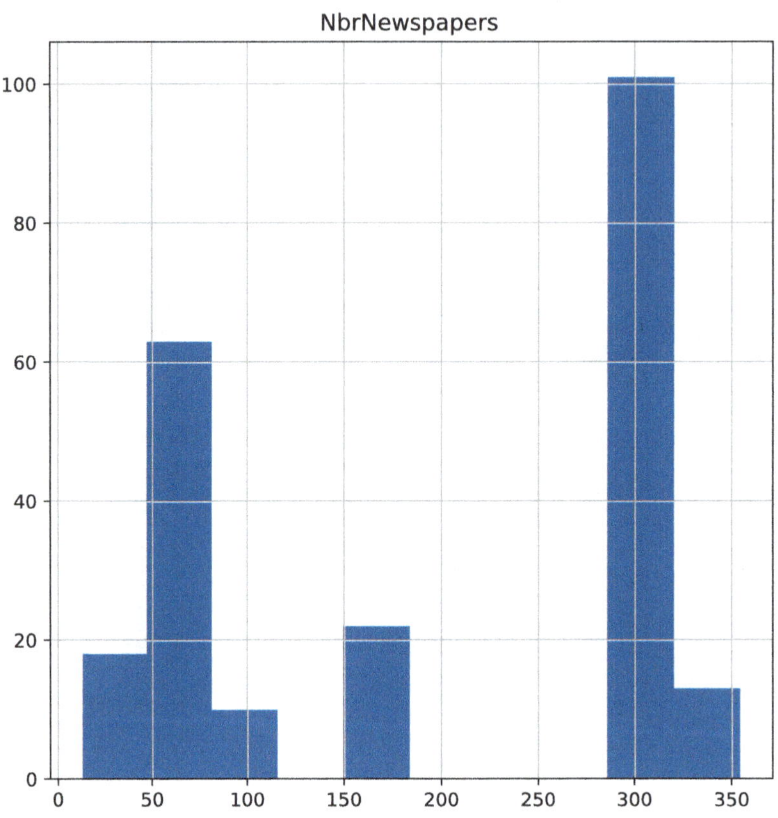


```
#barplots

#compute data
paymenttype_counts = subscriptions.PaymentType.value_counts()
paymenttype_counts

#-# PaymentType
#-# BT    211
#-# DD     16
#-# Name: count, dtype: int64

#show all the methods and attributes
```

```
# dir(paymenttype_counts)
# see an _index attribute and a values attribute

plt.bar(x=list(paymenttype_counts.index),
        height=paymenttype_counts.values)
plt.show()
```

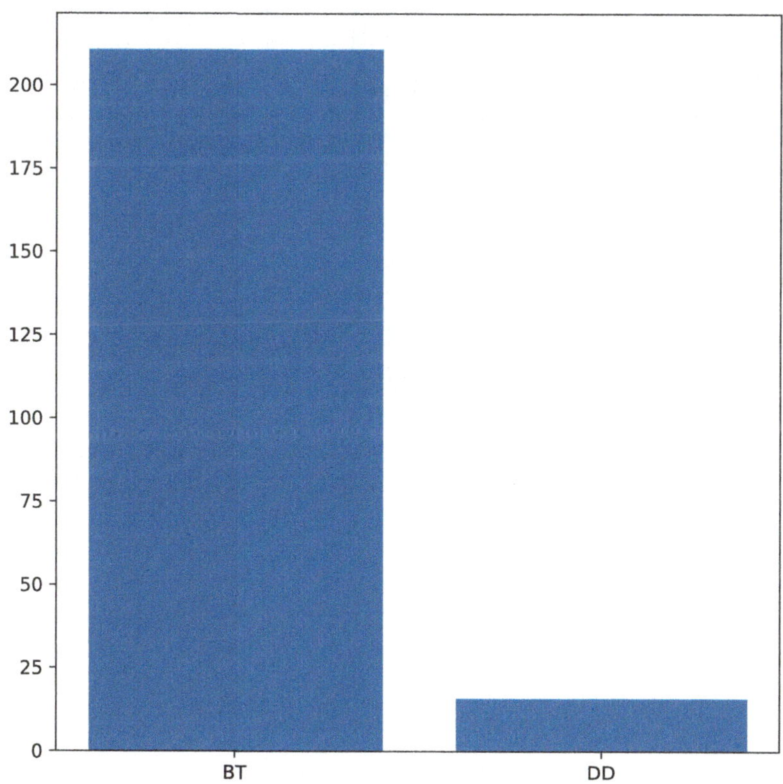


```
#line plots
plt.plot(subscriptions['NbrNewspapers'])
plt.show()
```

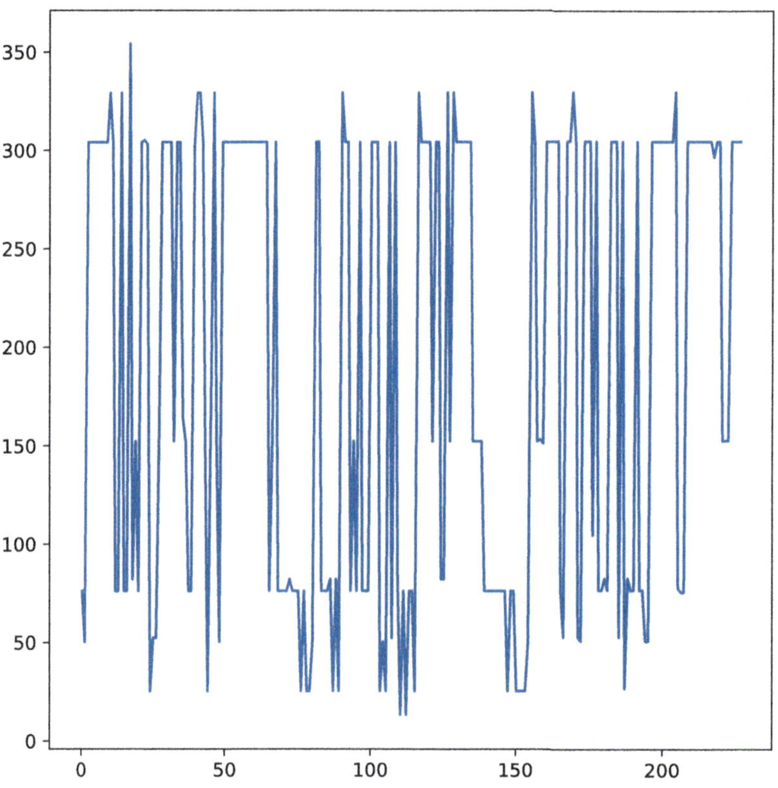


```
#scatter plots
plt.scatter(subscriptions['NbrNewspapers'],
            subscriptions['TotalPrice'] )
plt.show()
```

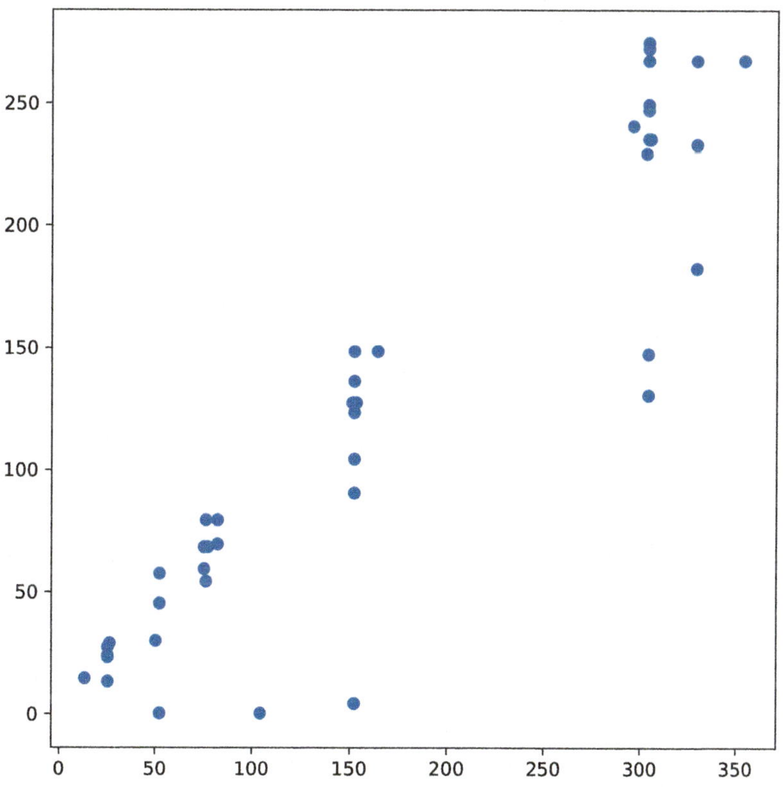


```
#draw a regression line:
import seaborn as sns
sns.lmplot(x='NbrNewspapers',
          y='TotalPrice',
          data=subscriptions, fit_reg=True)
```

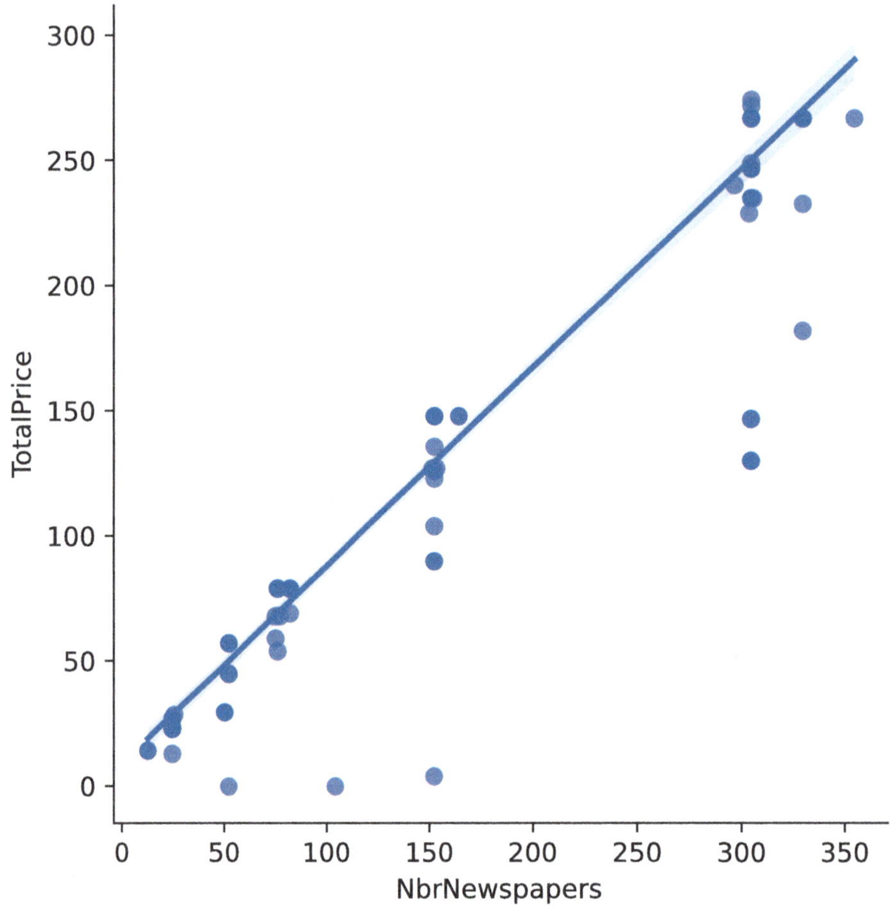


```
plt.show()
```

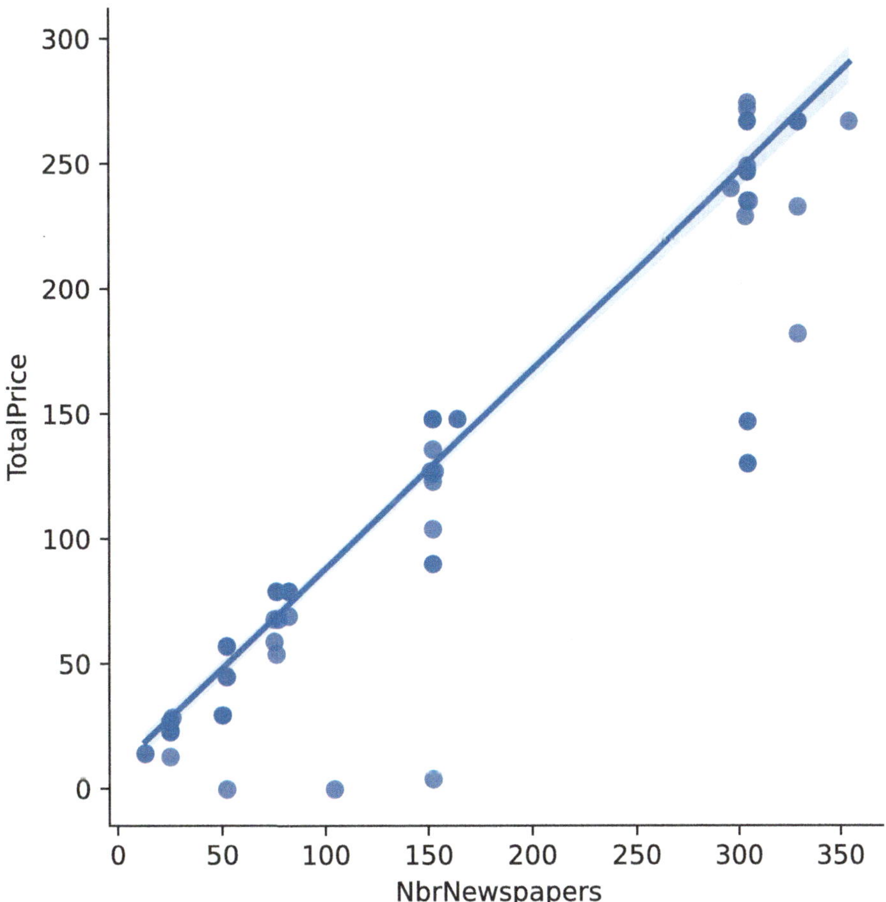


```
#min of a variable
np.min(subscriptions['NbrNewspapers'])

#-# 13

#or
subscriptions['NbrNewspapers'].min()

#-# 13

#min of a variable
np.max(subscriptions['NbrNewspapers'])
```

```
#-# 354

#or
subscriptions['NbrNewspapers'].max()

#-# 354

#mean of a variable
np.mean(subscriptions['NbrNewspapers'])

#-# 194.1409691629956

# or
subscriptions['NbrNewspapers'].mean()

#-# 194.1409691629956

#variance
np.var(subscriptions['NbrNewspapers'])

#-# 13719.504356769972

#or
subscriptions['NbrNewspapers'].var()

#-# 13780.210128260105

#standard deviation
np.std(subscriptions['NbrNewspapers'])

#-# 117.13028795648874

#or
subscriptions['NbrNewspapers'].std()

#-# 117.3891397372862

#correlations
subscriptions['TotalPrice'].corr(subscriptions['NbrNewspapers'])

#-# 0.9588972716472457

#or
#note we are using ~ to negate a boolean pandas series here
np.corrcoef(subscriptions['TotalPrice'][~ subscriptions['TotalPrice'].isna()],
            subscriptions['NbrNewspapers'][~ subscriptions['TotalPrice'].isna()])

#-# array([[1.        , 0.95889727],
#-#        [0.95889727, 1.        ]])
```

```
######NUMPY

NbrNewspapers = subscriptions.NbrNewspapers.to_numpy()
NetNewspaperPrice = subscriptions.NetNewspaperPrice.to_numpy()

#methods
# dir(NbrNewspapers)


#number of dimensions
NbrNewspapers.ndim

#-# 1

#data type
NbrNewspapers.dtype

#-# dtype('int64')

#maximum
NbrNewspapers.max()

#-# 354

#minimum
NbrNewspapers.min()

#-# 13

#variance
NbrNewspapers.var()

#-# 13719.504356769972

#mean
NbrNewspapers.mean()

#-# 194.1409691629956

#length
NbrNewspapers.size

#-# 227

len(NbrNewspapers)

#-# 227
```

```
#shape
NbrNewspapers.shape

#-# (227,)

#standard deviation
NbrNewspapers.std()

#-# 117.13028795648874

#correlation
#~ negates booleans
np.corrcoef(NbrNewspapers[~np.isnan(NetNewspaperPrice)],
            NetNewspaperPrice[~np.isnan(NetNewspaperPrice)])

#-# array([[ 1.        , -0.40082136],
#-#        [-0.40082136,  1.        ]])
```

10.3 PostgreSQL

```
--sample of the data (say 5 records):
select * from subscriptions limit 5;
#-#   subscriptionid customerid productid pattern  startdate
#-# 1        1000024    1150045         8 1111110 18/01/2010
#-# 2        1000082    1150046         8 1111110 14/01/2010
#-# 3         100012      89085         8 1111110 01/01/2008
#-# 4         100013      89085         8 1111110 02/01/2007
#-# 5         100016      89087         8 1111110 01/01/2008
#-#      enddate nbrnewspapers nbrstart renewaldate paymenttype
#-# 1 17/04/2010            76       25  17/03/2010          BT
#-# 2 12/03/2010            50       25  03/03/2010          BT
#-# 3 30/12/2008           304       10  21/11/2008          BT
#-# 4 31/12/2007           304       25  01/12/2007          BT
#-# 5 30/12/2008           304       10  21/11/2008          BT
#-#   paymentstatus paymentdate formulaid grossformulaprice
#-# 1          Paid  27/01/2010      8552           79.0000
#-# 2          Paid  11/02/2010     10017           51.9737
#-# 3          Paid  12/12/2007       875          249.0000
#-# 4          Paid  28/12/2006       874          235.0000
#-# 5          Paid  12/12/2007       875          249.0000
#-#   netformulaprice netnewspaperprice productdiscount
#-# 1            79.0          1.039474               0
```

```
#-# 2          29.6          0.592000          0
#-# 3         249.0          0.811842          0
#-# 4         235.0          0.773026          0
#-# 5         249.0          0.811842          0
#-#   formuladiscount totaldiscount totalprice totalcredit
#-# 1          0.0000        0.0000       79.0         0.0
#-# 2         22.3737       22.3737       29.6         0.0
#-# 3          0.0000        0.0000      246.8        -2.2
#-# 4          0.0000        0.0000      235.0         0.0
#-# 5          0.0000        0.0000      246.8        -2.2
```

```
--columns:
select column_name
from information_schema.columns
where table_name = 'subscriptions'
limit 10;
```

```
#-#           column_name
#-# 1            nbrstart
#-# 2       nbrnewspapers
#-# 3   grossformulaprice
#-# 4     netformulaprice
#-# 5   netnewspaperprice
#-# 6     productdiscount
#-# 7     formuladiscount
#-# 8       totaldiscount
#-# 9          totalprice
#-# 10        totalcredit
```

```
--number of input rows
select count(*) from subscriptions;
```

```
#-#   count
#-# 1   227
```

```
--number of input rows for which the value of the column is not null
select count(totalprice) from subscriptions;
```

```
#-#   count
#-# 1   217
```

```
--number of missing values in a given column:
select count(*) - count(totalprice) from subscriptions;
--select count(*) from subscriptions where totalprice is null; --slower

#-#   ?column?
#-# 1       10


--number of columns:
select count(*)
from (select column_name
      from information_schema.columns
      where table_name = 'subscriptions') as a;

#-#   count
#-# 1    21


--Remember that a select query can return rows in a different order each
--time, regardless of how they are stored. If we want to have
--a guaranteed order, we need to use the order by clause
--The default order direction is ascending (asc)
select customerid, totalprice
from subscriptions
order by totalprice
limit 10;

#-#    customerid totalprice
#-# 1     1120343        0.0
#-# 2      968445        0.0
#-# 3       89989        4.0
#-# 4     1150113       13.0
#-# 5      908515       14.3
#-# 6      138977       14.3
#-# 7      673006       22.9
#-# 8       52794       22.9
#-# 9      303317       22.9
#-# 10     455525       22.9


--descending order
select customerid, totalprice
from subscriptions
where totalprice is not null
```

```
order by totalprice desc
limit 10;

#-#    customerid totalprice
#-# 1      785441     274.44
#-# 2      649604     271.96
#-# 3      675279     267.00
#-# 4     1132498     267.00
#-# 5      892534     267.00
#-# 6      325943     267.00
#-# 7       83885     267.00
#-# 8      191542     267.00
#-# 9     1111604     267.00
#-# 10     809659     267.00


--frequencies
select paymentstatus, count(*)
from subscriptions
group by paymentstatus;

#-#   paymentstatus count
#-# 1      Not Paid    12
#-# 2          Paid   215


--min, avg, max, sum
select min(totalprice),
       avg(totalprice),
       max(totalprice),
       sum(totalprice)
from subscriptions;

#-#   min      avg    max      sum
#-# 1   0 163.0524 274.44 35382.36


--variance and standard deviation
select variance(totalprice),
       stddev(totalprice)
from subscriptions;

#-#   variance   stddev
#-# 1 9654.953 98.25962
```

```
--correlation
select corr(totalprice,nbrnewspapers)
from subscriptions;

#-#        corr
#-# 1 0.9588973


--OLS regression
--first column is Y and second is X
select regr_intercept(totalprice,nbrnewspapers),
       regr_slope(totalprice,nbrnewspapers),
       regr_r2(totalprice,nbrnewspapers)
from subscriptions;

#-#   regr_intercept regr_slope  regr_r2
#-# 1       8.761727  0.7953881 0.919484
```

Up until now we have used standard aggregate functions. Next we will use ordered-set aggregate functions.

```
--mode
select mode() within group (order by totalprice)
from subscriptions;

#-#   mode
#-# 1  267


--percentiles
--there exists percentile_cont (continuous) and percentile_disc (discrete)
--the former interpolates values and the latter returns a value from the data
select
min(totalprice),
percentile_cont(0.01) within group (order by totalprice) as percentile_1,
percentile_cont(0.25) within group (order by totalprice) as first_quartile,
percentile_cont(0.50) within group (order by totalprice) as median,
percentile_cont(0.75) within group (order by totalprice) as third_quartile,
percentile_cont(0.99) within group (order by totalprice) as percentile_99,
max(totalprice)
from subscriptions;

#-#   min percentile_1 first_quartile median third_quartile
```

```
#-# 1   0          5.44           79   148          267
#-#   percentile_99     max
#-# 1             267 274.44
```

Chapter 11

Missing Values

11.1 R

```
if (!require("imputeMissings")) {
    install.packages("imputeMissings", repos = "https://cran.rstudio.com/",
        quiet = FALSE)
    require("imputeMissings")
}
```

```
#-# Loading required package: imputeMissings
```

```
# Compute the values on a training dataset and
# impute them on new data. This is very
# convenient in predictive contexts. For example:

# define training data
(train <- data.frame(v_int = as.integer(c(3, 3, 2,
    5, 1, 2, 4, 6)), v_num = as.numeric(c(4.1, NA,
    12.2, 11, 3.4, 1.6, 3.3, 5.5)), v_fact = as.factor(c("one",
    "two", NA, "two", "two", "one", "two", "two")),
    stringsAsFactors = FALSE))
```

```
#-#   v_int v_num v_fact
#-# 1     3   4.1    one
#-# 2     3    NA    two
#-# 3     2  12.2   <NA>
#-# 4     5  11.0    two
#-# 5     1   3.4    two
```

```
#-# 6      2   1.6    one
#-# 7      4   3.3    two
#-# 8      6   5.5    two

# Compute values on train data randomForest
# method
values <- compute(train, method = "randomForest")
# median/mode method
(values2 <- compute(train))

#-# $v_int
#-# [1] 3
#-#
#-# $v_num
#-# [1] 4.1
#-#
#-# $v_fact
#-# [1] "two"

# define new data
(newdata <- data.frame(v_int = as.integer(c(1, 1, 2,
    NA)), v_num = as.numeric(c(1.1, NA, 2.2, NA)),
    v_fact = as.factor(c("one", "one", "one", NA)),
    stringsAsFactors = FALSE))

#-#   v_int v_num v_fact
#-# 1     1   1.1    one
#-# 2     1    NA    one
#-# 3     2   2.2    one
#-# 4    NA    NA   <NA>

# locate the NA's
is.na(newdata)

#-#      v_int v_num v_fact
#-# [1,] FALSE FALSE  FALSE
#-# [2,] FALSE  TRUE  FALSE
#-# [3,] FALSE FALSE  FALSE
#-# [4,]  TRUE  TRUE   TRUE

# how many missings per variable?
colSums(is.na(newdata))

#-#  v_int  v_num v_fact
#-#      1      2      1
```

```
# Impute on newdata
impute(newdata, object = values)  #using randomForest values

#-#      v_int    v_num v_fact
#-# 1 1.00000 1.100000    one
#-# 2 1.00000 4.065563    one
#-# 3 2.00000 2.200000    one
#-# 4 2.61826 4.065563    one

impute(newdata, object = values2)  #using median/mode values

#-#   v_int v_num v_fact
#-# 1     1   1.1    one
#-# 2     1   4.1    one
#-# 3     2   2.2    one
#-# 4     3   4.1    two

# One can also impute directly in newdata without
# the compute step
impute(newdata)

#-#   v_int v_num v_fact
#-# 1     1  1.10    one
#-# 2     1  1.65    one
#-# 3     2  2.20    one
#-# 4     1  1.65    one

# In data mining it may be useful to have
# indicators for the variables imputations. These
# indicators may be predictive. To create these
# indicators, use flag=TRUE

# Flag parameter
impute(newdata, flag = TRUE)

#-#   v_int v_num v_fact v_int_flag v_num_flag v_fact_flag
#-# 1     1  1.10    one          0          0           0
#-# 2     1  1.65    one          0          1           0
#-# 3     2  2.20    one          0          0           0
#-# 4     1  1.65    one          1          1           1
```

11.2 Python

```
# There are several values in Python that can be used to denote missing data:
#     None: there is no value
#     nan: there is a value, but it is not a number
#     na: there is a value but it is not available
#     null: there is a value and it is null

# Different modules use different conventions.

#####################list###########################

# The default value for missing data in built-in python objects
# is None

a = [1,2,3,None,5]

#Check which values are missing

[x is None for x in a]
#-# [False, False, False, True, False]

#####################numpy array####################
# Numerical Python: numpy

# Missing data is 'unkown yet existing data'. It is a valid value, but is Not A Number (NAN),
and has a similar interpretation in R.
# This means that operations involving missing data will return a missing value.

#The missing data value of choice in numpy is np.nan.
#The main function to detect missings is np.isnan()

import numpy as np
a = np.array([1,2,np.nan,3])
sum(a)

#-# nan

a.sum()

#-# nan

np.isnan(a)

#-# array([False, False,  True, False])
```

```
#numpy does not have na, nor null values. It can have None, which is the standard missing data type in Python, but None can only be of type object, and nan can be of type float, which is more efficient, hence the choice to use nan.

a = np.array([1,2,None,3])
a.dtype #type is object

#-# dtype('O')

a = np.array([1,2,np.nan,3])
a.dtype #type is float

#-# dtype('float64')

#Let's see how long it takes to compute the sum of a large object array and float array (say, 10 times)
import numpy as np
import datetime

for dtype in ['object', 'float']:
    print("dtype =", dtype)
    start = datetime.datetime.now()
    for i in range(10):
        a = np.arange(10000000, dtype=dtype).sum()
    print(datetime.datetime.now() - start)

#-# dtype = object
#-# 0:00:02.856769
#-# dtype = float
#-# 0:00:00.078614

# Because of this speed difference numpy favors nan as a missing value.

# Remember that Nan is a float; there is no equivalent for integers, strings, or other types.


#the following will not work:
# a = np.array([1,2,np.nan,3],dtype=np.int)


####################pandas dataframe################
import pandas as pd
pd.__version__

#-# '2.2.2'
```

```
# pandas is built on top of numpy, so it also uses nan
# we can use np.isnan() on a dataframe
df = pd.DataFrame([[1,np.nan,3],[4,5,6]])
np.isnan(df)

#-#        0      1      2
#-# 0  False   True  False
#-# 1  False  False  False

# however, it does not have a .isnan() method.
# It does have a .isna() mehod (for consistency with R's data.frame)
df.isna()

#-#        0      1      2
#-# 0  False   True  False
#-# 1  False  False  False

df.notna()

#-#       0      1     2
#-# 0  True  False  True
#-# 1  True   True  True

# There is also the is.null() method. It does exactly the same thing
# as .isna(())
df.isnull()

#-#        0      1      2
#-# 0  False   True  False
#-# 1  False  False  False

df.notnull()

#-#       0      1     2
#-# 0  True  False  True
#-# 1  True   True  True

# What happens when np.nan and None are mixed?
df = pd.DataFrame([[1,np.nan,3],[4,5,None]])
df

#-#    0    1    2
#-# 0  1  NaN  3.0
#-# 1  4  5.0  NaN

#pandas will convert None to nan
df.dtypes
```

```
#-# 0      int64
#-# 1    float64
#-# 2    float64
#-# dtype: object

#There is no Nan representation in pandas for strings, booleans, or integer values. Pandas
will cast the entire column from boolean to object, and from integer to float, if NaN are
present. Object columns are not promoted.
#Regardless of this casting, if one subsets the df to extract the NaN, it will be a float.


# How can we handle missing values?
# Two very useful methods are .dropna() and .fillna()

#dropna drops full rows or columns
#the default is to drop all rows in which ANY value is null

df = pd.DataFrame([[1,np.nan,3],[4,5,None],[7,8,9],[10,11,12],[np.nan,np.nan,np.nan]])
df

#-#       0     1     2
#-# 0   1.0   NaN   3.0
#-# 1   4.0   5.0   NaN
#-# 2   7.0   8.0   9.0
#-# 3  10.0  11.0  12.0
#-# 4   NaN   NaN   NaN

df.dropna()

#-#       0     1     2
#-# 2   7.0   8.0   9.0
#-# 3  10.0  11.0  12.0

df.dropna(axis=0)

#-#       0     1     2
#-# 2   7.0   8.0   9.0
#-# 3  10.0  11.0  12.0

#drop columns as follows:
df.dropna(axis=1)

#-# Empty DataFrame
#-# Columns: []
#-# Index: [0, 1, 2, 3, 4]
```

```
#drop rows in which ALL values are missings
df.dropna(how='all')

#-#       0     1     2
#-# 0   1.0   NaN   3.0
#-# 1   4.0   5.0   NaN
#-# 2   7.0   8.0   9.0
#-# 3  10.0  11.0  12.0

#drop rows with a minimum number of 2 non-null values
df.dropna(thresh=2)

#-#       0     1     2
#-# 0   1.0   NaN   3.0
#-# 1   4.0   5.0   NaN
#-# 2   7.0   8.0   9.0
#-# 3  10.0  11.0  12.0

#filling NA values (this will return a copy of the data)
df

#-#       0     1     2
#-# 0   1.0   NaN   3.0
#-# 1   4.0   5.0   NaN
#-# 2   7.0   8.0   9.0
#-# 3  10.0  11.0  12.0
#-# 4   NaN   NaN   NaN

# fill with 0
df.fillna(0)

#-#       0     1     2
#-# 0   1.0   0.0   3.0
#-# 1   4.0   5.0   0.0
#-# 2   7.0   8.0   9.0
#-# 3  10.0  11.0  12.0
#-# 4   0.0   0.0   0.0

#fill with mean
df.mean()

#-# 0    5.5
#-# 1    8.0
#-# 2    8.0
#-# dtype: float64
```

```
df.fillna(df.mean()) #all columns

#-#      0     1     2
#-# 0   1.0   8.0   3.0
#-# 1   4.0   5.0   8.0
#-# 2   7.0   8.0   9.0
#-# 3  10.0  11.0  12.0
#-# 4   5.5   8.0   8.0

df.fillna(df.mean().loc[[0,2]]) #specific columns

#-#      0     1     2
#-# 0   1.0   NaN   3.0
#-# 1   4.0   5.0   8.0
#-# 2   7.0   8.0   9.0
#-# 3  10.0  11.0  12.0
#-# 4   5.5   NaN   8.0

df.fillna(df.mean().loc[[1]]) #specific column (correct! need to retain column name)

#-#      0     1     2
#-# 0   1.0   8.0   3.0
#-# 1   4.0   5.0   NaN
#-# 2   7.0   8.0   9.0
#-# 3  10.0  11.0  12.0
#-# 4   NaN   8.0   NaN

df.fillna(df.mean().loc[1]) #specific column (wrong!)

#-#      0     1     2
#-# 0   1.0   8.0   3.0
#-# 1   4.0   5.0   8.0
#-# 2   7.0   8.0   9.0
#-# 3  10.0  11.0  12.0
#-# 4   8.0   8.0   8.0

# Note that NaN's do not compare but None's do
#nan is a value but it is unknown and not a number
np.nan == np.nan

#-# False

#None means there is no value
None == None

#-# True
```

```
df[1]

#-# 0     NaN
#-# 1     5.0
#-# 2     8.0
#-# 3    11.0
#-# 4     NaN
#-# Name: 1, dtype: float64

df[1] == np.nan

#-# 0    False
#-# 1    False
#-# 2    False
#-# 3    False
#-# 4    False
#-# Name: 1, dtype: bool

# descriptive statistics
# in contrast to numpy, taking the sum of a column
# containing nan does not result in nan
# Pandas sets the nan to 0 and then computes the sum.
df[1].sum()

#-# 24.0

np.array([np.nan]).sum()

#-# nan

pd.DataFrame([np.nan]).sum()

#-# 0    0.0
#-# dtype: float64

# Non null values per column:
df.info()

#-# <class 'pandas.core.frame.DataFrame'>
#-# RangeIndex: 5 entries, 0 to 4
#-# Data columns (total 3 columns):
#-#  #   Column  Non-Null Count  Dtype
#-# ---  ------  --------------  -----
#-#  0   0       4 non-null      float64
#-#  1   1       3 non-null      float64
#-#  2   2       3 non-null      float64
#-# dtypes: float64(3)
#-# memory usage: 248.0 bytes
```

```
# Are any of the values missing per column?
df.isna().any()

#-# 0    True
#-# 1    True
#-# 2    True
#-# dtype: bool

#Are any of the values missing?
df.isna().any().any()

#-# True

#How many missings per column?
df.isna().sum()

#-# 0    1
#-# 1    2
#-# 2    2
#-# dtype: int64

#How many missings in total?
df.isna().sum().sum()

#-# 5
```

11.3 PostgreSQL

Missing values in PostgreSQL are denoted by `null` . Consider the following table:

```
drop table if exists a;


create table a (col1 int, col2 text, col3 int);


insert into a values (1,'a',3), (null,'b',4), (null,null,5), (2,null,6);


select * from a;

#-# col1 col2 col3
#-# 1     a    3
#-#       b    4
```

```
#-#            5
#-# 2          6
```

The following query will return `null` because a null value means that it is unknown. We do not know the value of the first null and we do not know the value of the second null and the values may be different.

```
select null = null;
```

```
#-# ?column?
```

Similarly, the following query will return `null`. The null value might be equal to 1, but we cannot be sure.

```
select null = 1;
```

```
#-# ?column?
```

To do comparisons when `null` values are involved we use the `is` operator.

```
select null is null;
```

```
#-#   ?column?
#-# 1     TRUE
```

```
select col1 from a where col1 is not null;
```

```
#-#   col1
#-# 1    1
#-# 2    2
```

```
--Remember, that ordinary operators will not work
select * from a where col1 != null;
```

```
#-# [1] col1 col2 col3
#-# <0 rows> (or 0-length row.names)
```

To count the number of missing values in a column we use the following trick. `Count(*)` counts all the records (even if all columns in a row are null) and `count(column)` counts the non-missing values:

```
select count(*)-count(col1) from a;

#-#   ?column?
#-# 1        2
```

The above query is much less expensive than the following query, which uses a subsetting operation: `select count(*) from a where col1 is not null;` . The `coalesce` function returns the first of its arguments that is not null. Null is returned only if all arguments are null. The function is often used to substitute a default value for null values when data is retrieved.

```
select coalesce(null,1,2,null);

#-#   coalesce
#-# 1        1
```

```
select coalesce(col1,col3) from a;

#-#   coalesce
#-# 1        1
#-# 2        4
#-# 3        5
#-# 4        2
```

Null values can be imputed with the mean value of that column as follows:

```
select coalesce(col1,(select avg(col1) from a))
from a;

#-#   coalesce
#-# 1      1.0
#-# 2      1.5
#-# 3      1.5
#-# 4      2.0
```

Chapter 12

Operators

The main types of operators are: arithmetic operators, comparison (relational) operators, assignment operators, logical operators, membership operators and identity operators.

12.1 R

```
# Consider the following two variables:
(x <- 1:5)

#-# [1] 1 2 3 4 5

(y <- 3)

#-# [1] 3

################################ Relational
################################ operators
`?`("<")
x < y

#-# [1]  TRUE  TRUE FALSE FALSE FALSE

x <= y

#-# [1]  TRUE  TRUE  TRUE FALSE FALSE

x > y
```

```
#-# [1] FALSE FALSE FALSE  TRUE  TRUE

x >= y

#-# [1] FALSE FALSE  TRUE  TRUE  TRUE

x == y  # note the double =

#-# [1] FALSE FALSE  TRUE FALSE FALSE

x != y

#-# [1]  TRUE  TRUE FALSE  TRUE  TRUE

x %in% y  #which elements of x appear in y?

#-# [1] FALSE FALSE  TRUE FALSE FALSE

y %in% x  #which elements of y appear in x?

#-# [1] TRUE

any(x > 0)  #is any value in x larger than 0?

#-# [1] TRUE

all(x > 0)  #are all values in x larger than 0?

#-# [1] TRUE

any(x > 2)

#-# [1] TRUE

all(x > 2)

#-# [1] FALSE

############################### Logical operators
############################### && and || are
############################### called `double
############################### form' and & and |
############################### are called `single
############################### form' logical
############################### operators.

x == 3 & y == 3  #and
```

```
#-# [1] FALSE FALSE  TRUE FALSE FALSE

x == 3 && y == 3  #double form only evaluates first element of a vector

#-# Error in x == 3 && y == 3: 'length = 5' in coercion to 'logical(1)'

x == 3 | y == 3  #or

#-# [1] TRUE TRUE TRUE TRUE TRUE

x == 3 || y == 3  #double form only evaluates first element of a vector

#-# Error in x == 3 || y == 3: 'length = 5' in coercion to 'logical(1)'

# Missing values (NA) values are regarded as
# non-comparable even to themselves and will
# always return NA instead of TRUE or FALSE.
(y <- NA)

#-# [1] NA

y == 5

#-# [1] NA

# So why would you use the double form? It seems
# useless.  We would use the double form for
# reasons of efficiency.  Evaluation proceeds
# only until the result is determined for the
# double form, whereas for the single form
# everything will be evaluated. Therefore the
# long form is more efficient.

# define fun1 to always return 5
fun1 <- function() {
    cat("fun1 executed \n")
    return(5)
}
# define fun2 to always return 6
fun2 <- function() {
    cat("fun2 executed  \n")
    return(6)
}

fun1() == 5 | fun2() == 6  # we see that both functions were executed
```

```
#-# fun1 executed
#-# fun2 executed
#-# [1] TRUE

fun1() == 5 || fun2() == 6  # we see that only fun1 is executed

#-# fun1 executed
#-# [1] TRUE

# Only fun1 is executed because only one of the
# two conditions needs to be TRUE and since the
# first condition is already TRUE we already know
# the answer.
```

12.2 Python

```
a = 7
b = 3

########################################
#arithmetic operators:
a + b
#-# 10

a - b

#-# 4

a * b

#-# 21

a / b

#-# 2.3333333333333335

a // b #floor division, divide and remove decimals. If one of the operands is negative it
is rounded away from zero

#-# 2

a % b #modulus: divide and return remainder

#-# 1
```

```
a ** b #exponent

#-# 343

########################################
#comparison operators:

a == b

#-# False

a != b

#-# True

a > b

#-# True

a < b

#-# False

a >= b

#-# True

a <= b

#-# False

########################################
#assignment operators

a = 7
b = 3

a += b #add AND, same as a = a + b
a

#-# 10

a -= b #subtract AND, same as a = a - b
a

#-# 7

a *= b #multiply AND, same as a = a * b
a
```

```
#-# 21

a /= b #divide AND, same as a = a / b
a

#-# 7.0

a %= b #moduls AND, same as a = a % b
a

#-# 1.0

a **= b #exponent AND, same as a = a ** b
a

#-# 1.0

a //= b #floor dvision AND, same as a = a // b
a

#-# 0.0

##########################################
#logical operators
a = 7
b = 3

a==7 and b==3

#-# True

a==6 or b==3

#-# True

not(a==6 or b==3)

#-# False

##########################################
#membership operators

a = 3
b = [1,2,3,4]

a in b

#-# True
```

```
a not in b

#-# False

##########################################
#identity operators


a is b #is evaluates to true if the names point to the same object

#-# False

a = 400
b = a

a is b

#-# True

a == b

#-# True

a = 400
b = 400

a is b # see section on memory monitoring and management

#-# False

a == b

#-# True
```

12.3 PostgreSQL

Arithmetic operators

```
select 7 + 3;

#-#   ?column?
#-# 1       10
```

```
select 7 - 3;

#-#   ?column?
#-# 1        4
```

```
select 7 * 3;

#-#   ?column?
#-# 1       21
```

```
select 7.0/3.0;

#-#   ?column?
#-# 1 2.333333
```

```
select 7.0%3.0; -- modulo: divide and return remainder

#-#   ?column?
#-# 1        1
```

```
select 7.0^3.0; --exponent

#-#   ?column?
#-# 1      343
```

```
select @ -5; --absolute value

#-#   ?column?
#-# 1        5
```

```
select |/ 4; --square root

#-#   ?column?
#-# 1        2
```

Comparison operators

```
select 7 = 3; --equal operator is single =

#-#   ?column?
#-# 1    FALSE

select 7 != 3; --not equal

#-#   ?column?
#-# 1     TRUE

select 7 <> 3; --not equal, same as previous line

#-#   ?column?
#-# 1     TRUE

select 7 < 3;

#-#   ?column?
#-# 1    FALSE

select 7 <= 3;

#-#   ?column?
#-# 1    FALSE

select 7 > 3;

#-#   ?column?
#-# 1     TRUE

select 7 >= 3;

#-#   ?column?
#-# 1     TRUE

select 7 between 7 and 7;

#-#   ?column?
#-# 1     TRUE
```

```
select 7 >= 6 and 7 <=8; --same as previous line

#-#   ?column?
#-# 1     TRUE


--Ordinary comparison operators yield null,
--not true or false, when an input is null,
--because it is not known what null represents
--For example, null might be 7 and so it will return null;
select 7 = null;

#-#   ?column?
#-# 1       NA


--To avoid this use:
select 7 IS DISTINCT FROM null;

--'is distinct from' behaves as if null were a normal data value and not unknown, and
--
-- is equivalent to <> for non-null inputs:
-- returns false if both inputs are null, select null IS DISTINCT FROM null;
-- returns true if only one input is null

--Behavior for 'is not distinct from' is similar.

#-#   ?column?
#-# 1     TRUE


--To verify if a value is null use:
select 7 is null;

#-#   ?column?
#-# 1    FALSE


select 7 is not null;

#-#   ?column?
#-# 1     TRUE
```

Logical operators

```
select 7 = 7 or 7 = 3;

#-#   ?column?
#-# 1     TRUE
```

```
select 7 = 7 and 7 = 3;

#-#   ?column?
#-# 1    FALSE
```

```
select 7 = 7 and not 7 = 3; --not can be used with any logical operator

#-#   ?column?
#-# 1     TRUE
```

Membership operators

```
select 7 in (select 7);

#-#   ?column?
#-# 1     TRUE
```

```
select 7 not in (select 7);

#-#   ?column?
#-# 1    FALSE
```

Chapter 13

Conditional Processing

13.1 R

```
# Consider the following self explanatory if then
# construct:
x <- 4

if (x <= 2) {
    print("Smaller than or equal to 2")
} else if (x == 3) {
    print("Equal to 3")
} else {
    print("Greater than 3")
}

#-# [1] "Greater than 3"

# Note that && and || go with if()

# If x is a vector we need to use ifelse()
(x <- 1:5)

#-# [1] 1 2 3 4 5

ifelse(x == 4, 1, 0)

#-# [1] 0 0 0 1 0

# Note that & and | go with ifelse()
```

13.2 Python

```
#For single values

x = 4

if (x <= 2):
    print("<= 2")
elif (x==3):
    print("== 3")
else:
    print("> 3")
#-# > 3

# short form on a single line:
print("<= 2") if x <= 2 else print("== 3") if x==3 else print("> 3")

#-# > 3

#short form is harder to read so it is best to keep it to a single if and else

#For arrays

import numpy as np
x = np.arange(5)
x

#-# array([0, 1, 2, 3, 4])


np.where(x == 3, x, 0)

#-# array([0, 0, 0, 3, 0])
```

13.3 PostgreSQL

```
drop table if exists a;


create table a (col1 int);
```

```
insert into a values (0),(1),(2),(3),(4),(5);
```

```
select * from a;
#-#   col1
#-# 1    0
#-# 2    1
#-# 3    2
#-# 4    3
#-# 5    4
#-# 6    5
```

```
select col1,
       case when col1 <= 1 then 'small'
            when col1 in (2,3) then 'medium'
            when col1 = 4 then 'large'
            else 'super large'
        end
from a;

#-#   col1        case
#-# 1    0       small
#-# 2    1       small
#-# 3    2      medium
#-# 4    3      mcdium
#-# 5    4       large
#-# 6    5 super large
```

The case expression does not evaluate subexpressions that are not needed to determine the result. For example, to avoid division by zero we can use the following query.

```
select col1,
       case when col1 != 0 then 5/col1
       end
from a;

#-#   col1 case
#-# 1    0   NA
#-# 2    1    5
#-# 3    2    2
#-# 4    3    1
```

```
#-# 5     4     1
#-# 6     5     1
```

In pl/pgsql we can also use `case when - when - else - end case`. Alternatively we can use `if - elsif - else - end if`. The keyword `elsif` can also be spelled `elseif`. We provide examples immediately below.

```
do $$
declare
    x int;
begin
    x = 4;
    case
        when x <= 2 then
            raise notice 'Smaller than or equal to 2';
        when x = 3 then
            raise notice 'Equal to 3';
        else
            raise notice 'Greater than 3';
    end case;
end $$

#-# NOTICE:  Greater than 3
```

```
do $$
declare
    x int;
begin
    x = 4;
    if x <= 2 then
        raise notice 'Smaller than or equal to 2';
    elsif x = 3 then
        raise notice 'Equal to 3';
    else
        raise notice 'Greater than 3';
    end if;
end $$

#-# NOTICE:  Greater than 3
```

Chapter 14

Timing Code

14.1 R

If we want to make our code more efficient, we want to measure how long different parts take. There are two ways to do that.

```
# How long does one second take?
start <- Sys.time()
Sys.sleep("1")
round(Sys.time() - start)

#-# Time difference of 1 secs

# or
system.time(Sys.sleep("1"))

#-#    user  system elapsed
#-#   0.000   0.000   1.003
```

14.2 Python

```
import datetime
import time

#how long do three seconds take?
start = datetime.datetime.now()
```

```
time.sleep(3) #sleep for three seconds

print(datetime.datetime.now() - start)
#-# 0:00:03.013969

#or

import timeit

#execute the code 4 times and report the total time
timeit.timeit(stmt='time.sleep(1)',
              setup = 'import time',
              number = 4)

#-# 4.013514416990802

#other example:
timeit.timeit(stmt='np.arange(1000000, dtype=float).sum()',
              setup = 'import numpy as np',
              number = 20)

#-# 0.024836792144924402
```

14.3 PostgreSQL

Three easy ways to measure how long a query takes are the `now()` function, `explain analyze` and `pg_stat_statements` .

now()

We can measure how long a query takes by printing the current time before and after a query.

```
select now();

#-#                     now
#-# 1 2024-11-30 00:22:29


--add 1+1 and sleep 2 seconds
select 1+1, pg_sleep(2);
```

```
#-#   ?column?  pg_sleep
#-# 1        2 blob[0 B]
```

```
select now();
```

```
#-#                      now
#-# 1 2024-11-30 00:22:31
```

explain analyze:

Another way to determine how long a query takes is to use the query plan. A query plan details how postgres is going to execute a query. If we use `explain` without analyze, then we get a description of how postgres is going to execute the query and an estimate of how expensive the query is. In very simple queries, only the cost is given. Below we present an example:

```
explain select 1+1, pg_sleep(2);
```

```
#-# QUERY PLAN
#-# Result (cost=0.00..0.01 rows=1 width=8)
```

We see that the estimated cost of retrieving the first row is 0.00 (in arbitrary units determined by the planner's cost parameters), the cost of retrieving all the rows is 0.01, the estimated number of rows resulting from the query is one row, and the average width of a row is 8 bytes wide. Note that the query is not executed. Postgres merely estimates the cost and uses the latest information that it has about the objects involved (Postgres keeps and periodically updates statistics about tables). When we use `explain analyze` , Postgres does execute the statement (and discards the output information) and we get the actual run time and row counts along with the same estimates that a plain `explain` shows. Note that insert, update and create actually changes data.

```
explain analyze select 1+1, pg_sleep(2);
```

```
#-# QUERY PLAN
#-# Result (cost=0.00..0.01 rows=1 width=8) (actual time=2071.426..2071.427 rows=1 loops=1)
#-# Planning Time: 0.021 ms
```

```
#-# Execution Time: 2071.437 ms
```

The actual time values are in milliseconds of real time, and the cost estimates are in arbitrary units. The number of loops refers to the number of times the action (in this case the entire query) was executed. The planning time is the time it took to generate and optimize the query plan. The execution time is the time to actually execute the plan, excluding planning time, but including executor start-up and shut-down time. That is one of the reasons why it is a little higher than the actual time (i.e., 2071.427 vs 2071.437).

The `explain analyze` way of measuring execution time has the caveat that output rows are not delivered to the client, and therefore network transmission costs and input and ouput time is not included. Therefore, it is sometimes recommended to use the `now()` approach as demonstrated in the beginning of this section.

pg_stat_statements

`Pg_stat_statements` is an external module that records how long each query takes. See Section 5.3 for how to load the module and how to query the data.

Chapter 15

Iteration

15.1 R

Instead of copy pasting code multiple times and changing it slightly, we use loops. This will make our code shorter and less error-prone. The 'for loop' is to be used when the number of iterations is known before executing the loop. Otherwise we can use the 'while or repeat loops'.

```
########### Loop types

# Consider three different loop constructs that
# print 10 numbers to the screen.

# For loop
for (i in 1:10) {
    print(i)
}

#-# [1] 1
#-# [1] 2
#-# [1] 3
#-# [1] 4
#-# [1] 5
#-# [1] 6
#-# [1] 7
#-# [1] 8
#-# [1] 9
#-# [1] 10
```

```
# While loop
i <- 0
while (i < 10) {
    i <- i + 1
    print(i)
}

#-# [1] 1
#-# [1] 2
#-# [1] 3
#-# [1] 4
#-# [1] 5
#-# [1] 6
#-# [1] 7
#-# [1] 8
#-# [1] 9
#-# [1] 10

# Repeat loop
i <- 0
repeat {
    i <- i + 1
    print(i)
    if (i == 10)
        break
}

#-# [1] 1
#-# [1] 2
#-# [1] 3
#-# [1] 4
#-# [1] 5
#-# [1] 6
#-# [1] 7
#-# [1] 8
#-# [1] 9
#-# [1] 10

############ Storing values inside loops

# Example 1:

# Loops are very slow. There is a way to make
```

```r
# them faster: preallocation. If we do not
# preallocate, R will, in each iteration: (1)
# copy the vector, and (2) append one value.
# Preallocation avoids this and is a lot faster.
# Before using a loop, we always need to ask
# ourselves if we really need it. If we are not
# putting a lot of code in our loop then probably
# there is a vectorized version of what we want
# to do. For example, consider the loop below.
# It simply stores the values 1 to 10000000 in an
# integer vector.  Of course we know that we can
# do that by simply doing x <- 1:10000000. We
# have included the three alternatives just
# below:

# slow version
start <- Sys.time()
x <- integer()
for (i in 1:1e+07) {
    x[i] <- i
}
(duration1 <- Sys.time() - start)

#-# Time difference of 1.482063 secs

# faster version (use with preallocation)
start <- Sys.time()
x <- integer(1e+07)
for (i in 1:1e+07) {
    x[i] <- i
}
(duration2 <- Sys.time() - start)

#-# Time difference of 0.2822661 secs

# Preallocation makes our code this many times
# faster:
as.numeric(duration1)/as.numeric(duration2)

#-# [1] 5.250587

# fastest version (use vectorized function)
start <- Sys.time()
x <- 1:1e+07
(duration3 <- Sys.time() - start)
```

```
#-# Time difference of 0.0002698898 secs

# Using the vectorized solution in this case
# makes our code this many times faster:
as.numeric(duration2)/as.numeric(duration3)

#-# [1] 1045.857

########### Applying functions to the columns of
########### data.frames.

df1 <- data.frame(a = c(1, 2), b = c(3, 4), c = c(5,
    6))
df1

#-#   a b c
#-# 1 1 3 5
#-# 2 2 4 6

# column sums and means
colSums(df1)

#-#  a  b  c
#-#  3  7 11

colMeans(df1)

#-#   a   b   c
#-# 1.5 3.5 5.5

# sapply
sapply(df1, sum)

#-#  a  b  c
#-#  3  7 11

# lapply (usually not what we want)
lapply(df1, sum)

#-# $a
#-# [1] 3
#-#
#-# $b
#-# [1] 7
#-#
#-# $c
#-# [1] 11
```

```
# for loop
for (i in 1:ncol(df1)) {
   print(sum(df1[, i]))
}

#-# [1] 3
#-# [1] 7
#-# [1] 11

########### Applying functions to lists

# We could use a loop, but we can also use the
# following two functions: lapply do.call

# Consider the following list
df1 <- data.frame(a = c(1, 2), b = c(3, 4), c = c(5,
   6))
df2 <- data.frame(a = c(7, 8), b = c(9, 10), c = c(11,
   12))

(l <- list(df1, df2))

#-# [[1]]
#-#   a b c
#-# 1 1 3 5
#-# 2 2 4 6
#-#
#-# [[2]]
#-#   a  b  c
#-# 1 7  9 11
#-# 2 8 10 12

# Suppose that we want to stack df1 and df2 We
# would rather use do.call and not use lapply
# Example:

# lapply applies a function over a list
lapply(l, rbind)

#-# [[1]]
#-#   a b c
#-# 1 1 3 5
#-# 2 2 4 6
```

```
#-#
#-# [[2]]
#-#    a  b  c
#-# 1  7  9 11
#-# 2  8 10 12

# That is equivalent to
list(rbind(l[[1]]), rbind(l[[2]]))

#-# [[1]]
#-#   a b c
#-# 1 1 3 5
#-# 2 2 4 6
#-#
#-# [[2]]
#-#    a  b  c
#-# 1  7  9 11
#-# 2  8 10 12

# do.call calls a function with a list of
# arguments
do.call(rbind, l)

#-#    a  b  c
#-# 1  1  3  5
#-# 2  2  4  6
#-# 3  7  9 11
#-# 4  8 10 12

# The latter is equivalent to
rbind(l[[1]], l[[2]])

#-#    a  b  c
#-# 1  1  3  5
#-# 2  2  4  6
#-# 3  7  9 11
#-# 4  8 10 12

# Hence it makes no sense to combine rbind and
# lapply.  However, lapply could be useful for
# other things, such as:
lapply(l, colMeans)
```

```
#-# [[1]]
#-#   a   b   c
#-# 1.5 3.5 5.5
#-#
#-# [[2]]
#-#    a    b    c
#-#  7.5  9.5 11.5

############ Error handling

# Consider the following values
vals <- list(1, 8, 4, -1, "one", 0, 10)

# We are going to loop through it.  In each
# iteration we compute the logarithm

for (i in vals) {
    cat("log(", i, ")=", log(i), "\n")
}

#-# log( 1 )= 0
#-# log( 8 )= 2.079442
#-# log( 4 )= 1.386294

#-# Warning in log(i): NaNs produced

#-# log( -1 )= NaN

#-# Error in log(i): non-numeric argument to mathematical function

# The loop exits early without going through all
# the values. It produces a warning when i=-1 and
# an error when i='one'.

# If we would have been doing some heavy
# computations in our loop and we would have it
# run overnight, we would find an error message
# in the morning.  It would be much better if R
# would simply skip the error and move on to the
# next iteration. R would do as much iterations
# as possible and we can fix the errors
# afterwards.  Essentially we are telling R to
# keep going and skip iterations that produce an
# error so we can investigate the errors later,
```

```
# as opposed to when they are produced.

# Skipping errors can be accomplished with the
# try function as follows:

for (i in vals) {
    try(cat("log(", i, ")=", log(i), "\n"))
}

#-# log( 1 )= 0
#-# log( 8 )= 2.079442
#-# log( 4 )= 1.386294

#-# Warning in log(i): NaNs produced

#-# log( -1 )= NaN
#-# Error in log(i) : non-numeric argument to mathematical function
#-# log( 0 )= -Inf
#-# log( 10 )= 2.302585

# In some cases we want some more power. We might
# want to write our own error or warning
# handlers.  For example, we may want to add 1 to
# i when i=-1.  If we want to do that we can use
# the tryCatch function.

for (i in vals) {
    tryCatch(cat("log(", i, ")=", log(i), "\n"), error = function(x) {
        cat("log(", i, ")=ERROR :", conditionMessage(x),
            "\n")
    }, warning = function(x) {
        cat("log(", i, ")=WARNING :", conditionMessage(x),
            "/// Compute log(", i, "+1) instead=",
            log(i + 1), "\n")
    })
}

#-# log( 1 )= 0
#-# log( 8 )= 2.079442
#-# log( 4 )= 1.386294
#-# log( -1 )=WARNING : NaNs produced /// Compute log( -1 +1) instead= -Inf
#-# log( one )=ERROR : non-numeric argument to mathematical function
#-# log( 0 )= -Inf
#-# log( 10 )= 2.302585
```

15.2 Python

```
#########WHILE LOOP

# basic while loop
x = 0
while x < 10:
    x += 1
    print(x)
#-# 1
#-# 2
#-# 3
#-# 4
#-# 5
#-# 6
#-# 7
#-# 8
#-# 9
#-# 10


# while loop with break and continue statements
x = 0
while x < 10:
    x +- 1
    if x == 3: continue #skip, jump to start of while loop
    if x == 8: break #stop the loop
    print(x)

#-# 1
#-# 2
#-# 4
#-# 5
#-# 6
#-# 7

#Note, there is also a 'pass' statement. It does nothing and is often
#used as a placeholder for future code.

# while loop as a repeat loop
x = 0
while True:
    x += 1
```

```
    print(x)
    if x == 10: break #stop the loop

#-# 1
#-# 2
#-# 3
#-# 4
#-# 5
#-# 6
#-# 7
#-# 8
#-# 9
#-# 10

#Note: there is also an else block to while loops.
#This is out of the scope, of this book.

#########FOR LOOP

#basic for loop
for x in [1,2,3,4,5,6,7,8,9,10]:
    print(x)

#-# 1
#-# 2
#-# 3
#-# 4
#-# 5
#-# 6
#-# 7
#-# 8
#-# 9
#-# 10

#for loop with continue and break statements
for x in [1,2,3,4,5,6,7,8,9,10]:
    if x == 3: continue #skip, jump to start of while loop
    if x == 8: break #stop the loop
    print(x)

#-# 1
#-# 2
#-# 4
#-# 5
```

```
#-# 6
#-# 7

#Note, the object does not have to be a list:
#example with tuple:
for x in (1,2,3,4):
    print(x)

#-# 1
#-# 2
#-# 3
#-# 4

#example with dictionary:
for (key,value) in {'a':1,'b':2,'c':3}.items():
    print(key,value)

#-# a 1
#-# b 2
#-# c 3

# Unpacking tuples
# What happens in "for target in object"?
# In first iteration, this assignment: target = first element of object
# In second iteration, this assignment: target = second element of object
# ...

# Python has a mechanism called unpacking:
(a,b) = (1,2)
a,b #remember that a,b is syntactic sugar for (a,b)

#-# (1, 2)

# This also happens in a loop:
for (a,b) in [(1,2),(3,4),(5,6)]:
    print(a,b)

#-# 1 2
#-# 3 4
#-# 5 6

###############LOOP HELPERS:

######RANGE:

# range() is an iterable.
```

```
# What are iterables?
# Iterable objects are sequences that are stored in memory or generated
# one item at a time in an iteration operation. They respond to the
# iter call and advance in response to next calls.
# Example of an iterable (a string):

s = 'hello'
s_iter = iter(s)
s_iter

#-# <str_iterator object at 0x33f609e10>

next(s_iter)

#-# 'h'

next(s_iter)

#-# 'e'

next(s_iter)

#-# 'l'

next(s_iter)

#-# 'l'

next(s_iter)

#-# 'o'

# When an iterable's values are not stored all at once in memory,
# but produced as requested in an iteration they are called
# generators. Generators can save memory by deferring results as
# needed.

# Every generator is an iterator, but not every iterator is a generator.
# Iterators are created with the iter call and are a more general concept
# than generators. A generator is built by calling a function that has
# at least one yield function.
# We can use the iterator protocol directly when we need to extend a Python object as an
object that can be iterated over.
# However, in most cases, we are best suited to use yield to define a function
# that returns a generator. We will see more information about generators
# in the section on functions.
```

```
# in Python 3.x the range iterable is a generator (in Python 2.x it was not.)

range(10)

#-# range(0, 10)

list(range(10))

#-# [0, 1, 2, 3, 4, 5, 6, 7, 8, 9]

for x in range(10): #generate next number in next iteration
    print(x)

#-# 0
#-# 1
#-# 2
#-# 3
#-# 4
#-# 5
#-# 6
#-# 7
#-# 8
#-# 9

for x in list(range(10)): #generate all numbers first, then iterate
    print(x)

#-# 0
#-# 1
#-# 2
#-# 3
#-# 4
#-# 5
#-# 6
#-# 7
#-# 8
#-# 9

#change a list
l = [1,2,3,4]
for x in range(len(l)):
    l[x] += 10
print(l)
```

```
#-# [11, 12, 13, 14]

######ZIP:

#zip takes two or more sequences and returns tuples that pair the  items in those sequences,
just like a zipper

a = [1,2,3,4]
b = [5,6,7,8]
list(zip(a,b))

#-# [(1, 5), (2, 6), (3, 7), (4, 8)]

for x in zip(a,b):
    print(x)

#-# (1, 5)
#-# (2, 6)
#-# (3, 7)
#-# (4, 8)


######MAP:
#map applies a function to an iterable, similar to the apply family in R
import numpy as np
list(map(np.mean,[(1,2),(2,3),(4,4)]))

#-# [1.5, 2.5, 4.0]

#other example (to show that map returns an iterator, not a list)
res = map(abs,[-1,2,-3])
next(res)

#-# 1

next(res)

#-# 2

next(res)

#-# 3

######ENUMERATE:
#gets the item and counter

#manual counter:
```

```
word = 'hello'
counter = 0 #initialize counter
l = [None] * len(word) #initialize list
for item in word:
    l[counter] = item
    counter += 1 #counter
l

# # ['h', 'e', 'l', 'l', 'o']

#with enumerate
word = 'hello'
l = [None] * len(word) #initialize list
for (counter, item) in enumerate(word):
    l[counter] = item
l

#-# ['h', 'e', 'l', 'l', 'o']

######FILTER:
def foo(x):
    l = ['a', 'e', 'i', 'o', 'u']
    if (x in l):
        return True
    else:
        return False

list(filter(foo,['a','b','c','i']))

#-# ['a', 'i']

#different from map:
list(map(foo, ['a','b','c','i']))

#-# [True, False, False, True]

#########COMPREHENSIONS
#Preliminaries:
#an iterable is an object that supports the iter call
#an iterator is the returned object after applying the iter function

#example
iterable = [1,2,3]
iterator = iter(iterable)
next(iterator)
```

```
#-# 1

# Consider the following loop:
l =  [1,2,3]
for i in range(len(l)):
    l[i] += 10
l

#-# [11, 12, 13]

# A shorter way is to do this with a list comprehension:
# This looks like a backward for loop
l =  [1,2,3]
l = [x + 10  for x in l]
l

#-# [11, 12, 13]

#note that this makes a new list
#the for loop does not


#if clauses
l =  [1,2,3]
l = [x + 10  for x in l if x != 2]
l

#-# [11, 13]

#we can make a generator out of
#a list comprehension by using parentheses
l = (x + 10  for x in l if x != 2)
next(l)

#-# 21
```

15.3 PostgreSQL

There are three main loop constructs: `loop` , `while` , `for` (and `foreach`).

Create toy data:

```
drop table if exists a;


--create an empty table called a with two columns
create table a (
    col_a integer,
    col_b integer);


--insert some data
insert into a (col_a, col_b)
values (1, 2),
       (1, 2),
       (4, 5),
       (4, 5);
```

Loop:

The `continue` statement skips what comes after it, if the condition is true, and returns to the top of the loop. The `exit` statement tells the loop when to stop.

```
DO $$
DECLARE
    counter int = 0; --initialize the variable
BEGIN
    LOOP

        counter = counter + 1;
        CONTINUE WHEN counter = 5; --return to top of loop when counter = 5
        RAISE NOTICE '%', counter;
        EXIT WHEN counter = 10;

    END LOOP;
END $$

#-# NOTICE:  1
#-# NOTICE:  2
#-# NOTICE:  3
#-# NOTICE:  4
#-# NOTICE:  6
#-# NOTICE:  7
#-# NOTICE:  8
```

```
#-# NOTICE:  9
#-# NOTICE:  10
```

While:

The `while` loop statement executes until a condition evaluates to false.

```
DO $$
DECLARE
    counter int = 0; --initialize the variable
BEGIN
    WHILE counter < 10 LOOP

        counter = counter + 1;
        CONTINUE WHEN counter = 5; --return to top of loop when counter = 5
        RAISE NOTICE '%', counter;

    END LOOP;
END $$
```

```
#-# NOTICE:  1
#-# NOTICE:  2
#-# NOTICE:  3
#-# NOTICE:  4
#-# NOTICE:  6
#-# NOTICE:  7
#-# NOTICE:  8
#-# NOTICE:  9
#-# NOTICE:  10
```

For:

The `for` loop is the most common loop statement. Below we provide an example to loop through a range of integers.

```
DO $$
BEGIN
    FOR counter IN 1..10 LOOP

        CONTINUE WHEN counter = 5; --return to top of loop when counter = 5
        RAISE NOTICE '%', counter;
```

```
    END LOOP;
END $$

#-# NOTICE:  1
#-# NOTICE:  2
#-# NOTICE:  3
#-# NOTICE:  4
#-# NOTICE:  6
#-# NOTICE:  7
#-# NOTICE:  8
#-# NOTICE:  9
#-# NOTICE:  10
```

Below we present an example of a `for` loop for looping through a query result. We use the `record` type here, which matches the structure of the result. Individual columns can be accessed with the dot notation as shown below.

```
DO $$
DECLARE
    rec record;
BEGIN
    FOR rec IN (select * from a) LOOP

        RAISE NOTICE '% %', rec.col_a, rec.col_b;

    END LOOP;
END $$

#-# NOTICE:  1 2
#-# NOTICE:  1 2
#-# NOTICE:  4 5
#-# NOTICE:  4 5
```

We can also `for` loop through the result of a dynamic query. We use a dynamic query if we do not know the exact query before run-time. In a dynamic query we concatenate parts of the query that are known, denoted by strings, with variables that take on values when we run the code. Concatenation happens with `||`, and if unsure, one can always print the query itself to the screen with a `raise notice`. Consider, for example, the following nested loop, in which the inner loop uses a dynamic query. In the outer loop we are selecting the column names present in table `a`. In the inner loop we are then using those column names in the query. Specifically, thanks to the dynamic query, the inner loop runs `select col_a from a` and `select col_b from a` as opposed to `select 'col_a' from a` and `select 'col_b' from a`. The latter would not work, because the result would be `'col_a'` and `'col_b'`, i.e., constants, as opposed to returning the values in these columns.

```
DO $$
DECLARE
    val text;
    col text;
    query text;
BEGIN

    FOR col IN (select column_name from information_schema.columns where table_name = 'a')
LOOP
        query = 'select distinct ' || col || ' from a';
        FOR val IN EXECUTE query LOOP

            RAISE NOTICE '% %', col, val;

        END LOOP;
    END LOOP;
END $$

#-# NOTICE:  col_a 4
#-# NOTICE:  col_a 1
#-# NOTICE:  col_b 5
#-# NOTICE:  col_b 2
```

Foreach:

Finally, if we wish to loop through the elements of an array, we use `foreach`. This allows us to loop through the elements inside the column of a single row, as opposed to looping through records.

```
DO $$
DECLARE
    counter int;
BEGIN
    FOREACH counter IN ARRAY ARRAY[1,2,3,4,6,7,8,9,10] LOOP
```

```
        CONTINUE WHEN counter = 5; --return to top of loop when counter = 5
        RAISE NOTICE '%', counter;

    END LOOP;
END $$

#-# NOTICE:  1
#-# NOTICE:  2
#-# NOTICE:  3
#-# NOTICE:  4
#-# NOTICE:  6
#-# NOTICE:  7
#-# NOTICE:  8
#-# NOTICE:  9
#-# NOTICE:  10
```

We can also select from an array in a table.

```
--create a to table
drop table if exists c;


create table c  (
    a integer array
);


insert into c values (array[1,2,3,4,5,6,7,8,9,10]);


DO $$
DECLARE
    counter int;
BEGIN
    FOREACH counter IN ARRAY (select a from c) LOOP

        RAISE NOTICE '%', counter;

    END LOOP;
END $$

#-# NOTICE:  1
#-# NOTICE:  2
```

```
#-# NOTICE:  3
#-# NOTICE:  4
#-# NOTICE:  5
#-# NOTICE:  6
#-# NOTICE:  7
#-# NOTICE:  8
#-# NOTICE:  9
#-# NOTICE:  10
```

Cleaning up:

```
drop table a;
```

```
drop table c;
```

Chapter 16

Creating Dummy Variables

Many algorithms cannot handle categorical variables. Whenever we have a variable with nominal values one option is to transform that variable to dummy, also called indicator, variables. Consider the dataset in Table 16.1. The result of the dummy transformation is displayed in Table 16.2.

Table 16.1: Categorical variables

CustomerID	OwnsCar	lifeCategory
5012953	y	youth
230329	n	mid
254823	n	mid
1943860	y	sen
82942	y	sen

Table 16.2: Dummy variables

CustomerID	OwnsCarYes	OwnsCarNo	lifeYouth	lifeMid	lifeSen
5012953	1	0	1	0	0
230329	0	1	0	1	0
254823	0	1	0	1	0
1943860	1	0	0	0	1
82942	1	0	0	0	1

The dataset in Table 16.2 is, however, not very efficient. We could remove one category of each original variable without losing any information. For example, 'owns car' is either yes or no, so if we would delete the 'owns car: no' column, then we would still know if the customer owns a car or not by looking at the 'owns car: yes' column. If 'owns car: yes' equals 1 then the customer owns a car, otherwise the customer does not. The same goes for life category. We can remove one column without losing any information (e.g., 'lifeSen'). For predictive analytics it is unimportant as to which column to delete. The deleted categories will be represented by the intercept in a regression. If we remove the columns, 'lifeSen' and 'owns car: no' the intercept will represent seniors without a car. Table 16.3 represents an example of the final step in the creation of our dummy variables and represents the most efficient representation of our data. The columns that we remove are called reference variables.

Table 16.3: Dummy variables without reference variables

CustomerID	OwnsCarYes	lifeYouth	lifeMid
5012953	1	1	0
230329	0	0	1
254823	0	0	1
1943860	1	0	0
82942	1	0	0

16.1 R

```
# Create dummies manually
(x <- data.frame(ID = c(1, 1, 2, 2, 3, 3), V1 = c(1,
    2, 3, 4, 4, 4)))

#-#   ID V1
#-# 1  1  1
#-# 2  1  2
#-# 3  2  3
#-# 4  2  4
#-# 5  3  4
#-# 6  3  4

x[, 3] <- ifelse(x$V1 == 1, 1, 0)
x[, 4] <- ifelse(x$V1 == 2, 1, 0)
x[, 5] <- ifelse(x$V1 == 3, 1, 0)
x[, 6] <- ifelse(x$V1 == 4, 1, 0)
x
```

```
#-#   ID V1 V3 V4 V5 V6
#-# 1  1  1  1  0  0  0
#-# 2  1  2  0  1  0  0
#-# 3  2  3  0  0  1  0
#-# 4  2  4  0  0  0  1
#-# 5  3  4  0  0  0  1
#-# 6  3  4  0  0  0  1
```

```
(names(x)[3:6] <- c("V1_1", "V1_2", "V1_3", "V1_4"))
```

```
#-# [1] "V1_1" "V1_2" "V1_3" "V1_4"
```

```
# Create dummy variables automatically
if (!require("dummy")) {
    install.packages("dummy", repos = "https://cran.rstudio.com/",
        quiet = TRUE)
    require("dummy")  #same as library(dummy)
}
```

```
#-# Loading required package: dummy
#-# dummy 0.1.3
#-# dummyNews()
```

```
(x <- data.frame(ID = c(1, 1, 1, 1, 2, 2, 2), V1 = as.character(c(1,
    2, 3, 4, 4, 4, 4)), V2 = as.factor(c(1, 2, 3, 4,
    4, 4, 4))))
```

```
#-#   ID V1 V2
#-# 1  1  1  1
#-# 2  1  2  2
#-# 3  1  3  3
#-# 4  1  4  4
#-# 5  2  4  4
#-# 6  2  4  4
#-# 7  2  4  4
```

```
(x <- dummy(x))
```

```
#-#   V1_1 V1_2 V1_3 V1_4 V2_1 V2_2 V2_3 V2_4
#-# 1    1    0    0    0    1    0    0    0
#-# 2    0    1    0    0    0    1    0    0
#-# 3    0    0    1    0    0    0    1    0
#-# 4    0    0    0    1    0    0    0    1
#-# 5    0    0    0    1    0    0    0    1
#-# 6    0    0    0    1    0    0    0    1
#-# 7    0    0    0    1    0    0    0    1
```

```
# Removing reference variables:
x$V2_4 <- x$V1_4 <- NULL

x

#-#   V1_1 V1_2 V1_3 V2_1 V2_2 V2_3
#-# 1    1    0    0    1    0    0
#-# 2    0    1    0    0    1    0
#-# 3    0    0    1    0    0    1
#-# 4    0    0    0    0    0    0
#-# 5    0    0    0    0    0    0
#-# 6    0    0    0    0    0    0
#-# 7    0    0    0    0    0    0

# train and test

# suppose we would make dummies on train and
# estimate a model
(train <- data.frame(ID = c(1, 1, 1, 1, 2, 2, 2), V1 = as.character(c(1,
    2, 3, 4, 4, 4, 4)), V2 = as.factor(c(1, 2, 3, 4,
    4, 4, 4))))

#-#   ID V1 V2
#-# 1  1  1  1
#-# 2  1  2  2
#-# 3  1  3  3
#-# 4  1  4  4
#-# 5  2  4  4
#-# 6  2  4  4
#-# 7  2  4  4

colnames(dummy(train))

#-# [1] "V1_1" "V1_2" "V1_3" "V1_4" "V2_1" "V2_2" "V2_3" "V2_4"

# then we make dummies on test, and deploy the
# model
(test <- data.frame(ID = c(1, 1, 1, 1, 2, 2, 2), V1 = as.character(c(0,
    21, 3, 4, 10, 4, 11)), V2 = as.factor(c(1, 2, 3,
    4, 5, 7, 20))))

#-#   ID V1 V2
#-# 1  1  0  1
#-# 2  1 21  2
```

```
#-# 3  1  3  3
#-# 4  1  4  4
#-# 5  2 10  5
#-# 6  2  4  7
#-# 7  2 11 20

colnames(dummy(test))

#-#  [1] "V1_0"  "V1_10" "V1_11" "V1_21" "V1_3"  "V1_4"  "V2_1"
#-#  [8] "V2_2"  "V2_3"  "V2_4"  "V2_5"  "V2_7"  "V2_20"

# we have more dummies here and that would break
# the model

# we can use the object parameter to only compute
# dummies for categories available in train

colnames(dummy(test, object = categories(train)))

#-# [1] "V1_1" "V1_2" "V1_3" "V1_4" "V2_1" "V2_2" "V2_3" "V2_4"
```

16.2 Python

```
#consider this toy data frame
import numpy as np
import pandas as pd
df = pd.DataFrame({'A': ['a', 'b', 'c'],
                   'B': ['b', np.nan, 'c'],
                   'C': [1, 2, 3]})
df
#-#    A    B  C
#-# 0  a    b  1
#-# 1  b  NaN  2
#-# 2  c    c  3

df.info()

#-# <class 'pandas.core.frame.DataFrame'>
#-# RangeIndex: 3 entries, 0 to 2
#-# Data columns (total 3 columns):
#-#  #   Column  Non-Null Count  Dtype
```

```
#-# ---  ------  --------------  -----
#-#  0    A       3 non-null      object
#-#  1    B       2 non-null      object
#-#  2    C       3 non-null      int64
#-# dtypes: int64(1), object(2)
#-# memory usage: 200.0+ bytes

#make dummies of all columns of type object
pd.get_dummies(df)

#-#    C    A_a    A_b    A_c    B_b    B_c
#-# 0  1   True  False  False   True  False
#-# 1  2  False   True  False  False  False
#-# 2  3  False  False   True  False   True

#select only certain columns to create dummies for
#note that other columns are retained
pd.get_dummies(df,
               columns=['B'])

#-#    A  C    B_b    B_c
#-# 0  a  1   True  False
#-# 1  b  2  False  False
#-# 2  c  3  False   True

#drop the the first category of each variable
pd.get_dummies(df,
               columns=['B'],
               drop_first=True)

#-#    A  C    B_c
#-# 0  a  1  False
#-# 1  b  2  False
#-# 2  c  3   True

#create dummies for NAs
pd.get_dummies(df,
               columns=['B'],
               drop_first=True,
               dummy_na=True)

#-#    A  C    B_c  B_nan
#-# 0  a  1  False  False
#-# 1  b  2  False   True
#-# 2  c  3   True  False
```

```
# Now consider the situation where we trained a model on
# a data frame called train.
# We then get new data (test) and there are new categories.
# If we would simply apply the get_dummies function,
# we would get different columns.

#train
train = pd.DataFrame({'A': ['a', 'b', 'a'],
                      'C': [1, 2, 3]})
train

#-#   A  C
#-# 0  a  1
#-# 1  b  2
#-# 2  a  3

pd.get_dummies(train,columns=['A'])

#-#   C    A_a    A_b
#-# 0  1   True  False
#-# 1  2  False   True
#-# 2  3   True  False

#test (category b is not there, and there are two new
#      categories, c and d)
test = pd.DataFrame({'A': ['a', 'c', 'd'],
                     'C': [1, 2, 3]})
test

#-#   A  C
#-# 0  a  1
#-# 1  c  2
#-# 2  d  3

pd.get_dummies(test,columns=['A'])

#-#   C    A_a    A_c    A_d
#-# 0  1   True  False  False
#-# 1  2  False   True  False
#-# 2  3  False  False   True

#the problem is that train and test have different dummy variables

#Solution:
#first extract the unique values of train.A and make a categorical type
```

```
#this is very similar to a factor in R
train_A_categorical_type = pd.CategoricalDtype(categories=train.A.unique(),ordered=True)

train_A_categorical_type

#-# CategoricalDtype(categories=['a', 'b'], ordered=True, categories_dtype=object)

#then apply that type to test.A
test.A.dtype #type object

#-# dtype('O')

test["A"] = test["A"].astype(train_A_categorical_type)

test.A.dtype #type categorical

#-# CategoricalDtype(categories=['a', 'b'], ordered=True, categories_dtype=object)

#then create dummies
pd.get_dummies(test,columns=['A'])

#-#    C    A_a    A_b
#-# 0  1   True  False
#-# 1  2  False  False
#-# 2  3  False  False

#now our models will not complain about the different columns
```

16.3 PostgreSQL

Create some toy data:

```
drop table if exists a;


create table a (
    cat_variable text);


insert into a (cat_variable)
values ('a'),
       ('b'),
```

```
    ('a'),
    ('c');
```

```
select * from a;
```

```
#-#   cat_variable
#-# 1            a
#-# 2            b
#-# 3            a
#-# 4            c
```

Creating dummies manually:

```
alter table a
    add column cat_variable_a int,
    add column cat_variable_b int,
    add column cat_variable_c int;
```

```
select * from a;
```

```
#-#   cat_variable cat_variable_a cat_variable_b cat_variable_c
#-# 1            a             NA             NA             NA
#-# 2            b             NA             NA             NA
#-# 3            a             NA             NA             NA
#-# 4            c             NA             NA             NA
```

```
update a set (cat_variable_a, cat_variable_b, cat_variable_c) = (0,0,0);
```

```
select * from a;
```

```
#-#   cat_variable cat_variable_a cat_variable_b cat_variable_c
#-# 1            a              0              0              0
#-# 2            b              0              0              0
#-# 3            a              0              0              0
#-# 4            c              0              0              0
```

```
update a set cat_variable_a = 1
where cat_variable = 'a';
```

```
update a set cat_variable_b = 1
where cat_variable = 'b';


update a set cat_variable_c = 1
where cat_variable = 'c';


select * from a;

#-#   cat_variable cat_variable_a cat_variable_b cat_variable_c
#-# 1            a              1              0              0
#-# 2            a              1              0              0
#-# 3            b              0              1              0
#-# 4            c              0              0              1
```

Creating dummies automatically:

```
alter table a
    drop column cat_variable_a,
    drop column cat_variable_b,
    drop column cat_variable_c;


select * from a;

#-#   cat_variable
#-# 1            a
#-# 2            a
#-# 3            b
#-# 4            c



DO $$
DECLARE
    category text;
    query1 text;
    query2 text;
    query3 text;
BEGIN

    --make a copy of a, for two reasons:
        --have a backup in case something goes wrong
```

```
    --it is used in the for-clause and therefore in an active query when we alter it
  drop table if exists dummies;
  create table dummies as select cat_variable from a;

  FOR category IN (select distinct cat_variable from a) LOOP

    query1 = 'alter table dummies add column cat_variable_' || category || ' int';
    execute query1;

    query2 = 'update dummies set cat_variable_' || category || ' = 0';
    execute query2;

    query3 = 'update dummies set cat_variable_' || category || ' = 1
              where cat_variable = ''' || category || '''';
    --the four quotes at the end of query 3:
      --first quote starts the string
       --second quote escapes the next one
       --third quote is the quote that gets added at the end of category
      --fourth quote ends the string
    execute query3;

  END LOOP;

END $$;


select * from dummies;
#-# cat_variable cat_variable_a cat_variable_b cat_variable_c
#-#            a              1              0              0
#-#            a              1              0              0
#-#            b              0              1              0
#-#            c              0              0              1


drop table if exists a;


drop table if exists dummies;
```

It is important to note that PostgreSQL has a maximum of 1600 columns per table, so creating dummies in PostgreSQL might not be the best course of action if you have more than 1600 categorical values. If creating the dummies in R or Python is not an option for you, one solution may be to use a Postgres array.

Chapter 17

Aggregating

17.1 R

```
# Create a data frame
(x <- data.frame(ID = c(1, 1, 1, 1, 2, 2, 2), V1 = c(1,
    2, 3, 4, 4, 4, 4), V2 = c(1, 2, 3, 4, 4, 4, 4)))

#-#   ID V1 V2
#-# 1  1  1  1
#-# 2  1  2  2
#-# 3  1  3  3
#-# 4  1  4  4
#-# 5  2  4  4
#-# 6  2  4  4
#-# 7  2  4  4

`?`(aggregate)

# sum
aggregate(x[, names(x) != "ID"], by = list(ID = x$ID),
    sum)

#-#   ID V1 V2
#-# 1  1 10 10
#-# 2  2 12 12

# counts
aggregate(x[, names(x) != "ID"], by = list(x$ID), length)
```

```
#-#   Group.1 V1 V2
#-# 1       1  4  4
#-# 2       2  3  3

# Notice the difference in the by argument
# between the first and last aggregate

# first or last observation
aggregate(x[, names(x) != "ID"], by = list(x$ID), head,
    n = 1)

#-#   Group.1 V1 V2
#-# 1       1  1  1
#-# 2       2  4  4

aggregate(x[, names(x) != "ID"], by = list(x$ID), tail,
    n = 1)

#-#   Group.1 V1 V2
#-# 1       1  4  4
#-# 2       2  4  4

# aggregating with multiple functions (e.g., min
# and max):
aggregate(x[, names(x) != "ID"], by = list(ID = x$ID),
    function(x) c(min = min(x), max = max(x)))

#-#   ID V1.min V1.max V2.min V2.max
#-# 1  1      1      4      1      4
#-# 2  2      4      4      4      4
```

17.2 Python

```
import warnings
warnings.simplefilter(action='ignore', category=FutureWarning)

import pandas as pd

#create a daframe
df = pd.DataFrame({'ID': [1,1,1,1,2,2,2],
                   'V1': [1,2,3,4,4,4,4],
```

```
                 'V2': [1,2,3,4,4,4,4]})
df
#-#    ID  V1  V2
#-# 0   1   1   1
#-# 1   1   2   2
#-# 2   1   3   3
#-# 3   1   4   4
#-# 4   2   4   4
#-# 5   2   4   4
#-# 6   2   4   4

# help(df.groupby)

#compute the sum per ID (ID will be index)
x = df.groupby(by='ID').sum()
x

#-#     V1  V2
#-# ID
#-# 1   10  10
#-# 2   12  12

#change names:
x.columns = ['V1_sum','V2_sum']
x

#-#     V1_sum  V2_sum
#-# ID
#-# 1       10      10
#-# 2       12      12

#compute the sum per ID (with as_index=False, ID will be a column)
x = df.groupby(by='ID', as_index=False).sum()
x.rename(columns={'V1':'V1_sum','V2':'V2_sum'}, inplace=True)
x

#-#    ID  V1_sum  V2_sum
#-# 0   1      10      10
#-# 1   2      12      12

#counts
df.groupby(by='ID').count()

#-#     V1  V2
#-# ID
```

```
#-# 1     4   4
#-# 2     3   3
```

```
df.groupby(by='ID').size()
```

```
#-# ID
#-# 1     4
#-# 2     3
#-# dtype: int64
```

```
#first
df.groupby(by='ID').first()
```

```
#-#     V1  V2
#-# ID
#-# 1    1   1
#-# 2    4   4
```

```
#last
df.groupby(by='ID').last()
```

```
#-#     V1  V2
#-# ID
#-# 1    4   4
#-# 2    4   4
```

```
#head (first n, say 2)
df.groupby(by='ID').head(2)
```

```
#-#    ID  V1  V2
#-# 0   1   1   1
#-# 1   1   2   2
#-# 4   2   4   4
#-# 5   2   4   4
```

```
#tail (last n, say 2)
df.groupby(by='ID').tail(2)
```

```
#-#    ID  V1  V2
#-# 2   1   3   3
#-# 3   1   4   4
#-# 5   2   4   4
#-# 6   2   4   4
```

```
#nth (e.g., second)
df.groupby(by='ID').nth(2)
```

```
#-#    ID  V1  V2
#-# 2   1   3   3
#-# 6   2   4   4

#Mutiple functions:
x= df.groupby('ID').agg(['min','max'])
x

#-#     V1      V2
#-#    min max min max
#-# ID
#-# 1    1   4   1   4
#-# 2    4   4   4   4

#same as:
x= df.groupby('ID').aggregate(['min','max'])
x

#-#     V1      V2
#-#    min max min max
#-# ID
#-# 1    1   4   1   4
#-# 2    4   4   4   4

#To make single level columns
#first flatten the columns with ravel to single level
#then join individual elements with "separator".join()
x.columns = ["_".join(y) for y in np.array(x.columns).ravel()]
x

#-#     V1_min  V1_max  V2_min  V2_max
#-# ID
#-# 1        1       4       1       4
#-# 2        4       4       4       4

#Alternatively, to make single level columns:
#Expecting new_column_name = ('selection', aggfunc)
x= df.groupby('ID').aggregate(min_V1=('V1', min),
                              max_V1=('V1', max),
                              min_V2=('V2', min),
                              max_V2=('V2', max))
x

#-#     min_V1  max_V1  min_V2  max_V2
#-# ID
```

```
#-# 1          1        4        1        4
#-# 2          4        4        4        4

#aggregation by two or more columns:
#create a daframe
df = pd.DataFrame({'ID1': [1,1,1,1,2,2,2],
                   'ID2': [1,2,1,2,1,2,1],
                   'V1': [1,2,3,4,4,4,4],
                   'V2': [1,2,3,4,4,4,4]})
df

#-#    ID1  ID2  V1  V2
#-# 0    1    1   1   1
#-# 1    1    2   2   2
#-# 2    1    1   3   3
#-# 3    1    2   4   4
#-# 4    2    1   4   4
#-# 5    2    2   4   4
#-# 6    2    1   4   4

df.groupby(['ID1','ID2']).sum()

#-#          V1  V2
#-# ID1 ID2
#-# 1   1     4   4
#-#     2     6   6
#-# 2   1     8   8
#-#     2     4   4

#if we do not want the groupings ax (multi-)index.
df.groupby(['ID1','ID2'], as_index=False).sum()

#-#    ID1  ID2  V1  V2
#-# 0    1    1   4   4
#-# 1    1    2   6   6
#-# 2    2    1   8   8
#-# 3    2    2   4   4
```

17.3 PostgreSQL

Consider the following data. It has an `id` and two additional columns.

```
drop table if exists a;


create table a (id int, col1 int, col2 int);


insert into a values (1,4,8), (1,5,9), (2,6,10), (2,7,11);


select * from a;

#-#   id col1 col2
#-# 1  1    4    8
#-# 2  1    5    9
#-# 3  2    6   10
#-# 4  2    7   11
```

To aggregate a table, we use the `group by` clause. For example, let's compute the sum of the first column and the average of the second column by id:

```
select id, sum(col1), avg(col2)
from a
group by id;

#-#   id sum  avg
#-# 1  2  13 10.5
#-# 2  1   9  8.5
```

Now, suppose we want only the records for which `sum(col1)=9` . We can subset the result in two ways. The long way uses a subquery approach with a where clause:

```
select *
from (select id, sum(col1) as sum, avg(col2) as avg
      from a
      group by id) as t1
where sum = 9;

#-#   id sum avg
#-# 1  1   9 8.5
```

The short way uses the `having` clause.

```
select id, sum(col1), avg(col2)
from a
group by id
having sum(col1) = 9;

#-#   id sum avg
#-# 1  1   9 8.5
```

All the aggregation functions that we present in Section 10.3 can be used in combination with a `group by` clause.

Chapter 18

Merging

18.1 R

```
# Merging 2 data frames ?merge

# Create two data frames
(x <- data.frame(ID = c(1, 1, 2, 2, 3, 3), V1 = c(1,
    2, 3, 4, 4, 4), V2 = c(1, 2, 3, 4, 4, 4)))

#-#   ID V1 V2
#-# 1  1  1  1
#-# 2  1  2  2
#-# 3  2  3  3
#-# 4  2  4  4
#-# 5  3  4  4
#-# 6  3  4  4

(y <- data.frame(ID = c(2, 2, 3, 3, 4, 4), V3 = c(1,
    2, 3, 4, 4, 4), V4 = c(1, 2, 3, 4, 4, 4)))

#-#   ID V3 V4
#-# 1  2  1  1
#-# 2  2  2  2
#-# 3  3  3  3
#-# 4  3  4  4
#-# 5  4  4  4
#-# 6  4  4  4
```

```
(x_by <- aggregate(x[, names(x) != "ID"], by = list(ID = x$ID),
    sum))

#-#   ID V1 V2
#-# 1  1  3  3
#-# 2  2  7  7
#-# 3  3  8  8

(y_by <- aggregate(y[, names(y) != "ID"], by = list(y$ID),
    sum))

#-#   Group.1 V3 V4
#-# 1       2  3  3
#-# 2       3  7  7
#-# 3       4  8  8

# You can name a column like this:
names(y_by)[1] <- "ID"
# or you can list(ID=x$ID) as for x_by

str(x_by)

#-# 'data.frame': 3 obs. of  3 variables:
#-#  $ ID: num  1 2 3
#-#  $ V1: num  3 7 8
#-#  $ V2: num  3 7 8

str(y_by)

#-# 'data.frame': 3 obs. of  3 variables:
#-#  $ ID: num  2 3 4
#-#  $ V3: num  3 7 8
#-#  $ V4: num  3 7 8

# Inner Join
merge(x_by, y_by, by = "ID")

#-#   ID V1 V2 V3 V4
#-# 1  2  7  7  3  3
#-# 2  3  8  8  7  7

# Left outer join
merge(x_by, y_by, by = "ID", all.x = TRUE)
```

```
#-#   ID V1 V2 V3 V4
#-# 1  1  3  3 NA NA
#-# 2  2  7  7  3  3
#-# 3  3  8  8  7  7

# Right outer join
merge(x_by, y_by, by = "ID", all.y = TRUE)

#-#   ID V1 V2 V3 V4
#-# 1  2  7  7  3  3
#-# 2  3  8  8  7  7
#-# 3  4 NA NA  8  8

# Full outer join
merge(x_by, y_by, by = "ID", all = TRUE)

#-#   ID V1 V2 V3 V4
#-# 1  1  3  3 NA NA
#-# 2  2  7  7  3  3
#-# 3  3  8  8  7  7
#-# 4  4 NA NA  8  8

# Merging multiple data frames

# create a third dataset
(z <- data.frame(ID = c(2, 2, 3, 3, 4, 4), V5 = c(1,
    2, 3, 4, 4, 4), V6 = c(1, 2, 3, 4, 4, 4)))

#-#   ID V5 V6
#-# 1  2  1  1
#-# 2  2  2  2
#-# 3  3  3  3
#-# 4  3  4  4
#-# 5  4  4  4
#-# 6  4  4  4

(z_by <- aggregate(z[, names(z) != "ID"], by = list(ID = z$ID),
    sum))

#-#   ID V5 V6
#-# 1  2  3  3
#-# 2  3  7  7
#-# 3  4  8  8
```

```
# Approach 1: Use a loop (the bad approach,
# correct but slower)
datalist <- list(x_by, y_by, z_by)
for (i in 1:length(datalist)) {
    if (i == 1)
        intermediate <- datalist[[1]]
    if (i > 1)
        intermediate <- merge(intermediate, datalist[[i]],
            by = "ID")
}
intermediate

#-#   ID V1 V2 V3 V4 V5 V6
#-# 1  2  7  7  3  3  3  3
#-# 2  3  8  8  7  7  7  7

# Approach 2: Reduce (the good approach) ?Reduce

# The Reduce function successively combines the
# elements of a given vector. To see the process
# in action, set accumulate=TRUE
str(datalist)

#-# List of 3
#-#  $ :'data.frame': 3 obs. of  3 variables:
#-#   ..$ ID: num [1:3] 1 2 3
#-#   ..$ V1: num [1:3] 3 7 8
#-#   ..$ V2: num [1:3] 3 7 8
#-#  $ :'data.frame': 3 obs. of  3 variables:
#-#   ..$ ID: num [1:3] 2 3 4
#-#   ..$ V3: num [1:3] 3 7 8
#-#   ..$ V4: num [1:3] 3 7 8
#-#  $ :'data.frame': 3 obs. of  3 variables:
#-#   ..$ ID: num [1:3] 2 3 4
#-#   ..$ V5: num [1:3] 3 7 8
#-#   ..$ V6: num [1:3] 3 7 8

Reduce(function(x, y) merge(x, y, by = "ID"), datalist,
    accumulate = TRUE)

#-# [[1]]
#-#   ID V1 V2
#-# 1  1  3  3
```

```
#-# 2  2  7  7
#-# 3  3  8  8
#-#
#-# [[2]]
#-#   ID V1 V2 V3 V4
#-# 1  2  7  7  3  3
#-# 2  3  8  8  7  7
#-#
#-# [[3]]
#-#   ID V1 V2 V3 V4 V5 V6
#-# 1  2  7  7  3  3  3  3
#-# 2  3  8  8  7  7  7  7
```

```
# To keep only the final merge drop the
# accumulate (default is accumulate=FALSE)
Reduce(function(x, y) merge(x, y, by = "ID"), datalist)
```

```
#-#   ID V1 V2 V3 V4 V5 V6
#-# 1  2  7  7  3  3  3  3
#-# 2  3  8  8  7  7  7  7
```

18.2 Python

```
import pandas as pd

#create two daframes
x = pd.DataFrame({'ID': [1,1,2,2,3,3],
                  'V1': [1,2,3,4,4,4],
                  'V2': [1,2,3,4,4,4]})
x
#-#    ID  V1  V2
#-# 0   1   1   1
#-# 1   1   2   2
#-# 2   2   3   3
#-# 3   2   4   4
#-# 4   3   4   4
#-# 5   3   4   4

y = pd.DataFrame({'ID': [2,2,3,3,4,4],
                  'V3': [1,2,3,4,4,4],
```

```
                    'V4': [1,2,3,4,4,4]})
y

#-#    ID  V3  V4
#-# 0   2   1   1
#-# 1   2   2   2
#-# 2   3   3   3
#-# 3   3   4   4
#-# 4   4   4   4
#-# 5   4   4   4

x_by = x.groupby('ID',as_index=False).sum()
x_by.rename(columns={'V1':'V1_sum','V2':'V2_sum'}, inplace=True)
x_by

#-#    ID  V1_sum  V2_sum
#-# 0   1       3       3
#-# 1   2       7       7
#-# 2   3       8       8

y_by = y.groupby('ID',as_index=False).sum()
y_by.rename(columns={'V3':'V3_sum','V4':'V4_sum'}, inplace=True)
y_by

#-#    ID  V3_sum  V4_sum
#-# 0   2       3       3
#-# 1   3       7       7
#-# 2   4       8       8

#Inner join
pd.merge(left=x_by,
         right=y_by,
         how='inner',
         on='ID')

#-#    ID  V1_sum  V2_sum  V3_sum  V4_sum
#-# 0   2       7       7       3       3
#-# 1   3       8       8       7       7

#full outer join
pd.merge(left=x_by,
         right=y_by,
         how='outer',
         on='ID')
```

```
#-#    ID  V1_sum  V2_sum  V3_sum  V4_sum
#-# 0   1     3.0     3.0     NaN     NaN
#-# 1   2     7.0     7.0     3.0     3.0
#-# 2   3     8.0     8.0     7.0     7.0
#-# 3   4     NaN     NaN     8.0     8.0

#left outer join
pd.merge(left=x_by,
         right=y_by,
         how='left',
         on='ID')

#-#    ID  V1_sum  V2_sum  V3_sum  V4_sum
#-# 0   1       3       3     NaN     NaN
#-# 1   2       7       7     3.0     3.0
#-# 2   3       8       8     7.0     7.0

#right outer join
pd.merge(left=x_by,
         right=y_by,
         how='right',
         on='ID')

#-#    ID  V1_sum  V2_sum  V3_sum  V4_sum
#-# 0   2     7.0     7.0       3       3
#-# 1   3     8.0     8.0       7       7
#-# 2   4     NaN     NaN       8       8

# pd.merge is the underlying function for all join behavior.
# pd.DataFrame.merge and pd.DataFrame.join both use pd.merge.

# The last pd.merge query is equivalent to the following
# pd.DataFrame.merge query:
x_by.merge(y_by,
           how='right',
           on='ID')

#-#    ID  V1_sum  V2_sum  V3_sum  V4_sum
#-# 0   2     7.0     7.0       3       3
#-# 1   3     8.0     8.0       7       7
#-# 2   4     NaN     NaN       8       8

# pd.DataFrame.join is a shortcut/convenience to (i.e., it has other defaults) merging on
```

```
index to index, or index to column.
# This is not of interest to us.
```

18.3 PostgreSQL

Create some toy data:

```
drop table if exists a;
```

```
drop table if exists b;
```

```
drop table if exists c;
```

```
create table a (id int, col_a int);
```

```
create table b (id int, col_b int);
```

```
create table c (id int, col_c int);
```

```
insert into a values (1,100),(2,200),(3,300);
```

```
insert into b values (2,400),(3,500),(4,600);
```

```
insert into c values (1,700),(3,800),(4,900);
```

```
select * from a;
```

```
#-#   id col_a
#-# 1  1   100
#-# 2  2   200
#-# 3  3   300
```

```
select * from b;
```

```
#-#   id col_b
#-# 1  2   400
#-# 2  3   500
#-# 3  4   600
```

```
select * from c;
```

```
#-#   id col_c
#-# 1  1   700
#-# 2  3   800
#-# 3  4   900
```

Single inner join

```
select *
from a
inner join b on a.id = b.id;
```

```
#-#   id col_a id col_b
#-# 1  2   200  2   400
#-# 2  3   300  3   500
```

Single left outer join:

```
select *
from a
left outer join b on a.id = b.id;
```

```
#-#   id col_a id col_b
#-# 1  1   100 NA    NA
#-# 2  2   200  2   400
#-# 3  3   300  3   500
```

Single right outer join:

```
select *
from a
right outer join b on a.id = b.id;
```

```
#-#   id col_a id col_b
```

```
#-# 1  2   200  2   400
#-# 2  3   300  3   500
#-# 3 NA    NA  4   600
```

Single full outer join:

```
select *
from a
full outer join b on a.id = b.id;

#-#   id col_a id col_b
#-# 1  1   100 NA    NA
#-# 2  2   200  2   400
#-# 3  3   300  3   500
#-# 4 NA    NA  4   600


--if we wish to have a single id column that has all the values:
select *, coalesce(a.id,b.id)
from a
full outer join b on a.id = b.id;

#-#   id col_a id col_b coalesce
#-# 1  1   100 NA    NA        1
#-# 2  2   200  2   400        2
#-# 3  3   300  3   500        3
#-# 4 NA    NA  4   600        4
```

Multi-join:

```
--Multiple joins
--Reading and writing multiple joins can be confusing
--In the query below, it appears that there is first
--an inner join between table a and b, and then
--a right outer join between table a and c.
--That is not what actually happens.
--Postgres indeed first joins a and b, but then
--does something else.
--What then does a multi-join query do?
--Postgres incrementally performs single joins
--between two tables at a time.
--Each single join generates a single intermediate table
--that is then joined to the next table.
```

```
select *
from a
inner join b on a.id = b.id
right outer join c on a.id = c.id;

--The steps are:
--Step 1: table a and b are joined, call it a_b
--Step 2: table a_b and c are joined

--The confusion stems from the table reference
--in the on-clause. It is not so that the second
--join merges with table a because a.id is used
--in the on-clause. The 'a.' in 'a.id' is there
--to identify the right column in the intermediate
--table (which contains both a.id and b.id).
```

```
#-#   id col_a id col_b id col_c
#-# 1 NA    NA NA    NA  1   700
#-# 2  3   300  3   500  3   800
#-# 3 NA    NA NA    NA  4   900
```

Chapter 19

Stacking

19.1 R

```
df1 <- data.frame(a = c(1, 2), b = c(3, 4), c = c(5,
    6))
df1
```

```
#-#   a b c
#-# 1 1 3 5
#-# 2 2 4 6
```

```
df2 <- data.frame(a = c(7, 8), b = c(9, 10), c = c(11,
    12))
df2
```

```
#-#   a  b  c
#-# 1 7  9 11
#-# 2 8 10 12
```

```
rbind(df1, df2)
```

```
#-#   a  b  c
#-# 1 1  3  5
#-# 2 2  4  6
#-# 3 7  9 11
#-# 4 8 10 12
```

19.2 Python

```
import pandas as pd
df1 = pd.DataFrame({'col1': [1,2], 'col2':[3,4]})
df2 = pd.DataFrame({'col1': [5,6], 'col2':[7,8]})
print(df1)
#-#    col1  col2
#-# 0     1     3
#-# 1     2     4

print(df2)

#-#    col1  col2
#-# 0     5     7
#-# 1     6     8

print(pd.concat([df1, df2]))

#-#    col1  col2
#-# 0     1     3
#-# 1     2     4
#-# 0     5     7
#-# 1     6     8
```

19.3 PostgreSQL

The result of two or more queries can be combined when the queries are union compatible. This means that they need to return the same columns and compatible data types. Below we will provide examples of three ways to stack queries: `union` , `intersect` , `except` .

Create toy data:

```
--create an empty table called a with two columns
create table a (
    col_a integer,
    col_b integer);
```

```
--insert some data
insert into a (col_a, col_b)
values (1, 2),
       (1, 2),
       (4, 5),
       (4, 5);


--create an empty table called b with two columns
create table b (
    col_a integer,
    col_b integer);


--insert some data
insert into b (col_a, col_b)
values  (1, 2),
        (1, 2),
        (10, 11);


select * from a;

#-#   col_a col_b
#-# 1     1     2
#-# 2     1     2
#-# 3     4     5
#-# 4     4     5


select * from b;

#-#   col_a col_b
#-# 1     1     2
#-# 2     1     2
#-# 3    10    11
```

We now have two tables, a and b, which can be combined as follows. `Union all` appends the result of the second query to the result of the first query. If we also wish to eliminate duplicates we can use `union` .

```
select * from a
union all
select * from b;
```

```
#-#   col_a col_b
#-# 1     1     2
#-# 2     1     2
#-# 3     4     5
#-# 4     4     5
#-# 5     1     2
#-# 6     1     2
#-# 7    10    11
```

```
select * from a
union
select * from b;
```

```
#-#   col_a col_b
#-# 1     1     2
#-# 2     4     5
#-# 3    10    11
```

`Intersect all` returns all rows that appear in both the first and second query. If we also want to remove duplicates we can use `intersect`.

```
--there are two rows with (1,2) in both a and b
select * from a
intersect all
select * from b;
```

```
#-#   col_a col_b
#-# 1     1     2
#-# 2     1     2
```

```
select * from a
intersect
select * from b;
```

```
#-#   col_a col_b
#-# 1     1     2
```

`Except all` returns the rows that are in the result of the first query but not in the result of the second query. If we wish to remove duplicates, we would use `except`.

```
--there are two records with (4,5) in a
select * from a
except all
select * from b;

#-#   col_a col_b
#-# 1     4     5
#-# 2     4     5
```

```
select * from a
except
select * from b;

#-#   col_a col_b
#-# 1     4     5
```

Note that we can chain as many commands as we want. For example: `query1 union query2 intersect query3` . It is always recommended to add parentheses to avoid unwanted ordering effects. For example: `(query1 union query2) intersect query3` .

Chapter 20

Working with Dates

20.1 R

```
# When we read in data, dates are read in as a
# character vector. The function as.Date()
# creates a Date object. Most systems store dates
# internally as the number of days (numeric
# vector) since some origin. When using as.Date
# on a numeric vector we need to set the origin.
# The origin on this system is '1970/01/01'
help(as.Date)

# This is how you find out what the origin is:
Sys.Date() - as.integer(Sys.Date())

#-# [1] "1970-01-01"

# This is Today's date:
Sys.Date()

#-# [1] "2024-10-23"

# Converting an integer requires an origin:
as.Date(10, origin = "1970/01/01")

#-# [1] "1970-01-11"
```

```
# formats %d day as a number (e.g., 11) %a
# abbreviated weekday (e.g., MON) %A
# unabbreviated weekday (e.g., MONDAY)\t
# %m\tmonth as a number (e.g., 06) %b abbreviated
# month (e.g., JUN) %B\tunabbreviated month
# (e.g., JUNE) %y 2-digit year (e.g., 20)
# %Y\t4-digit year (e.g., 2020)

# More information: help(strftime)
# help(ISOdatetime)

# Specifying a date format:
f <- "%d/%m/%Y"

# Subtraction of two dates as Date object using
# the format:
as.Date("02/01/1970", format = f) - as.Date("01/01/1970",
    format = f)

#-# Time difference of 1 days

# Subtraction of two dates as numeric objects:
as.numeric(as.Date("02/01/1970", format = f)) - as.numeric(as.Date("01/01/1970",
    format = f))

#-# [1] 1

# Adding zero days to the origin should be 0:
as.numeric(as.Date(0, origin = "1970/01/01"))

#-# [1] 0

# To go before 1970/01/01 use negative numbers

# Read in the data with dates as characters
URL_subs <- "http://hde.onl/subscriptions.txt"

subscriptions <- read.table(URL_subs, header = TRUE,
    sep = ";", colClasses = c("character", "character",
        "character", "character", "character", "character",
        "integer", "integer", "character", "factor",
        "factor", "character", "character", "numeric",
        "numeric", "numeric", "numeric", "numeric",
        "numeric", "numeric", "numeric"))
```

```
# Transform the dates in the subscriptions data
# frame First look at the data
str(subscriptions, vec.len = 0.7)

#-# 'data.frame': 227 obs. of  21 variables:
#-#  $ SubscriptionID   : chr  "1000024" ...
#-#  $ CustomerID       : chr  "1150045" ...
#-#  $ ProductID        : chr  "8"
#-#  $ Pattern          : chr  "1111110" ...
#-#  $ StartDate        : chr  "18/01/2010" ...
#-#  $ EndDate          : chr  "17/04/2010" ...
#-#  $ NbrNewspapers    : int  76 50 ...
#-#  $ NbrStart         : int  25 25 ...
#-#  $ RenewalDate      : chr  "17/03/2010" ...
#-#  $ PaymentType      : Factor w/ 2 levels "BT","DD": 1 1 ...
#-#  $ PaymentStatus    : Factor w/ 2 levels "Not Paid","Paid": 2 2 ...
#-#  $ PaymentDate      : chr  "27/01/2010" ...
#-#  $ FormulaID        : chr  "8552" ...
#-#  $ GrossFormulaPrice: num  79 ...
#-#  $ NetFormulaPrice  : num  79 29.6 ...
#-#  $ NetNewspaperPrice: num  1.04 ...
#-#  $ ProductDiscount  : num  0 0 ...
#-#  $ FormulaDiscount  : num  0 ...
#-#  $ TotalDiscount    : num  0 ...
#-#  $ TotalPrice       : num  79 29.6 ...
#-#  $ TotalCredit      : num  0 0 ...

head(subscriptions$StartDate)

#-# [1] "18/01/2010" "14/01/2010" "01/01/2008" "02/01/2007"
#-# [5] "01/01/2008" "02/01/2007"

# Get the positions of the date variables
(vars <- which(names(subscriptions) %in% c("StartDate",
    "EndDate", "PaymentDate", "RenewalDate")))

#-# [1]  5  6  9 12

# Transform to dates
subscriptions[, vars] <- sapply(vars, function(vars) {
    as.Date(subscriptions[, vars], format = "%d/%m/%Y")
}, simplify = FALSE)
# Note: in this case 'simplify' means simplify
```

```
# the result to a numeric vector
str(subscriptions, vec.len = 0.7)

#-# 'data.frame': 227 obs. of  21 variables:
#-#  $ SubscriptionID   : chr  "1000024" ...
#-#  $ CustomerID       : chr  "1150045" ...
#-#  $ ProductID        : chr  "8" ...
#-#  $ Pattern          : chr  "1111110" ...
#-#  $ StartDate        : Date, format: "2010-01-18" ...
#-#  $ EndDate          : Date, format: "2010-04-17" ...
#-#  $ NbrNewspapers    : int  76 50 ...
#-#  $ NbrStart         : int  25 25 ...
#-#  $ RenewalDate      : Date, format: "2010-03-17" ...
#-#  $ PaymentType      : Factor w/ 2 levels "BT","DD": 1 1 ...
#-#  $ PaymentStatus    : Factor w/ 2 levels "Not Paid","Paid": 2 2 ...
#-#  $ PaymentDate      : Date, format: "2010-01-27" ...
#-#  $ FormulaID        : chr  "8552" ...
#-#  $ GrossFormulaPrice: num  79 ...
#-#  $ NetFormulaPrice  : num  79 29.6 ...
#-#  $ NetNewspaperPrice: num  1.04 ...
#-#  $ ProductDiscount  : num  0 0 ...
#-#  $ FormulaDiscount  : num  0 ...
#-#  $ TotalDiscount    : num  0 ...
#-#  $ TotalPrice       : num  79 29.6 ...
#-#  $ TotalCredit      : num  0 0 ...

head(subscriptions$StartDate)

#-# [1] "2010-01-18" "2010-01-14" "2008-01-01" "2007-01-02"
#-# [5] "2008-01-01" "2007-01-02"

# Reading in dates directly (as opposed to
# changing them afterwards) what is the current
# default date format?
Sys.Date()

#-# [1] "2024-10-23"

# looks like it is %Y-%m-%d

# Currently all the dates are character vectors
# The date format in our data is %d/%m/%Y
# (e.g.,'27/01/2010')
```

```
# If we use Date, values are not imported
# adequately. Let's try it. Look at StartDate
subscriptions <- read.table(URL_subs, header = TRUE,
    sep = ";", colClasses = c("integer", "integer",
        "character", "character", "Date", "character",
        "integer", "integer", "character", "factor",
        "factor", "character", "integer", "numeric",
        "numeric", "numeric", "numeric", "numeric",
        "numeric", "numeric", "numeric"))
str(subscriptions, vec.len = 0.7)

#-# 'data.frame': 227 obs. of  21 variables:
#-#  $ SubscriptionID   : int  1000024 1000082 ...
#-#  $ CustomerID       : int  1150045 1150046 ...
#-#  $ ProductID        : chr  "8" ...
#-#  $ Pattern          : chr  "1111110" ...
#-#  $ StartDate        : Date, format: "0018-01-20" ...
#-#  $ EndDate          : chr  "17/04/2010" ...
#-#  $ NbrNewspapers    : int  76 50 ...
#-#  $ NbrStart         : int  25 25 ...
#-#  $ RenewalDate      : chr  "17/03/2010" ...
#-#  $ PaymentType      : Factor w/ 2 levels "BT","DD": 1 1 ...
#-#  $ PaymentStatus    : Factor w/ 2 levels "Not Paid","Paid": 2 2 ...
#-#  $ PaymentDate      : chr  "27/01/2010" ...
#-#  $ FormulaID        : int  8552 10017 ...
#-#  $ GrossFormulaPrice: num  79 ...
#-#  $ NetFormulaPrice  : num  79 29.6 ...
#-#  $ NetNewspaperPrice: num  1.04 ...
#-#  $ ProductDiscount  : num  0 0 ...
#-#  $ FormulaDiscount  : num  0 ...
#-#  $ TotalDiscount    : num  0 ...
#-#  $ TotalPrice       : num  79 29.6 ...
#-#  $ TotalCredit      : num  0 0 ...

head(subscriptions$StartDate)

#-# [1] "0018-01-20" "0014-01-20" "0001-01-20" "0002-01-20"
#-# [5] "0001-01-20" "0002-01-20"

# StartDate clearly read incorrectly

# Take care of default date format
f <- "%d/%m/%Y"
```

```
setClass("fDate")
setAs(from = "character", to = "fDate", def = function(from) as.Date(from,
    format = f))

# Let's use fDate instead of Date for StartDate
# Look at StartDate
subscriptions <- read.table(URL_subs, header = TRUE,
    sep = ";", colClasses = c("integer", "integer",
        "character", "character", "fDate", "character",
        "integer", "integer", "character", "factor",
        "factor", "character", "integer", "numeric",
        "numeric", "numeric", "numeric", "numeric",
        "numeric", "numeric", "numeric"))
str(subscriptions, vec.len = 0.7)

#-# 'data.frame': 227 obs. of  21 variables:
#-#  $ SubscriptionID   : int  1000024 1000082 ...
#-#  $ CustomerID       : int  1150045 1150046 ...
#-#  $ ProductID        : chr  "8" ...
#-#  $ Pattern          : chr  "1111110" ...
#-#  $ StartDate        : Date, format: "2010-01-18" ...
#-#  $ EndDate          : chr  "17/04/2010" ...
#-#  $ NbrNewspapers    : int  76 50 ...
#-#  $ NbrStart         : int  25 25 ...
#-#  $ RenewalDate      : chr  "17/03/2010" ...
#-#  $ PaymentType      : Factor w/ 2 levels "BT","DD": 1 1 ...
#-#  $ PaymentStatus    : Factor w/ 2 levels "Not Paid","Paid": 2 2 ...
#-#  $ PaymentDate      : chr  "27/01/2010" ...
#-#  $ FormulaID        : int  8552 10017 ...
#-#  $ GrossFormulaPrice: num  79 ...
#-#  $ NetFormulaPrice  : num  79 29.6 ...
#-#  $ NetNewspaperPrice: num  1.04 ...
#-#  $ ProductDiscount  : num  0 0 ...
#-#  $ FormulaDiscount  : num  0 ...
#-#  $ TotalDiscount    : num  0 ...
#-#  $ TotalPrice       : num  79 29.6 ...
#-#  $ TotalCredit      : num  0 0 ...

head(subscriptions$StartDate)

#-# [1] "2010-01-18" "2010-01-14" "2008-01-01" "2007-01-02"
#-# [5] "2008-01-01" "2007-01-02"

# StartDate is correct now
```

In sum, dates are read in as characters. We can transform them afterwards, but it's more efficient to read them in correctly the first time. We can use the `Date` class if the dates are stored in the default format. If they are not we need to define our own class and use it when reading in data.

20.2 Python

```
# A date is not a separate data type in Python.
# However, we can import the datetime module to work with dates
# as date objects.

import warnings
warnings.simplefilter(action='ignore')

import datetime as dt

#the main types are
# date
# time
# datetime
# timedelta (difference between two dates, times or datetimes)
# tzinfo (time zone info), and timezone
# and they are immutable

#create a date object:
x = dt.date(2023,10,11)
type(x)
#-# <class 'datetime.date'>

print(x)

#-# 2023-10-11

#create a datetime object
#(year, month, day, hour, minute, second, microsecond):
x = dt.datetime(2023,10,11,0,0,0,0)
type(x)

#-# <class 'datetime.datetime'>

print(x)

#-# 2023-10-11 00:00:00
```

```
#create a time object:
x = dt.time(hour=0,minute=0,second=0,microsecond=0)
type(x)

#-# <class 'datetime.time'>

print(x)

#-# 00:00:00

#display the current datetime:
x = dt.datetime.now()
print(x)

#-# 2024-11-29 19:22:34.152233

#Useful attributes of datetime:

x.year

#-# 2024

x.month

#-# 11

x.day

#-# 29

x.hour

#-# 19

x.minute

#-# 22

x.second

#-# 34

x.microsecond

#-# 152233
```

```
#FORMATTING DATE OBJECTS WITH STRING FORMAT TIME (strftime)

#x.strftime()

#DAY
# %a      weekday short
x.strftime('%a')

#-# 'Fri'

# %A      weekday full
x.strftime('%A')

#-# 'Friday'

# %w      weekday as number (0 is Sunday)
x.strftime('%w')

#-# '5'

# %d      day of month (01-31)
x.strftime('%d')

#-# '29'

# %j      day number of year 001-366
x.strftime('%j')

#-# '334'

#WEEK
# %U      week number of year (Sunday first day of week) 00-53
x.strftime('%U')

#-# '47'

# %W      week number of year (Monday first day of week) 00-53
x.strftime('%W')

#-# '48'

#MONTH
# %b      month name short
x.strftime('%b')

#-# 'Nov'

# %B      month name full
x.strftime('%B')
```

```
#-# 'November'

# %m      month as number 01-12
x.strftime('%m')

#-# '11'

#YEAR
# %y      year short with century
x.strftime('%y')

#-# '24'

# %Y      year full
x.strftime('%Y')

#-# '2024'

#HOUR
# %H      hour 00-23
x.strftime('%H')

#-# '19'

# %I      hour 00-12
x.strftime('%I')

#-# '07'

# %p      AM/PM
x.strftime('%p')

#-# 'PM'

#MINUTE
# %M      minute 00-59
x.strftime('%M')

#-# '22'

#SECOND
# %S      second 00-59
x.strftime('%S')

#-# '34'

#MICROSECOND (one millionth of a second)
# %f      microsecond 000000-999999
x.strftime('%f')
```

```
#-# '152233'

#To get the milliseconds, divide the microseconds by 1000:
int(x.strftime('%f'))/1000

#-# 152.233

#COMBINED USE (example):
x.strftime('%m/%d/%Y')

#-# '11/29/2024'

#To do computations, or use time in models, it is often
#useful to have time as the number of seconds since an origin.
#The convention is to use 1970 Jan 1 00:00:00 Universal Time Coordinated as the origin.
#The number of seconds since this origin is called epoch time, POSIX (Portable Operating
System Interface) time, unix epoch time, unix time. #In the datetime package it is called
'timestamp'.
#Epoch is the zero moment, and is the start of the decade in which the unix operating system
was invented.
#Let's calculate the epoch time, assuming we are in the UTC timezone.
sometime = dt.datetime.now(tz=dt.timezone.utc)
epoch = dt.datetime(1970, 1, 1, 0, 0, 0, tzinfo=dt.timezone.utc)
int((sometime - epoch).total_seconds())

#-# 1732926154

#short way:
int(dt.datetime.timestamp(sometime))

#-# 1732926154

#go from a timestamp (epoch time) to a datetime
timestamp = int(dt.datetime.timestamp(sometime))
dt.datetime.fromtimestamp(timestamp)

#-# datetime.datetime(2024, 11, 29, 19, 22, 34)

dt.datetime.fromtimestamp(timestamp, tz= dt.timezone.utc)

#-# datetime.datetime(2024, 11, 30, 0, 22, 34, tzinfo=datetime.timezone.utc)

#To get the time as number of seconds (as opposed to datetime),
#the origin is midnight of the same day. Example:
sometime = dt.datetime.now()
midnight = sometime.replace(hour=0, minute=0, second=0, microsecond=0)
int((sometime - midnight).total_seconds())
```

```
#-# 69754

#other useful methods of datetime objects
x = dt.datetime.now()
x.date()

#-# datetime.date(2024, 11, 29)

x.weekday()

#-# 4

x.time()

#-# datetime.time(19, 22, 34, 210335)

#timezones (naive vs aware)
naive_datetime = dt.datetime.now()
naive_datetime

#-# datetime.datetime(2024, 11, 29, 19, 22, 34, 215403)

#make it aware of the timezone we are in (say UTC-5)
aware_datetime = naive_datetime.replace(tzinfo = dt.timezone(dt.timedelta(hours=-5)))
#aware_datetime


#Now show the time in UTC
aware_datetime.astimezone(tz=dt.timezone.utc)

#-# datetime.datetime(2024, 11, 30, 0, 22, 34, 215403, tzinfo=datetime.timezone.utc)

#It is recommended to always
#1) use 'aware' objects
#2) work in UTC and do timezone conversion to local timezone as a last step


#pandas
import pandas as pd

subscriptions = pd.read_table('http://hde.onl/subscriptions.txt',
                              delimiter=';')
subscriptions.dtypes #StartDate is of type object (i.e., string)
```

```
#-# SubscriptionID          int64
#-# CustomerID              int64
#-# ProductID               int64
#-# Pattern                 int64
#-# StartDate              object
#-# EndDate                object
#-# NbrNewspapers           int64
#-# NbrStart                int64
#-# RenewalDate            object
#-# PaymentType            object
#-# PaymentStatus          object
#-# PaymentDate            object
#-# FormulaID               int64
#-# GrossFormulaPrice     float64
#-# NetFormulaPrice       float64
#-# NetNewspaperPrice     float64
#-# ProductDiscount       float64
#-# FormulaDiscount       float64
#-# TotalDiscount         float64
#-# TotalPrice            float64
#-# TotalCredit           float64
#-# dtype: object
```

```
subscriptions[['StartDate']]
```

```
#-#       StartDate
#-# 0    18/01/2010
#-# 1    14/01/2010
#-# 2    01/01/2008
#-# 3    02/01/2007
#-# 4    01/01/2008
#-# ..          ...
#-# 222  13/11/2006
#-# 223  02/03/2010
#-# 224  02/03/2010
#-# 225  02/03/2010
#-# 226  02/03/2010
#-#
#-# [227 rows x 1 columns]
```

```
#now tell pandas to parse StartDate as a date
subscriptions = pd.read_table('http://hde.onl/subscriptions.txt',
                              delimiter=';',
                              parse_dates = ['StartDate'],
```

```
                                infer_datetime_format = True
                                )
#An alternative to infer_datetime_format = True is dayfirst = True in #this case.

subscriptions.dtypes

#-# SubscriptionID                 int64
#-# CustomerID                     int64
#-# ProductID                      int64
#-# Pattern                        int64
#-# StartDate             datetime64[ns]
#-# EndDate                       object
#-# NbrNewspapers                  int64
#-# NbrStart                       int64
#-# RenewalDate                   object
#-# PaymentType                   object
#-# PaymentStatus                 object
#-# PaymentDate                   object
#-# FormulaID                      int64
#-# GrossFormulaPrice            float64
#-# NetFormulaPrice              float64
#-# NetNewspaperPrice            float64
#-# ProductDiscount              float64
#-# FormulaDiscount              float64
#-# TotalDiscount                float64
#-# TotalPrice                   float64
#-# TotalCredit                  float64
#-# dtype: object

subscriptions['StartDate']

#-# 0      2010-01-18
#-# 1      2010-01-14
#-# 2      2008-01-01
#-# 3      2007-01-02
#-# 4      2008-01-01
#-#           ...
#-# 222    2006-11-13
#-# 223    2010-03-02
#-# 224    2010-03-02
#-# 225    2010-03-02
#-# 226    2010-03-02
#-# Name: StartDate, Length: 227, dtype: datetime64[ns]
```

```
type(subscriptions['StartDate'][0])

#-# <class 'pandas._libs.tslibs.timestamps.Timestamp'>

#pandas.Timestamp is the equivalent of the datetime.datetime object
#and is interchangeable in most cases
subscriptions['StartDate'].dt.year

#-# 0      2010
#-# 1      2010
#-# 2      2008
#-# 3      2007
#-# 4      2008
#-#        ...
#-# 222    2006
#-# 223    2010
#-# 224    2010
#-# 225    2010
#-# 226    2010
#-# Name: StartDate, Length: 227, dtype: int32

subscriptions['StartDate'].dt.month

#-# 0       1
#-# 1       1
#-# 2       1
#-# 3       1
#-# 4       1
#-#        ..
#-# 222    11
#-# 223     3
#-# 224     3
#-# 225     3
#-# 226     3
#-# Name: StartDate, Length: 227, dtype: int32

subscriptions['StartDate'].dt.day

#-# 0      18
#-# 1      14
#-# 2       1
#-# 3       2
#-# 4       1
#-#        ..
#-# 222    13
```

```
#-# 223     2
#-# 224     2
#-# 225     2
#-# 226     2
#-# Name: StartDate, Length: 227, dtype: int32
```

```
subscriptions['StartDate'].dt.weekday
```

```
#-# 0      0
#-# 1      3
#-# 2      1
#-# 3      1
#-# 4      1
#-#       ..
#-# 222    0
#-# 223    1
#-# 224    1
#-# 225    1
#-# 226    1
#-# Name: StartDate, Length: 227, dtype: int32
```

```
df = pd.DataFrame({'Seconds': [1614622968,1614622969,1614622970,1614622971,1614622972]})
df
```

```
#-#       Seconds
#-# 0  1614622968
#-# 1  1614622969
#-# 2  1614622970
#-# 3  1614622971
#-# 4  1614622972
```

```
#Change epoch time to date time
tstamp_df = pd.to_datetime(df['Seconds'],unit='s',utc=True).dt.tz_convert('US/Eastern')


#numpy also has datetimes and timedeltas
#they are called datetime64, because "datetime" is already taken by the datetime library
import numpy as np
#basic datetimes:
np.datetime64('2020-02-25')
```

```
#-# numpy.datetime64('2020-02-25')
```

```
np.datetime64('2020-02-25T03:30')
```

```
#-# numpy.datetime64('2020-02-25T03:30')
```

```
np.array(['2007-07-13', '2006-01-13', '2010-08-13'], dtype='datetime64')

#-# array(['2007-07-13', '2006-01-13', '2010-08-13'], dtype='datetime64[D]')

np.datetime64('2023-01-01') - np.datetime64('2020-01-01')

#-# numpy.timedelta64(1096,'D')


#More information:
#docs.scipy.org/doc/numpy/reference/arrays.datetime.html?highlight=date%20time%20types
```

20.3 PostgreSQL

The main date and time types in PostreSQL are `date`, `time`, `interval` (time interval), `timestamp` (date and time), and `timestamp with time zone`. These types can be specified in statements such as `create table` and `select` queries:

```
select date '2020-04-19';

#-#          date
#-# 1 2020-04-19


select time '10:23:54';

#-#        time
#-# 1 10:23:54


select interval '5 days'; --other options year, month, week, hour, minute, second

#-#   interval
#-# 1    5 days


select timestamp '2020-04-19 10:23:54';
```

For a timestamp with time zone the internally stored value is always in UTC (Universal Coordinated Time). If the input value does not state the time zone then it is assumed to be in the system's timezone and is converted to UTC using the offset of that timezone. When the timestamp with time zone is output, it is always converted from UTC to the system's time zone (i.e., displayed as local time).

```
set timezone to -4;


show timezone;

#-#    TimeZone
#-# 1       UTC


select timestamp with time zone '2020-04-19 10:23:54';

#--#                 timestamptz
#--# 2020-04-19 10:23:54-04:00
--(i.e., if we are in UTC-4 then the above would be stored as
--2020-04-19 14:23:54 and displayed as 2020-04-19 10:23:54-04:00)


select timestamptz '2020-04-19 10:23:54'; --same as previous line

#--#                 timestamptz
#--# 2020-04-19 10:23:54-04:00
```

If the input value does state the time zone then it is converted to UTC using the offset for that time zone. When the timestamp with time zone is output, it is always converted from UTC to the system's time zone (i.e., displayed as local time). Note that the hour is different:

```
select timestamp with time zone '2020-04-19 10:23:54-07:00'; --it is 10:23 locally and 17:23
in UTC

#--#                 timestamptz
#--# 2020-04-19 13:23:54-04:00

--(i.e., if we are in UTC-4 then the above would be 7h later in UTC and
--stored as such as 2020-04-19 17:23:54 and
--displayed as 2020-04-19 13:23:54-04:00)
```

To see the time in another time zone, we can use `at time zone` :

```
select timestamp with time zone '2020-04-19 10:23:54-07:00' as local,
    timestamp with time zone '2020-04-19 10:23:54-07:00' at time zone 'UTC' as utc;

#--#                  local                    utc
#--# 2020-04-19 13:23:54-04:00    2020-04-19 17:23:54

--Valid time zone names: select * from pg_timezone_names;
```

Special functions related to the current time and day:

```
select current_date;

#--# current_date
#--# 2020-04-19
```

```
select current_time;

#--# current_time
#--# 16:37:50.971078-04:00
```

```
select current_timestamp;

#--# current_timestamp
#--# 2020-04-19 16:38:00.675590-04:00
```

```
select now();

#--# now
#--# 2020-04-19 16:38:09.179440-04:00
```

```
select timestamp 'now';

#--# timestamp
#--# 2020-04-19 16:38:24.187413
```

```
select timestamp 'today';

#--# timestamp
#--# 2020-04-19 00:00:00
```

```
select timestamp 'tomorrow';

#--# timestamp
#--# 2020-04-20 00:00:00
```

```
select timestamp 'yesterday';

#--# timestamp
#--# 2020-04-18 00:00:00
```

Adding or subtracting time from a timestamp with interval

```
select current_timestamp, current_timestamp + interval '1 year' ;

#-#     current_timestamp            ?column?
#-# 1 2024-11-30 00:22:35 2025-11-30 00:22:35
```

```
select current_timestamp, current_timestamp + interval '1 month' ;

#-#     current_timestamp            ?column?
#-# 1 2024-11-30 00:22:35 2024-12-30 00:22:35
```

```
select current_timestamp, current_timestamp + interval '1 week' ;

#-#     current_timestamp            ?column?
#-# 1 2024-11-30 00:22:35 2024-12-07 00:22:35
```

```
select current_timestamp, current_timestamp + interval '1 day' ;

#-#     current_timestamp            ?column?
#-# 1 2024-11-30 00:22:35 2024-12-01 00:22:35
```

```
select current_timestamp, current_timestamp + interval '1 hour' ;
```

```
#-#     current_timestamp            ?column?
#-# 1 2024-11-30 00:22:35 2024-11-30 01:22:35
```

```
select current_timestamp, current_timestamp + interval '1 minute' ;
```

```
#-#     current_timestamp            ?column?
#-# 1 2024-11-30 00:22:35 2024-11-30 00:23:35
```

```
select current_timestamp, current_timestamp + interval '1 second' ;
```

```
#-#     current_timestamp            ?column?
#-# 1 2024-11-30 00:22:35 2024-11-30 00:22:36
```

Extracting parts from a timestamp

```
select extract(year from current_timestamp);
```

```
#-#   extract
#-# 1    2024
```

```
select extract(month from current_timestamp);
```

```
#-#   extract
#-# 1      11
```

```
select extract(week from current_timestamp);
```

```
#-#   extract
#-# 1      48
```

```
select extract(dow from current_timestamp); -- day of week (Monday 1, Sunday 7)
```

```
#-#   extract
#-# 1       6
```

```
select extract(doy from current_timestamp); -- day of year

#-#   extract
#-# 1     335

select extract(day from current_timestamp); --day of month

#-#   extract
#-# 1      30

select extract(hour from current_timestamp);

#-#   extract
#-# 1       0

select extract(minute from current_timestamp);

#-#   extract
#-# 1      22

select extract(second from current_timestamp);

#-#    extract
#-# 1 35.92898

select extract(milliseconds from current_timestamp); --takes seconds field, including fractional
parts, multiplied by 1000

#-#    extract
#-# 1 35943.36

select extract(microseconds from current_timestamp); --takes seconds field, including fractional
parts, multiplied by 1,000,000

#-#    extract
#-# 1 35956722
```

```
--date_part is equivalent to extract:
--Example:
select date_part('year', current_timestamp);

#-#   date_part
#-# 1      2024
```

Truncating to a specified precision

```
--truncate everything that is more precise than the year
select date_trunc('year', current_timestamp);

#--#                 date_trunc
#--# 2020-01-01 00:00:00-04:00
```

```
--truncate everything that is more precise than the month
select date_trunc('month', current_timestamp);

#--#                 date_trunc
#--# 2020-04-01 00:00:00-04:00
```

```
--truncate everything that is more precise than the week
select date_trunc('week', current_timestamp);

#--#                 date_trunc
#--# 2020-04-13 00:00:00-04:00
```

```
--truncate everything that is more precise than the day
select date_trunc('day', current_timestamp);

#--#                 date_trunc
#--# 2020-04-19 00:00:00-04:00
```

```
--truncate everything that is more precise than the hour
select date_trunc('hour', current_timestamp);

#--#                 date_trunc
#--# 2020-04-19 16:00:00-04:00
```

```
--truncate everything that is more precise than the minute
select date_trunc('minute', current_timestamp);

#--#                 date_trunc
#--# 2020-04-19 16:35:00-04:00


--truncate everything that is more precise than the
select date_trunc('second', current_timestamp);

#--#                 date_trunc
#--# 2020-04-19 16:35:11-04:00
```

Epoch

```
--select epoch: seconds since seconds since 1970-01-01 00:00:00+00
select extract(epoch from current_timestamp);

#-#      extract
#-# 1 1732926156


--Convert epoch to timestamp
select to_timestamp(extract(epoch from current_timestamp));

#-#          to_timestamp
#-# 1 2024-11-30 00:22:36
```

Casting

```
--Casting a string to a date:
select '2020/2/20' as String,
       '2020/2/20'::date Date;
--we can do computations with the date but not with the string

#-#      string       date
#-# 1 2020/2/20 2020-02-20
```

If the input format cannot be converted with simple casting we can use `to_date`. Options are listed here: https://www.postgresql.org/docs/14/functions-formatting.html

```
--This will not work: select '2020/20/2'::date;
select to_date('2020/20/2', 'YYYY/DD/MM');

#-#       to_date
#-# 1 2020-02-20
```

For details about the `to_timestamp` function see the link above.

Chapter 21

Creating Functions

21.1 R

Whenever we want to reuse a piece of code multiple times in the future we make a function. This will ensure minimal code maintenance.

```r
# Make a new function:

# functionname <- fuction(parametername){ code }

# Example:
MySum <- function(a, b) {
    c <- a + b
    c  #since this is the last line, c will be returned
}

MySum(1, 2)

#-# [1] 3

# This is identical:
MySum <- function(a, b) {
    c <- a + b
    return(c)
}

MySum(1, 2)

#-# [1] 3
```

```
# Everything we do in a function stays in the
# function, unless we make it global.

outerfunc <- function(a, b) {

    innerfunc <- function(a, b) {
        a + b
    }
    v <- 1
}

outerfunc(1, 2)  #Nothing is printed (it does return v but invisibly)

(d <- outerfunc(1, 2))

#-# [1] 1

# What comes next will not work.  R will complain
# that it cannot find the function and object
innerfunc(1, 2)

#-# Error in innerfunc(1, 2): could not find function "innerfunc"

v

#-# Error: object 'v' not found

# Make the innerfunc and v global
outerfunc <- function(a, b) {

    innerfunc <<- function(a, b) {
        a + b
    }
    v <<- 1
}

outerfunc(1, 2)
innerfunc(1, 2)

#-# [1] 3

v

#-# [1] 1
```

```
# However, this is generally considered bad
# practice. It's better to have a function return
# another function
outerfunc <- function() {

    innerfunc <- function(a, b) {
        a + b
    }
    v <- 1
    return(list(innerfunc, v))
}

f <- outerfunc()
f

#-# [[1]]
#-# function (a, b)
#-# {
#-#     a + b
#-# }
#-# <environment: 0x105f81940>
#-#
#-# [[2]]
#-# [1] 1

f[[1]](1, 2)

#-# [1] 3

f[[2]]

#-# [1] 1
```

21.2 Python

```
##################################
#def statement

# The def statement is what we use to define a function.
# The three examples below show the need for a return statement
```

```
#this will print but return None
def mySum(a,b):
  c = a+b
  print(c)

x = mySum(1,2)
#-# 3

print(x)

#-# None

#this will return None
def mySum1(a,b):
  c = a+b
  c

y = mySum1(1,2)
print(y)

#-# None

#This will return c
def mySum2(a,b):
  c = a+b
  return c #without return result will be None

z = mySum2(1,2)
print(z)

#-# 3

###################################
#Scope of visibility
#When we use a name (e.g., of a variable), Python searches the
#name in a namespace - a place where names live.
#Scope is a namespace in wich a name is visible and
#scope classification happens at assign time.
#In other words: scope is determined based on where the assignment happened

#Calling a function creates a new namespace (scope).

#There are three levels:
#A variable assigned in a def is local to that function.
#A variable assigned in an enclosing def is nonlocal to nested functions.
```

```
#A variable assigned outside all defs is global to the entire file.


#Names assigned inside a function definition are local.
v = 0
def innerfunc():
    v = 1
    return v
innerfunc()

#-# 1

v

#-# 0

#Make v global: visible outside the function (to the enclosing module (file))

v = 0
def innerfunc():
    global v #note the global
    v = 1
    return v
innerfunc()

#-# 1

v

#-# 1

#Similarly, when we have a nested function and want
#to make a local variable visible only in the enclosing function:

#v is local
def outerfunc():
    v = 0
    def innerfunc():
        v = 1
        return v
    innerfunc()
    return v

outerfunc()

#-# 0
```

```
#Make v nonlocal to innerfunc = make it available to the enclosing def statement: allows
functions to retain state
def outerfunc():
    v = 0
    def innerfunc():
        nonlocal v #note the nonlocal
        v = 1
        return v
    innerfunc()
    return v

outerfunc()

#-# 1

#Names defined outside a function are enclosing function locals (defined in an enclosing
def), or
#globals (defined at the level of our module/file), or built-ins
#Important: **name assignments** make the name local, but
    #subset assignments
    #modifying an object
#impact global objects in the global environment.
#example:

v = [1,2,3] #object in the global environment
def innerfunc():
    v[0] = 100 #subset assignment
    v.append(4) #append object
    return v
innerfunc()

#-# [100, 2, 3, 4]

v

#-# [100, 2, 3, 4]

#if you want to avoid changing v globally
v = [1,2,3]
def innerfunc():
    w = v.copy()
    w[0] = 100
    w.append(4)
    return w
innerfunc()
```

```
#-# [100, 2, 3, 4]

v

#-# [1, 2, 3]

##Names defined outside the function and not inside the function:
r = 99

def innerfunc():
    return r

innerfunc()

#-# 99

#Python will first search for the name inside the function,
#then in any enclosing functions, then inside the file (called module; global), then inside
built-ins (e.g., range, for). This is called the LEGB rule. It will stop when it has found
the name definition.

#It is the call to a function that creates the scope (every time the function is called),
not running the def statement.


##################################
#Defaults

#Arguments with defaults need to be defined after arguments
#without defaults:
def mySum(a,b=2):
  c = a+b
  return c

mySum(1)

#-# 3

mySum(1,3)

#-# 4

#Be careful with defaults
#Defaults are evaluated once when def is run,
#not each time the function is called.
```

```
#Functions are first-class citizens in Python,
#and that means they behave like other objects.
#The function is an object, and the default variables
#are attributes to the function object (and are stored in the
#function object).

# Consider what happens we set a default argument
# that is mutable, in this case, an empty list.
def foo(x=[]):
    x.append(1)
    return x

#Let's see what the value of the defaults is:
foo.__defaults__

#-# ([],)

foo()

#-# [1]

#Let's see what the value of the defaults is:
foo.__defaults__

#-# ([1],)

foo()

#-# [1, 1]

#Let's see what the value of the defaults is:
foo.__defaults__

#-# ([1, 1],)

# Note that the defaults and what is returned refer to the same
# object in memory.
id(foo.__defaults__[0]) == id(foo())

#-# True

# Note that the list is growing.

# There are two reasons for this:
# 1. the function header (the line on which
# the def satement is written) is executed only once; when the
# function is declared (in contrast the function body is run every time the function is
```

```
called.)
# 2. the default argument is a mutable object

# In other words, when we run foo(), x=[] is not re-run.
# The list object [] is created once, when the function is defined, and
# a reference to it is stored as an attribute of the function object, called __defaults__,
and a second reference is stored in x.

# Inside the function body, the [] object is mutated, and both __defaults__
# and x will continue pointing to [].

# Every time when the function is called, the arguments that are not
# specified in the call will then get the values from __defaults__.

# If this is not what we want, we can use an immutable object,
# such as the value None, a string, a number, ...


def foo(x=None):
    if x is None:
        x = []
    else:
        x
    x.append(1)
    return x

#Let's see what the value of the defaults is:
foo.__defaults__


foo()


#Let's see what the value of the defaults is:
foo.__defaults__


foo()


#Let's see what the value of the defaults is:
foo.__defaults__
```

```
#-# (None,)

# Note that the defaults and what is returned refer to different
# objects in memory.
id(foo.__defaults__[0]) == id(foo())

#-# False

# This is because x = None is only executed once, at function definition.
# Both x and __defaults__ point to the immutable object None.
# When x = [] happens, __defaults__ still points to None, and x starts
# pointing to [].

# Every time when the function is called, the arguments that are not
# specified in the call will then get the values from __defaults__.

# Since the function body is executed anew each time, and __defaults__
# will always be None, we always get a fresh
# new empty list if no argument was passed for x.




##################################
#*args, **kwargs
#the words args and kwargs are just conventions
#it could be *vars and **kvars, for example
#they allow us to have an unknown number of arguments and keyworded arguments
#note that if we use both args and kwargs,
#args need to be defined before kwargs, and both need to
#be defind after default parameters

def foo(*args,a):
    print('a:',a)
    for val in args:
        print(val)

foo(1,2,3,4,5,6, a=0)

#-# a: 0
#-# 1
#-# 2
#-# 3
#-# 4
```

```
#-# 5
#-# 6

def foo(a, **kwargs):
    print('a',a)
    for key,val in kwargs.items():
        print(key,val)

foo(a=1,b=2,c=3,d=4,e=5,f=6)

#-# a 1
#-# b 2
#-# c 3
#-# d 4
#-# e 5
#-# f 6

##################################
#docstring

def mySum(a,b):
    """This function computes the sum of two variables"""
    c = a+b
    return c

help(mySum)

#-# Help on function mySum in module __main__:
#-#
#-# mySum(a, b)
#-#     This function computes the sum of two variables

#Note; we use triple quotes so we can have text
#on multiple lines:

print(
"""
hello
world
"""
)

#-#
#-# hello
#-# world
```

```
#If we change the triple quote to single quotes, we will get an error.

##################################
#decorators
#Decorators wrap a function to modify its behavior.
#This is one way to avoid having if-then logic in a function.

def my_decorator(func):
    def wrapper():
        print("Something is happening before the function is called.")
        func()
        print("Something is happening after the function is called.")
    return wrapper

@my_decorator
def hello():
    print("Hello world")

hello()

#-# Something is happening before the function is called.
#-# Hello world
#-# Something is happening after the function is called.

#the @ approach is equivalent to

def hello():
    print("Hello world")

hello = my_decorator(hello)

hello()

#-# Something is happening before the function is called.
#-# Hello world
#-# Something is happening after the function is called.


##################################
#yield
#Yield sends a result to the caller (like the return statement),
#but remembers where it left off.
#This is often used in generators, so they can be resumed later to
#produce results over time.
```

```
def foo(x):
    for i in range(x):
        yield i


gen = foo(5)
next(gen)

#-# 0

next(gen)

#-# 1

next(gen)

#-# 2

next(gen)

#-# 3

next(gen)

#-# 4

###################################
#arguments

#Setting an argument such as mySum(a=1,b=2) is doing an assignment
# a = 1
# b = 2
# Everything we have learned about assignments applies to arguments
# Immutable (e.g., integers, strings) and mutable arguments (e.g., lists, dicts) are passed
by references / pointer, and never copied.

x = [1,5]
l = [1,5]

def change(a,b):
    #on this line both a and b are references to the assigned objects
    a = [10,50] #name assignment, recreates a, local
    b[0] = 100 #subset assignment, changes b, global

change(x,l)
```

```
#x has not changed, because name assignment made it local
x

#-# [1, 5]

#l has changed because not name assignment
l

#-# [100, 5]

#To avoid changing l:

l = [1,5]

change(x,l[:])

l

#-# [1, 5]

change(x,l)

l

#-# [100, 5]

###################################
#returning multiple results

def foo():
    q = 1
    s = 2
    return q,s #syntactic sugar for (q,s)

foo()

#-# (1, 2)

#q
#s

q,s = foo()

q

#-# 1
```

```
s

#-# 2

###################################
#Anonymous functions: lambda
#are expressions and not statements (like def), and can therefore
#appear in places where defs cannot appear (e.g., in a list, or function arguments)
f = lambda x: x**2
f(2)

#-# 4

f = lambda x,y: x + y
f(1,2)

#-# 3

f= lambda x,y=2: x + y
f(1)

#-# 3

#jump table (list of actions):
# list of three callable functions:
l = [lambda x: x ** 2,
     lambda x: x ** 3,
     lambda x: x ** 4]

l[0](2)

#-# 4

l[1](2)

#-# 8

l[2](2)

#-# 16

d = {'action1': (lambda x: x ** 2),
     'action2': (lambda x: x ** 3),
     'action3': (lambda x: x ** 4)}

d['action2'](2)

#-# 8
```

21.3 PostgreSQL

21.3.1 pgSQL functions

Single output

```
--with returns keyword
drop function if exists my_sum(a int, b int);

CREATE FUNCTION my_sum(a int, b int) RETURNS int
AS $$

    select a + b;

$$
LANGUAGE SQL;

select * from my_sum(1,2);

#--# my_sum
#--# 3

select my_sum(1,2);

#--# my_sum
#--# 3


--with out parameter
drop function if exists my_sum(in a int, in b int, out c int);

CREATE FUNCTION my_sum(in a int, in b int, out c int)
AS $$

    select a + b;

$$
LANGUAGE SQL;

select c from my_sum(1,2);
#--# c
#--# 3
```

```
--or
select * from my_sum(1,2);

#--# c
#--# 3

select my_sum(1,2);

#--# c
#--# 3
```

Multiple outputs

```
--with custom type
drop type if exists my_ints cascade;
create type my_ints as (c int, d int, e int);

drop function if exists my_sum2;

CREATE FUNCTION my_sum2(a int, b int) RETURNS my_ints
AS $$

    select a, b, a + b;

$$
LANGUAGE SQL;

select * from my_sum2(1,2)

#--# c d e
#--# 1 2 3


select my_sum2(1,2);

#--# my_sum2
#--# (1,2,3)
```

```
--with return table keyword

drop function if exists my_sum2;

CREATE FUNCTION my_sum2(a int, b int) RETURNS TABLE (c int, d int, e int)
AS $$

    select a, b, a + b;

$$
LANGUAGE SQL;

select * from my_sum2(1,2)

#--# c d e
#--# 1 2 3

select my_sum2(1,2);

#--# my_sum2
#--# (1,2,3)


--with out parameters:

drop function my_sum2;

CREATE FUNCTION my_sum2(IN a int, IN b int, OUT c int, OUT d int, OUT e int)
AS $$

    select a, b, a + b;

$$
LANGUAGE SQL;

select * from my_sum2(1,2)

#--# c d e
#--# 1 2 3

select my_sum2(1,2);

#--# my_sum2
```

```
#--# (1,2,3)
```

21.3.2 PL/pgSQL FUNCTIONS

Only the single output example with a return keyword is shown here. Other options are consistent with the examples above.

```
--with returns statement

drop function my_sum(a int, b int);

CREATE FUNCTION my_sum(a int, b int) RETURNS int
AS $$
DECLARE
    c int;
BEGIN
    c = a + b;
    RETURN c;
END; $$
LANGUAGE plpgsql;

select * from my_sum(1,2);

#--# my_sum
#--# 3

select my_sum(1,2);

#--# my_sum
#--# 3
```

In all cases, if multiple rows are to be returned, the modifier `setof` needs to be added to the `returns` keyword. For example, if multiple records of an integer column will be returned use `returns setof int`. The `setof` modifier does not need to be added in the case of `returns table`. In the case of `out` parameters, do add the `returns setof` and make sure the result type agrees with the output parameters.

21.3.3 Special Arguments

Inout

```
--inout
drop function my_sum(INOUT a int, IN b int);

CREATE FUNCTION my_sum(INOUT a int, IN b int)
AS $$
BEGIN
    a = a + b;
END; $$
LANGUAGE plpgsql;

select * from my_sum(1,2);

#--# a
#--# 3

select my_sum(1,2);

#--# my_sum
#--# 3
```

Variadic

```
--variadic: takes as input an undefined number of arguments as an array
--requirements:
    --all of same type
    --specified after all other in-arguments

drop function my_sum(VARIADIC alphabet int[]);

CREATE FUNCTION my_sum(VARIADIC alphabet int[]) RETURNS bigint
AS $$
    select sum(a)
    from unnest(alphabet) as a; --unnest expands an array to a set of rows
$$
LANGUAGE sql;

select my_sum(10,10,10,10,10,10);
```

```
#--# my_sum
#--# 60
```

21.3.4 Overloading

Overloading means that functions of different argument types can share a name. Functions are uniquely identified by the combination of their name and arguments. This can be dangerous at times.

There exists a `create or replace function` keyword. The `replace` option only works when we change the definition of the function. It does not work when we change the argument names, argument types or the return type of a function. If we tried, we would be creating a new separate function. Therefore, if we want to change argument names, argument types or the return type we have to `drop` the function or risk cluttering our environment with many functions with the same name.

21.3.5 Default Values

```
drop function my_sum(a int, b int);

CREATE FUNCTION my_sum(a int DEFAULT 4, b int DEFAULT 5) RETURNS int
AS $$

    select a + b;

$$
LANGUAGE SQL;

select * from my_sum();

#--# my_sum
#--# 9

select my_sum();

#--# my_sum
#--# 9
```

21.3.6 Procedures

Procedures are special functions. They are special in that they are easier to work with when we do not wish to return values, but instead create tables, insert values, or update values. We can do all of that in a normal function, but it will require us to return a value unnecessarily. Below is an example of a procedure. A `returns` keyword cannot be specified.

```
drop table if exists tbl;

create table tbl (a int);

drop procedure if exists insert_data;

CREATE PROCEDURE insert_data(a integer, b integer)
AS $$
INSERT INTO tbl VALUES (a),(b);
$$
LANGUAGE SQL;

--it can be called as follows:
CALL insert_data(1, 2);

select * from tbl;

#--# a
#--# 1
#--# 2
```

21.3.7 Querying all procedures and functions

```
SELECT format('%I.%I(%s)',
              ns.nspname,
              p.proname,
              pg_get_function_arguments(p.oid))
FROM pg_proc p INNER JOIN pg_namespace ns
ON (p.pronamespace = ns.oid)
WHERE ns.nspname = 'public';

#--# public.pg_stat_statements_reset(userid oid DEFAULT 0, dbid oid DEFAULT 0, queryid bigint
```

```
DEFAULT 0)
#--# public.dup(integer)
#--# public.insert_data2(a integer, b integer)
#--# public.foo(a integer, b integer)
#--# public.foo(a double precision, b double precision)
#--# public.insert_data2(a integer, b integer, c integer, d integer)
#--# public.my_sum2(a integer, b integer, OUT c integer, OUT d integer, OUT e integer)
#--# public.my_sum(VARIADIC alphabet integer[])
#--# public.insert_data(a integer, b integer)
```

Chapter 22

Creating Methods

22.1 R

In any Object-Oriented (OO) system there are classes and methods. A class decribes the attributes of an object and is also used to select methods. A method is a function that is part of a class. The term method is almost exclusively used in OO programming. In other words, a method is a function that behaves differently depending on the class of the input.

R has three OO systems: S3, S4 and Reference Classes (RC). S4 is a more formal version of S3 and will not be covered in this book. We will first cover S3 before we move on to RC.

S3 is a generic-function OO system. In Python, which implements message-passsing OO, messages (which are methods) are passed through to the objects, and the object then determines which function to use. In Python it is typical to see `someobject.shape` to get the shape (dimensions) of `someobject` . In R one would see `shape(someobject)` (if the shape function would exist in R) and `shape` would behave differently depending on the class of `someobject` Computations are executed via methods in both cases, but in R a special function, called generic function, decides which method to call, whereas in Python it is the object. R also has Reference Classes, the closest thing to Python's way of doing it.

22.1.1 S3

R possesses a generic function mechanism that can be used for an object-oriented programming style. The functions `plot`, `print`, `summary` and `predict` are all generic functions. Each generic function has associated with it a set of other functions, called methods, that have the same arguments as the generic function. Method dispatch takes place based on the class of the object supplied as an argument. If the class does not have a name, or R cannot find the associated method, it will call the default method.

Methods make a programmer's life easy. For example, regardless of the argument's class, one would use the `plot` function, to print to the screen, one would use `print`, to create a summary, one would use `summary`, and to create predictions, one would use `predict`. Consider the following code block.

```
# define two variables
integer_vector <- c(1, 1, 1, 2, 2, 2)
factor_vector <- as.factor(c(1, 1, 1, 2, 2, 2))

# Call the generic function called summary.
# summary behaves differently depending on
# whether it is called on a integer or a factor.
# R dispatches (uses) a different method
# (function) based on the class of the object the
# generic function is called on.
summary(integer_vector)

#-#    Min. 1st Qu.  Median    Mean 3rd Qu.    Max.
#-#     1.0     1.0     1.5     1.5     2.0     2.0

summary(factor_vector)

#-# 1 2
#-# 3 3

# In the case of the integer vector, R will not
# find a method called summary.integer, hence it
# calls summary.default. In the case of the
# factor vector, R does find a method called
# summary.factor and hence will use that method.
# We can skip the dispatching step and call the
# methods directly.
```

```
summary.default(integer_vector)

#-#    Min. 1st Qu.  Median    Mean 3rd Qu.    Max.
#-#     1.0     1.0     1.5     1.5     2.0     2.0

summary.factor(factor_vector)

#-# 1 2
#-# 3 3

# We can even force R to use a method that was
# not designed for the class. For example:

summary.factor(integer_vector)

#-# 1 2
#-# 3 3

# One can print all the methods associated with a
# generic function as follows:
apropos("summary\\.")

#-#  [1] "print.summary.table"     "print.summary.warnings"
#-#  [3] "summary.aov"             "summary.connection"
#-#  [5] "summary.data.frame"      "Summary.data.frame"
#-#  [7] "summary.Date"            "Summary.Date"
#-#  [9] "summary.default"         "Summary.difftime"
#-# [11] "summary.factor"          "Summary.factor"
#-# [13] "summary.glm"             "summary.lm"
#-# [15] "summary.manova"          "summary.matrix"
#-# [17] "Summary.numeric_version" "Summary.ordered"
#-# [19] "summary.POSIXct"         "Summary.POSIXct"
#-# [21] "summary.POSIXlt"         "Summary.POSIXlt"
#-# [23] "summary.proc_time"       "summary.srcfile"
#-# [25] "summary.srcref"          "summary.stepfun"
#-# [27] "summary.table"           "summary.warnings"

# Because the first argument is a regular
# expession we need to escape (\) the dot which
# is a metacharacter.  In R we always need to
# double backslashes.

# Now let's get back to how we are going to use
```

```
# method dispatching. Consider the following
# function called acquisitionModel.  Imagine that
# it creates and outputs a model.  The returned
# object has class 'acquisition'.

acquisitionModel <- function(x) {
    a <- "a model"
    class(a) <- "acquisition"
    a
}

(model <- acquisitionModel())

#-# [1] "a model"
#-# attr(,"class")
#-# [1] "acquisition"

# We now want to create a function called
# 'predict', because that is what the user is
# expecting.  We can find out if there exist
# already functions that are called predict by
# using 'apropos'.

apropos("predict\\.")

#-# [1] "predict.glm" "predict.lm"

# Indeed there are already several functions.
# Therefore, in order not to overwrite existing
# functions we will need to use method
# dispatching and create a new method by
# appending the class name to the generic
# function name (i.e., predict).  Since we have
# assigned the class 'acquisition' to our object,
# we call our function 'predict.acquisition'.

predict.acquisition <- function(object) {
    a <- "predictions from our model"
    a
}

predict(model)

#-# [1] "predictions from our model"
```

```
# As we can see, using predict instead of
# predict.acquisition correctly calls
# predict.acquisition.

# This is equivalent to:
predict.acquisition(model)

#-# [1] "predictions from our model"
```

22.1.2 RC (Reference Classes)

Reference classes are the closest thing to Python's programming style. In addition, they allow the user to avoid copy-on-modify (see more in the data.table Section).

```
# setRefClass returns a generator function for
# creating objects from a class
basetable <- setRefClass(Class = "basetable", fields = list(CustomerID = "character",
    MonetaryValue = "numeric", Recency = "numeric"))

# Create a new object using the generator
# function
a <- basetable$new(CustomerID = c("00123", "00124",
    "00125"), MonetaryValue = c(1000, 10, 5), Recency = c(10,
    20, 30))
a$MonetaryValue

#-# [1] 1000   10    5

a$MonetaryValue[1] <- 1200
a$MonetaryValue

#-# [1] 1200   10    5

# it is important to note that reference class
# objects are mutable they are not
# copied-on-modify

b <- a
b$MonetaryValue

#-# [1] 1200   10    5
```

```
a$MonetaryValue[1] <- 999
b$MonetaryValue

#-# [1] 999  10   5

# in other words, changing a also changes b, they
# point to the same value.  This is an advantage
# in that an object is only stored once, with
# multiple pointers to that some object. Changing
# a value in the object with be very fast.

# to make the objects behave a usual, one can use
# the copy() method

c <- a$copy()
c$MonetaryValue

#-# [1] 999  10   5

a$MonetaryValue[1] <- 100
b$MonetaryValue

#-# [1] 100  10   5

c$MonetaryValue

#-# [1] 999  10   5

# We can also create new methods next to new()
# and copy(), which are inherited from the
# Superclass envRefClass (note the <<-, which is
# required here)

# Here let's create a shape method (similar to
# dim in S3 and shape in Python)

basetable <- setRefClass(Class = "basetable", fields = list(CustomerID = "character",
    MonetaryValue = "numeric", Recency = "numeric"),
    methods = list(shape = function() {
        c(length(MonetaryValue), length(.self$getRefClass()$fields()))
    }))
a <- basetable$new(CustomerID = c("00123", "00124",
    "00125"), MonetaryValue = c(1000, 10, 5), Recency = c(10,
    20, 30))
```

```
a$shape()

#-# [1] 3 3

# Reference classes can be exploited to make
# large data engineering tasks more efficient,
# because copy-on-modify is avoided. This is the
# strategy used by the data.table package.
```

22.2 Python

```
########DEFINING A CLASS: the class statement

#The syntax for creating a class is as follows:

#class <ClassName>(superclass):
    #code follows


#If we do not specify a superclass that we want to inherit from
#the superclass will always be object. The lowercased word 'object'
#is not really an object, it is rather the name of a class, which
#is the root of all classes in Python.

# If we do not specify the word object when creating a class,
# then Python implicity inherits from the 'object' superclass.

# For example if we want to create a class called Person:

# This class definition...
class Person(object):
    pass

Person.__bases__
#-# (<class 'object'>,)

#... is equivalent to this class definition...
class Person():
    pass

Person.__bases__
```

```
#-# (<class 'object'>,)

#...and is equivalent to this class definition:
class Person:
    pass

Person.__bases__

#-# (<class 'object'>,)

#Gotcha:
#What we put in the parentheses in the class statement is
#not an argument as in a function.


########DEFINING A CLASS: the __init__ method

#So how do we pass in arguments?
#With the special __init__() method.
#object.__init__(self[, ...])
#The init method creates an instance of the class Person.
#The first required parameter is self.
#self is a special parameter (the name is not reserved, but self is a strong convention),
which is a reference to the instance itself. It allows
#us to access attributes and methods from inside the same instance.
#self needs to be the first argument in all methods

class Person:
    def __init__(self,firstname,lastname):
        self.firstname = firstname # create attribute
        self.lastname = lastname # create attribute

#create a person
a = Person("John","Doe")
a.firstname

#-# 'John'

a.lastname

#-# 'Doe'

#Gotcha: to find out what the arguments of a class are,
#look at the __init__ method. Whatever comes after self, are the arguments
#that you need to pass in to instantiate a class.
```

```
########DEFINING A CLASS: adding in other methods

from datetime import date

class Person:
    def __init__(self,firstname,lastname): #need firstname and lastname when instantiating
        self.firstname = firstname # create attribute
        self.lastname = lastname # create attribute
    def calculate_age(self,dob): #create method. Need dob when calling this method
        days_in_year = 365.2425
        age = int((date.today() - dob).days / days_in_year)
        return age


a = Person("John", "Doe")

a.calculate_age(date(year=1983,month=1,day=11))

#-# 41

######## DEFINING A CLASS: the __call__ method

# __call__ allows the class's instance to be called as a function:


class Person:
    def __init__(self,firstname,lastname): #need firstname and lastname when instantiating
        self.firstname = firstname # create attribute
        self.lastname = lastname # create attribute
    def calculate_age(self,dob): #create method. Need dob when calling this method
        days_in_year = 365.2425
        age = int((date.today() - dob).days / days_in_year)
        return age
    def __call__(self,anything): #method allowing instance to be called as a function
        print("Hello I am", self.firstname,"and I like",anything)


a = Person("John", "Doe")
a("biking") #__call__ method as a function.

#-# Hello I am John and I like biking
```

22.3 PostgreSQL

Postgres does not have an equivalent to classes.

Chapter 23

Speeding Up Code

23.1 R

The `data.table` package will speed up our code considerably. It is also more memory efficient because of passing-by-reference instead of passing-by-value (i.e., copying). In other words, it opens the door towards a shared-object system (as opposed to R's typical separate object system) and mutability. The `data.table` lets us choose whether we want a shared or separate object system. Moreover it allows shortcuts in our code, so we will have to do less typing. This makes our code easier to develop and maintain. However, we will need some time getting used to the different syntax. In the following code chunk we will cover the key programming statements.

```
# Install and load the data.table package
if (!require(data.table)) {
    install.packages("data.table")
    require(data.table)
}

#-# Loading required package: data.table
#-#
#-# Attaching package: 'data.table'
#-# The following object is masked from 'package:slam':
#-#
#-#     rollup

# Consider the following data frame
(df <- data.frame(V1 = c("a", "b", "a", "a", "b"),
    V2 = 1:5, V3 = c(6, 6, 7, 7, 8), stringsAsFactors = FALSE))
```

```
#-#   V1 V2 V3
#-# 1  a  1  6
#-# 2  b  2  6
#-# 3  a  3  7
#-# 4  a  4  7
#-# 5  b  5  8

# Now, consider the same data frame, but as a
# data table
(dt <- data.table(V1 = c("a", "b", "a", "a", "b"),
    V2 = 1:5, V3 = c(6, 6, 7, 7, 8)))

#-#        V1    V2    V3
#-#    <char> <int> <num>
#-# 1:      a     1     6
#-# 2:      b     2     6
#-# 3:      a     3     7
#-# 4:      a     4     7
#-# 5:      b     5     8

# note the difference in notation: the data table
# has colons next to the row names

# We can easily convert data frames to data
# tables.
(dt2 <- data.table(df))

#-#        V1    V2    V3
#-#    <char> <int> <num>
#-# 1:      a     1     6
#-# 2:      b     2     6
#-# 3:      a     3     7
#-# 4:      a     4     7
#-# 5:      b     5     8

# We can see all data tables in memory using
# tables() tables() is unrelated to table()
tables()

#-#    NAME NROW NCOL MB     COLS    KEY
#-# 1:   dt    5    3  0 V1,V2,V3 [NULL]
#-# 2:  dt2    5    3  0 V1,V2,V3 [NULL]
#-# Total: 0MB using type_size
```

```
# You may have noticed the empty column called
# KEY Setting a key (keying; indexing) can speed
# up operations on the data table.  Think of
# indexing in terms of a phone book. A phone book
# is indexed by name. Finding the phone number
# for a person is very easy. However, finding the
# name for a phone number is very hard, if not
# impossible. Indexing a data table is equivalent
# to sorting, and is out of the scope of this
# book.

# Let's look at the class of a data.table
class(dt)

#-# [1] "data.table" "data.frame"

class(df)

#-# [1] "data.frame"

# Note that a data table also is of class
# data.frame.  However, do not assume that code
# that would run on a data frame would run on a
# data.table.  While the data.table package has
# come a long way, we sometimes need different
# code to interact with a data.table.

######################################################## Subsetting
######################################################## a
######################################################## data.table
######################################################## (dt)
######################################################## vs
######################################################## a
######################################################## data.frame
######################################################## (df)
df

#-#   V1 V2 V3
#-# 1  a  1  6
#-# 2  b  2  6
#-# 3  a  3  7
#-# 4  a  4  7
#-# 5  b  5  8
```

```
dt

#-#        V1    V2    V3
#-#    <char> <int> <num>
#-# 1:      a     1     6
#-# 2:      b     2     6
#-# 3:      a     3     7
#-# 4:      a     4     7
#-# 5:      b     5     8

###################### by $-sign
df$V1

#-# [1] "a" "b" "a" "a" "b"

dt$V1  #note that dimensions are dropped just like in a df

#-# [1] "a" "b" "a" "a" "b"

df[df$V1 == "a", ]

#-#   V1 V2 V3
#-# 1  a  1  6
#-# 3  a  3  7
#-# 4  a  4  7

dt[V1 == "a", ]

#-#        V1    V2    V3
#-#    <char> <int> <num>
#-# 1:      a     1     6
#-# 2:      a     3     7
#-# 3:      a     4     7

###################### by name
df[, "V1"]

#-# [1] "a" "b" "a" "a" "b"

dt[, V1]

#-# [1] "a" "b" "a" "a" "b"

dt[, .(V1)]  #equivalent to drop=FALSE in df
```

```
#-#        V1
#-#    <char>
#-# 1:      a
#-# 2:      b
#-# 3:      a
#-# 4:      a
#-# 5:      b
```

```
dt[, list(V1)]  #equivalent to drop=FALSE in df, note that . is short for list
```

```
#-#        V1
#-#    <char>
#-# 1:      a
#-# 2:      b
#-# 3:      a
#-# 4:      a
#-# 5:      b
```

```
dt[, "V1"]
```

```
#-#        V1
#-#    <char>
#-# 1:      a
#-# 2:      b
#-# 3:      a
#-# 4:      a
#-# 5:      b
```

```
df[, c("V1", "V2")]
```

```
#-#   V1 V2
#-# 1  a  1
#-# 2  b  2
#-# 3  a  3
#-# 4  a  4
#-# 5  b  5
```

```
dt[, c("V1", "V2")]
```

```
#-#        V1    V2
#-#    <char> <int>
#-# 1:      a     1
#-# 2:      b     2
#-# 3:      a     3
```

```
#-# 4:      a     4
#-# 5:      b     5

dt[, .(V1, V2)]  #if we do not wish to quote the variable names

#-#         V1    V2
#-#     <char> <int>
#-# 1:      a     1
#-# 2:      b     2
#-# 3:      a     3
#-# 4:      a     4
#-# 5:      b     5

dt[, list(V1, V2)]  #same as previous line

#-#         V1    V2
#-#     <char> <int>
#-# 1:      a     1
#-# 2:      b     2
#-# 3:      a     3
#-# 4:      a     4
#-# 5:      b     5

###################### by indices

# for columns:
df[, 1]

#-# [1] "a" "b" "a" "a" "b"

df[, 1, drop = FALSE]

#-#   V1
#-# 1  a
#-# 2  b
#-# 3  a
#-# 4  a
#-# 5  b

df[, 1:2]

#-#   V1 V2
#-# 1  a  1
#-# 2  b  2
```

```
#-# 3  a  3
#-# 4  a  4
#-# 5  b  5
```

```
df[, c(1:2)]
```

```
#-#   V1 V2
#-# 1  a  1
#-# 2  b  2
#-# 3  a  3
#-# 4  a  4
#-# 5  b  5
```

```
dt[, 1]  #dimensions are not dropped
```

```
#-#        V1
#-#    <char>
#-# 1:      a
#-# 2:      b
#-# 3:      a
#-# 4:      a
#-# 5:      b
```

```
dt[, 1:2]
```

```
#-#        V1    V2
#-#    <char> <int>
#-# 1:      a     1
#-# 2:      b     2
#-# 3:      a     3
#-# 4:      a     4
#-# 5:      b     5
```

```
dt[, c(1:2)]
```

```
#-#        V1    V2
#-#    <char> <int>
#-# 1:      a     1
#-# 2:      b     2
#-# 3:      a     3
#-# 4:      a     4
#-# 5:      b     5
```

```
df[1]
```

```
#-#   V1
#-# 1  a
#-# 2  b
#-# 3  a
#-# 4  a
#-# 5  b

df[[1]]

#-# [1] "a" "b" "a" "a" "b"

dt[[1]]

#-# [1] "a" "b" "a" "a" "b"

# for rows
df[1:3, ]

#-#   V1 V2 V3
#-# 1  a  1  6
#-# 2  b  2  6
#-# 3  a  3  7

dt[1:3, ]

#-#         V1    V2    V3
#-#     <char> <int> <num>
#-# 1:       a     1     6
#-# 2:       b     2     6
#-# 3:       a     3     7

######################################################## Aggregating
######################################################## a
######################################################## data.table
######################################################## (dt)
######################################################## vs
######################################################## a
######################################################## data.frame
######################################################## (df)

# data.table syntax borrows from SQL as follows:
# dt[i,j,by] R: i j by SQL: where select/update
# group by
```

```
# Equivalent SQL syntax: SELECT j FROM dt WHERE i
# GROUP BY: by

# one by variable
aggregate(df$V2, by = list(V1 = df$V1), sum)

#-#   V1 x
#-# 1  a 8
#-# 2  b 7

dt[, sum(V2), by = V1]

#-#        V1    V1
#-#    <char> <int>
#-# 1:      a     8
#-# 2:      b     7

# multiple aggregation variables
aggregate(df[, c("V2", "V3")], by = list(V1 = df$V1),
    sum)

#-#   V1 V2 V3
#-# 1  a  8 20
#-# 2  b  7 14

dt[, .(sum(V2), sum(V3)), by = V1]

#-#        V1    V1    V2
#-#    <char> <int> <num>
#-# 1:      a     8    20
#-# 2:      b     7    14

# multiple by variables
aggregate(df[, "V2"], by = list(V1 = df$V1, V3 = df$V3),
    sum)

#-#   V1 V3 x
#-# 1  a  6 1
#-# 2  b  6 2
#-# 3  a  7 7
#-# 4  b  8 5

dt[, .(V2 = sum(V2)), by = .(V1, V3)]
```

```
#-#         V1    V3    V2
#-#     <char> <num> <int>
#-# 1:       a     6     1
#-# 2:       b     6     2
#-# 3:       a     7     7
#-# 4:       b     8     5

############################################################## Creating
############################################################## new
############################################################## variables
############################################################## in
############################################################## a
############################################################## data.table
############################################################## (dt)
############################################################## vs
############################################################## a
############################################################## data.frame
############################################################## (df)

# Creating new variables
df$V4 <- df$V2 + df$V3
dt$V4 <- df$V2 + df$V3

# or better, by reference:
dt

#-# Index: <V1>
#-#         V1    V2    V3    V4
#-#     <char> <int> <num> <num>
#-# 1:       a     1     6     7
#-# 2:       b     2     6     8
#-# 3:       a     3     7    10
#-# 4:       a     4     7    11
#-# 5:       b     5     8    13

dt[, V5 := V2 + V3]
dt

#-# Index: <V1>
#-#         V1    V2    V3    V4    V5
#-#     <char> <int> <num> <num> <num>
#-# 1:       a     1     6     7     7
#-# 2:       b     2     6     8     8
```

```
#-# 3:      a     3     7    10    10
#-# 4:      a     4     7    11    11
#-# 5:      b     5     8    13    13

# Note that there is no '<-' involved; we are
# creating a new variable by reference. This is a
# lot more efficient. If we use the '<-' we are
# copying the entire dt. If we use ':=' we are
# not.

# Removing variables
df

#-#   V1 V2 V3 V4
#-# 1  a  1  6  7
#-# 2  b  2  6  8
#-# 3  a  3  7 10
#-# 4  a  4  7 11
#-# 5  b  5  8 13

df$V4 <- NULL
df

#-#   V1 V2 V3
#-# 1  a  1  6
#-# 2  b  2  6
#-# 3  a  3  7
#-# 4  a  4  7
#-# 5  b  5  8

dt

#-# Index: <V1>
#-#        V1    V2    V3    V4    V5
#-#    <char> <int> <num> <num> <num>
#-# 1:      a     1     6     7     7
#-# 2:      b     2     6     8     8
#-# 3:      a     3     7    10    10
#-# 4:      a     4     7    11    11
#-# 5:      b     5     8    13    13

dt[, V4 := NULL]
dt
```

```
#-# Index: <V1>
#-#        V1    V2    V3    V5
#-#    <char> <int> <num> <num>
#-# 1:      a     1     6     7
#-# 2:      b     2     6     8
#-# 3:      a     3     7    10
#-# 4:      a     4     7    11
#-# 5:      b     5     8    13

######################################################## Merging
######################################################## data
######################################################## tables
######################################################## (dt)
######################################################## vs
######################################################## data
######################################################## frames
######################################################## (df)

# data frame
(df1 <- data.frame(V1 = c("a", "b"), V2 = 1:2, V3 = c(6,
    6)))

#-#   V1 V2 V3
#-# 1  a  1  6
#-# 2  b  2  6

(df2 <- data.frame(V1 = c("b", "c"), V4 = 3:4, V5 = c(7,
    8)))

#-#   V1 V4 V5
#-# 1  b  3  7
#-# 2  c  4  8

merge(df1, df2, by = "V1")

#-#   V1 V2 V3 V4 V5
#-# 1  b  2  6  3  7

merge(df1, df2, by = "V1", all = TRUE)

#-#   V1 V2 V3 V4 V5
#-# 1  a  1  6 NA NA
#-# 2  b  2  6  3  7
#-# 3  c NA NA  4  8
```

```
# data table
(dt1 <- data.table(V1 = c("a", "b"), V2 = 1:2, V3 = c(6,
   6)))

#-#        V1    V2    V3
#-#    <char> <int> <num>
#-# 1:      a     1     6
#-# 2:      b     2     6

(dt2 <- data.table(V1 = c("b", "c"), V4 = 3:4, V5 = c(7,
   8)))

#-#        V1    V4    V5
#-#    <char> <int> <num>
#-# 1:      b     3     7
#-# 2:      c     4     8

merge(dt1, dt2, by = "V1")

#-# Key: <V1>
#-#        V1    V2    V3    V4    V5
#-#    <char> <int> <num> <int> <num>
#-# 1:      b     2     6     3     7

merge(dt1, dt2, by = "V1", all = TRUE)

#-# Key: <V1>
#-#        V1    V2    V3    V4    V5
#-#    <char> <int> <num> <int> <num>
#-# 1:      a     1     6    NA    NA
#-# 2:      b     2     6     3     7
#-# 3:      c    NA    NA     4     8

######################################################## Reading
######################################################## in
######################################################## data
######################################################## as
######################################################## a
######################################################## data.table
######################################################## (dt)
######################################################## vs
######################################################## a
######################################################## data.frame
######################################################## (df)
```

```
URL_subs <- "http://hde.onl/subscriptions.txt"

# the usual way
subs1 <- read.table(URL_subs, header = TRUE, sep = ";")

# Using the data.table package If you have a
# large data set stored on disk, fread will be
# lightning fast compared to read.table
subs2 <- fread(URL_subs, header = TRUE, sep = ";")

class(subs2)

#-# [1] "data.table" "data.frame"

# If you don't want it to be a data.table You can
# transform it to a data.frame without incurring
# the copy-cost
setDF(subs2)
class(subs2)

#-# [1] "data.frame"

######################################################## rbinding
######################################################## elements
######################################################## in
######################################################## a
######################################################## list
######################################################## as
######################################################## a
######################################################## data.table
######################################################## (dt)
######################################################## vs
######################################################## a
######################################################## data.frame
######################################################## (df)

# data frame
df1 <- data.frame(a = c(1, 2), b = c(3, 4), c = c(5,
    6))
df2 <- data.frame(a = c(7, 8), b = c(9, 10), c = c(11,
    12))

(l <- list(df1, df2))
```

```
#-# [[1]]
#-#   a b c
#-# 1 1 3 5
#-# 2 2 4 6
#-#
#-# [[2]]
#-#   a  b  c
#-# 1 7  9 11
#-# 2 8 10 12

do.call(rbind, l)

#-#   a  b  c
#-# 1 1  3  5
#-# 2 2  4  6
#-# 3 7  9 11
#-# 4 8 10 12

# data table
dt1 <- data.table(a = c(1, 2), b = c(3, 4), c = c(5,
    6))
dt2 <- data.table(a = c(7, 8), b = c(9, 10), c = c(11,
    12))

(l <- list(dt1, dt2))

#-# [[1]]
#-#        a     b     c
#-#    <num> <num> <num>
#-# 1:     1     3     5
#-# 2:     2     4     6
#-#
#-# [[2]]
#-#        a     b     c
#-#    <num> <num> <num>
#-# 1:     7     9    11
#-# 2:     8    10    12

rbindlist(l)

#-#        a     b     c
#-#    <num> <num> <num>
#-# 1:     1     3     5
#-# 2:     2     4     6
```

```
#-# 3:      7     9    11
#-# 4:      8    10    12

######################################################## referencing
######################################################## vs
######################################################## copying
######################################################## Consider
######################################################## a
######################################################## dataframe
df1

#-#   a b c
#-# 1 1 3 5
#-# 2 2 4 6

# Copy df1
df2 <- df1
# Let's look at the memory locations.  Both are
# the same. It is actually a reference, and not a
# copy.  .Internal(inspect(df1)) #uncomment
# .Internal(inspect(df2)) #uncomment R copies on
# write (or more specifically copy-on-subassign)
df2[1, 2] <- 10
# .Internal(inspect(df2)) #uncomment

# Of course this copying is very inefficient
# data.table is designed to prevent this
dt1

#-#         a     b     c
#-#     <num> <num> <num>
#-# 1:      1     3     5
#-# 2:      2     4     6

# Copy dt1
dt2 <- dt1
# Let's look at the memory locations.  Both are
# the same. It is actually a reference, and not a
# copy.  .Internal(inspect(dt1)) #uncomment
# .Internal(inspect(dt2)) #uncomment data.table
# can avoid copying and instead use referencing
# when we use the := operator
dt2[1, b := 10]
dt2
```

```
#-#        a    b    c
#-#    <num> <num> <num>
#-# 1:     1   10    5
#-# 2:     2    4    6

# .Internal(inspect(dt2)) #uncomment of course,
# when we do that dt1 will also have changed:
dt1

#-#        a    b    c
#-#    <num> <num> <num>
#-# 1:     1   10    5
#-# 2:     2    4    6

# This makes the data.table package very
# powerful, especially when dealing with large
# data sets. However, care is required.  If we
# want base-type copying, we can use dt2[1,2] <-
# 10 or the copy function dt2 <- copy(dt1)
```

23.2 Python

Python is already very much optimized through its shared object system. If we need further speed-ups we can use `pyspark` , a Python API to Apache Spark. Apache Spark is the most actively developed open-source engine and a set of libraries for parallel data processing, on a single computer or a cluster of computers.

23.2.1 Spark's components

Spark consists of Low-level APIs (Resilient Distributed Datasets or RDDs, Distributed Variables), high-level APIs called Structured APIs (Datasets, DataFrames, SQL), and even higher-level APIs (Structured Streaming, Advanced Analytics, Libraries and Ecosystem). The higher-level systems use high-level systems, which in turn use the low-level systems.

In this book we will focus on the Structured APIs that are available in Python: DataFrames and SQL. Datasets are specific to Scala, another programming language and replace DataFrames in that language. The higher-level APIs are for narrower use-cases and because of their lack of generality we do not cover them in this book.

Some high-level APIs contain machine learning algorithms, which is not the topic of this book. Similarly, the low-level APIs are not covered in this book. They are automatically called by the high-level APIs and are only required to override high-level behavior.

23.2.2 How Spark speeds up data processing

Spark applications consist in a *driver* process and one or more *executor* processes. The driver process maintains information about the Spark application, responds to a user's code, and distributes work across the executors. The executors carry out their assigned work and report back to the driver. The *cluster manager* controls and allocates physical resources to Spark applications. If we are running everything on a single machine, as opposed to a cluster of machines, then we could call this the `local manager`, which is just to say a cluster of size one. Figure 23.1 is a visual representation of this system.

From this figure it is clear how Spark is able to speed up processing: through parallel processing. Key to this processing is to distribute or partition the data to have separate executor processes work on the different partitions. These partitions are subsets of the data and can be stored on different machines or a single machine. In this book we will work with Spark in local mode.

23.2.3 Installing pyspark locally

Step 1. Pyspark requires a Spark installation, which in turn requires Java. At the time of this writing the latest stable release is Spark 3.5.3, which runs on Java 8, 11, and 17. For the latest information see https://spark.apache.org/docs/latest/. We start the installation process by making sure Java 17 is on our computer. In the shell we type `java -version`, and find that Java is not installed. Next, we download Java 17 for our platform here: https://www.oracle.com/java/technologies/downloads/. Note that this requires one to create a free account. For Mac download *jdk-17.0.13_macos-aarch64_bin.dmg*, and for Windows, download *jdk-17.0.13_windows-x64_bin.exe*. We double click the installer, follow the prompts, and take note of the installation path if it is provided. On a Mac, after installing Java 17 we can verify if it visible in our system:

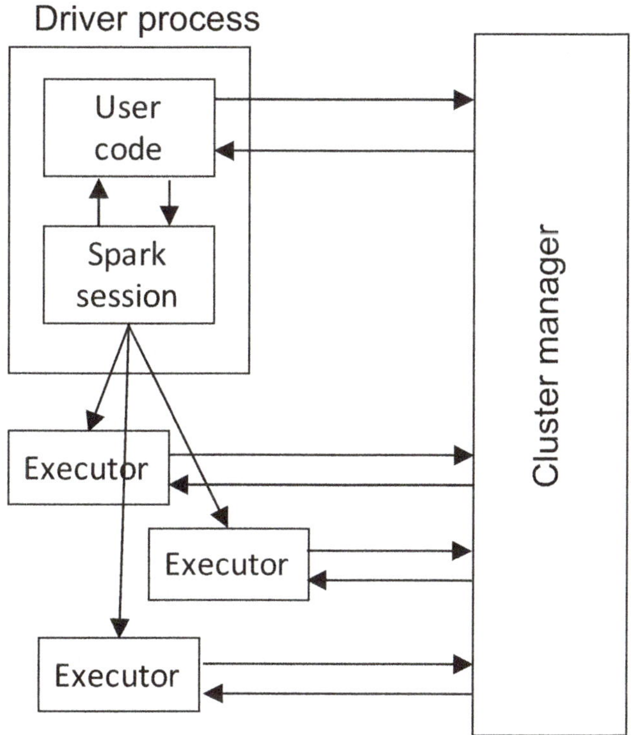

Figure 23.1: How Sparks Speeds up Processing

```
mb@Michels-MacBook-Pro-2 ~ % /usr/libexec/java_home -V
Matching Java Virtual Machines (1):
    17.0.13 (arm64) "Oracle Corporation" - "Java SE 17.0.13"
/Library/Java/JavaVirtualMachines/jdk-17.jdk/Contents/Home
```

There is no easy way to do this on a Windows machine but the path usually resembles Program Files > Java > jdk.... Next, let's verify if our computer is pointing to Java 17. This is especially important if we have multiple Java versions installed, or if our computer cannot find Java.

```
mb@Michels-MacBook-Pro-2 ~ % java -version
java version "17.0.13" 2024-10-15 LTS
Java(TM) SE Runtime Environment (build 17.0.13+10-LTS-268)
Java HotSpot(TM) 64-Bit Server VM (build 17.0.13+10-LTS-268, mixed mode, sharing)
```

Our computer does point to the correct Java version. However, for Spark we still need set the JAVA_HOME environment variable. On a Windows machine, add the JAVA_HOME environment variable using the system's point and click screens, and reboot the computer. The path needs to be the folder that contains the java executable. On a Mac or Linux machine, we can add it as follows to our terminal. On a Mac we do the following:

```
# Type the following in shell:
nano ~/.zshrc


#Add the path to your executable to the end of the file
#Make sure to use your path
export JAVA_HOME=/Library/Java/JavaVirtualMachines/jdk-17.jdk/Contents/Home

#Then type control o,
#Then type enter
#Then type control x
```

We then open up a new shell and verify the active version is still the correct version:

```
mb@Michels-MacBook-Pro-2 ~ % java -version
java version "17.0.13" 2024-10-15 LTS
Java(TM) SE Runtime Environment (build 17.0.13+10-LTS-268)
Java HotSpot(TM) 64-Bit Server VM (build 17.0.13+10-LTS-268, mixed mode, sharing)
```

We have successfuly installed Java 17 and have our system point to it when the keyword `java` is called.

Step 2. Next we download Apache Spark from `https://spark.apache.org/downloads.html`. We choose Spark release 3.5.3, pre-built for Apache Hadoop 3.3 and later as shown in Figure 23.2.
We make a new folder in our shell at a location of our choosing, for example `mkdir /server`, or `mkdir /Users/mb/Applications/server/`, and add the downloaded `.tgz` file to that folder. Next, on a Mac, we double click the file to unpack it. If we are on a Windows machine we may need to install 7-zip or WinRAR `https://www.win-rar.com/start.html` and right click the tgz file to extract its contents. Note that we may need to extract the resulting file another time if it is again an archive (e.g., tar, zip). The end-result should be a folder with several files

Download Apache Spark™

1. Choose a Spark release: 3.5.3 (Sep 24 2024)
2. Choose a package type: Pre-built for Apache Hadoop 3.3 and later
3. Download Spark: spark-3.5.3-bin-hadoop3.tgz

Figure 23.2: Downloading Spark

and subfolders. The only remaining task is then to tell our computer where it can find the software. On a Windows machine, we add three environment variables (SPARK_HOME, PYSPARK_PYTHON, PYSPARK_DRIVER_PYTHON) and paths using the system's point and click screens, and on a Mac machine we add these variables and corresponding paths to our `.zshrc` as follows (to find your python3 path, type `which python3` in your terminal; also note that some Windows users have reported that the python path should be simply the word *python*):

```
# Type the following in shell:
nano ~/.zshrc


#Add the following lines to the end of the file
export SPARK_HOME=/Users/mb/Applications/server/spark-3.5.3-bin-hadoop3
export PYSPARK_PYTHON=/Library/Frameworks/Python.framework/Versions/3.10/bin/python3
export PYSPARK_DRIVER_PYTHON=/Library/Frameworks/Python.framework/Versions/3.10/bin/python3

#Then type control o
#Then type enter
#Then type control x
```

Step 3. The penultimate step is to install `pyspark` in the shell as follows: `pip3 install pyspark` .

Step 4. Finally, we verify if the installation process was successful by opening a new shell and typing `pyspark` in the shell. Among other output, we will see a welcome message that looks like Figure 23.3. We quit by typing `exit()` .

If we are working in GitBash on Windows we might get a 'bad array subscript' error. This is a known bug. The solution is to type `pyspark` in Windows Command

```
mb@Michels-MacBook-Pro-2 ~ % pyspark
Python 3.10.10 (v3.10.10:aad5f6a891, Feb  7 2023, 08:47:40) [Clang 13.0.0 (clang-1300.0.29.30)] or
Type "help", "copyright", "credits" or "license" for more information.
24/10/24 10:59:29 WARN Utils: Your hostname, Michels-MacBook-Pro-2.local resolves to a loopback ac
24/10/24 10:59:29 WARN Utils: Set SPARK_LOCAL_IP if you need to bind to another address
Setting default log level to "WARN".
To adjust logging level use sc.setLogLevel(newLevel). For SparkR, use setLogLevel(newLevel).
24/10/24 10:59:30 WARN NativeCodeLoader: Unable to load native-hadoop library for your platform...
Welcome to
      ____              __
     / __/__  ___ _____/ /__
    _\ \/ _ \/ _ `/ __/  '_/
   /__ / .__/\_,_/_/ /_/\_\   version 3.5.3
      /_/

Using Python version 3.10.10 (v3.10.10:aad5f6a891, Feb  7 2023 08:47:40)
Spark context Web UI available at http://192.168.1.8:4040
Spark context available as 'sc' (master = local[*], app id = local-1729781970683).
SparkSession available as 'spark'.
>>> exit()
mb@Michels-MacBook-Pro-2 ~ %
```

Figure 23.3: Welcome to Spark

Prompt. Also note that it is not imperative that this works in the shell, as long as the pyspark module can be imported in python as shown in the following section.

Common errors and solutions:

- Error: Service 'sparkDriver' could not bind on a random free port.
  Solution: `pyspark -c spark.driver.bindAddress=127.0.0.1`

23.2.4 Main Operations

```
#The entry point into all functionality in Spark is the SparkSession

from pyspark.sql import SparkSession

#master: run in local model with 8 cores
#appName: name of app to show on the cluster UI
spark = SparkSession.builder \
    .master("local[8]") \
    .appName("my_app") \
    .getOrCreate()

spark
#-# <pyspark.sql.session.SparkSession object at 0x3493569b0>
```

```
spark.sparkContext

#-# <SparkContext master=local[8] appName=my_app>

##############################################################
#Reading data:

#download the data to your computer:
#http://hde.onl/subscriptions.csv

#automatically infer the column types
file_path = '/Users/mb/Documents/databook/subscriptions.csv'

subs = spark.read.csv(file_path,
                      header = True,
                      sep = ';',
                      inferSchema = True)
#or
#specify the column types

#The main types are:

#Integers:
# ByteType (1 byte)
# ShortType (2 bytes)
# IntegerType (4 bytes)
# LongType (8 bytes)

#Floats
# FloatType (32 bit, single precision float)
# DoubleType (64 bit, double precision float)
# DecimalType (128 bit)

#Strings
# StringType

#booleans
# BooleanType

#Time
# TimestampType
# DateType
```

```
from pyspark.sql.types import *

schema = StructType([
    StructField("SubscriptionID", StringType()),
    StructField("CustomerID", StringType()),
    StructField("ProductID", StringType()),
    StructField("Pattern", IntegerType()),
    StructField("StartDate", StringType()),
    StructField("EndDate", StringType()),
    StructField("NbrNewspapers", IntegerType()),
    StructField("NbrStart", IntegerType()),
    StructField("RenewalDate", StringType()),
    StructField("PaymentType", StringType()),
    StructField("PaymentStatus", StringType()),
    StructField("PaymentDate", StringType()),
    StructField("FormulaID", StringType()),
    StructField("GrossFormulaPrice", DoubleType()),
    StructField("NetFormulaPrice", DoubleType()),
    StructField("NetNewspaperPrice", DoubleType()),
    StructField("ProductDiscount", DoubleType()),
    StructField("FormulaDiscount", DoubleType()),
    StructField("TotalDiscount", DoubleType()),
    StructField("TotalPrice", DoubleType()),
    StructField("TotalCredit", DoubleType())
])

subs = spark.read.csv(file_path,
                      header = True,
                      sep = ';',
                      schema = schema)

#What type?
type(subs)

#-# <class 'pyspark.sql.dataframe.DataFrame'>

#Some more information:
#subs.show(5)


#subs.columns
```

```
# Creating data:

# Create pd_temp
import pandas as pd
import numpy as np
pd_table = pd.DataFrame(np.random.random(100))
type(pd_table)

#-# <class 'pandas.core.frame.DataFrame'>

# Create spark_temp from pd_table
spark_table = spark.createDataFrame(pd_table)
type(spark_table)

#-# <class 'pyspark.sql.dataframe.DataFrame'>

##############################################################
#DATAFRAME SYNTAX

####################Viewing data
subs.printSchema()

#-# root
#-#  |-- SubscriptionID: string (nullable = true)
#-#  |-- CustomerID: string (nullable = true)
#-#  |-- ProductID: string (nullable = true)
#-#  |-- Pattern: integer (nullable = true)
#-#  |-- StartDate: string (nullable = true)
#-#  |-- EndDate: string (nullable = true)
#-#  |-- NbrNewspapers: integer (nullable = true)
#-#  |-- NbrStart: integer (nullable = true)
#-#  |-- RenewalDate: string (nullable = true)
#-#  |-- PaymentType: string (nullable = true)
#-#  |-- PaymentStatus: string (nullable = true)
#-#  |-- PaymentDate: string (nullable = true)
#-#  |-- FormulaID: string (nullable = true)
#-#  |-- GrossFormulaPrice: double (nullable = true)
#-#  |-- NetFormulaPrice: double (nullable = true)
#-#  |-- NetNewspaperPrice: double (nullable = true)
#-#  |-- ProductDiscount: double (nullable = true)
#-#  |-- FormulaDiscount: double (nullable = true)
#-#  |-- TotalDiscount: double (nullable = true)
#-#  |-- TotalPrice: double (nullable = true)
#-#  |-- TotalCredit: double (nullable = true)
```

```
#subs.show(5)


####################
#selecting one or more columns and displaying the results
subs.select('TotalDiscount','TotalPrice').show()

#-# +-------------+----------+
#-# |TotalDiscount|TotalPrice|
#-# +-------------+----------+
#-# |          0.0|      79.0|
#-# |      22.3737|      29.6|
#-# |          0.0|     246.8|
#-# |          0.0|     235.0|
#-# |          0.0|     246.8|
#-# |          0.0|     235.0|
#-# |          0.0|     267.0|
#-# |          0.0|     267.0|
#-# |          0.0|     267.0|
#-# |         NULL|      NULL|
#-# |    21.957237|     267.0|
#-# |          0.0|     267.0|
#-# |          0.0|      79.0|
#-# |          0.0|      79.0|
#-# |    21.957237|     267.0|
#-# |          0.0|      79.0|
#-# |          0.0|      79.0|
#-# |    43.914306|     267.0|
#-# |     6.236868|      79.0|
#-# |         NULL|      NULL|
#-# +-------------+----------+
#-# only showing top 20 rows

#or
subs.select(subs.TotalDiscount,subs.TotalPrice).show()

#-# +-------------+----------+
#-# |TotalDiscount|TotalPrice|
#-# +-------------+----------+
#-# |          0.0|      79.0|
#-# |      22.3737|      29.6|
#-# |          0.0|     246.8|
#-# |          0.0|     235.0|
#-# |          0.0|     246.8|
```

```
#-# |          0.0|     235.0|
#-# |          0.0|     267.0|
#-# |          0.0|     267.0|
#-# |          0.0|     267.0|
#-# |         NULL|      NULL|
#-# |    21.957237|     267.0|
#-# |          0.0|     267.0|
#-# |          0.0|      79.0|
#-# |          0.0|      79.0|
#-# |    21.957237|     267.0|
#-# |          0.0|      79.0|
#-# |          0.0|      79.0|
#-# |    43.914306|     267.0|
#-# |     6.236868|      79.0|
#-# |         NULL|      NULL|
#-# +-------------+----------+
#-# only showing top 20 rows

####################
#Creating columns with withColumn
subs = subs.withColumn('TotalDiscountPlus1000', subs.TotalDiscount + 1000)
subs.select('TotalDiscountPlus1000').show(5)

#-# +---------------------+
#-# |TotalDiscountPlus1000|
#-# +---------------------+
#-# |               1000.0|
#-# |            1022.3737|
#-# |               1000.0|
#-# |               1000.0|
#-# |               1000.0|
#-# +---------------------+
#-# only showing top 5 rows

#This returns all the columns and the new column

#Alternatively we can use select
TotalDiscountPlus2000 = (subs.TotalDiscount + 2000).alias('TotalDiscountPlus2000')
subs = subs.select('*', TotalDiscountPlus2000)
subs.select('TotalDiscountPlus2000').show(5)

#-# +---------------------+
#-# |TotalDiscountPlus2000|
#-# +---------------------+
```

```
#-# |               2000.0|
#-# |            2022.3737|
#-# |               2000.0|
#-# |               2000.0|
#-# |               2000.0|
#-# +---------------------+
#-# only showing top 5 rows
```

```
#Or use selectExpr, which takes sql expressions as a string
subs = subs.selectExpr('*','TotalDiscount + 3000 as TotalDiscountPlus3000')
subs.select('TotalDiscountPlus3000').show(5)
```

```
#-# +---------------------+
#-# |TotalDiscountPlus3000|
#-# +---------------------+
#-# |               3000.0|
#-# |            3022.3737|
#-# |               3000.0|
#-# |               3000.0|
#-# |               3000.0|
#-# +---------------------+
#-# only showing top 5 rows
```

```
####################
#Subsetting data, filter takes either a boolean vector, or
#an expression that would follow the where clause in a sql expression
#as a string

#boolean vector

subs_subset = subs.filter(subs.TotalDiscount > 2)
subs.count()
```

```
#-# 227
```

```
subs_subset.count()
```

```
#-# 47
```

```
#sql string

subs_subset = subs.filter('TotalDiscount > 2')
subs_subset.count()
```

```
#-# 47
```

```
####################
#Aggregating

#need to apply the groupBy() method before using summary fuctions.
subs.groupBy().min('TotalDiscount').show()

#-# +------------------+
#-# |min(TotalDiscount)|
#-# +------------------+
#-# |               0.0|
#-# +------------------+

subs.groupBy().max('TotalDiscount').show()

#-# +------------------+
#-# |max(TotalDiscount)|
#-# +------------------+
#-# |             129.0|
#-# +------------------+

subs.groupBy().avg('TotalDiscount').show()

#-# +------------------+
#-# |avg(TotalDiscount)|
#-# +------------------+
#-# | 7.744266092165899|
#-# +------------------+

subs.groupBy().sum('TotalDiscount').show()

#-# +------------------+
#-# |sum(TotalDiscount)|
#-# +------------------+
#-# |       1680.505742|
#-# +------------------+

subs.groupBy().count().show()

#-# +-----+
#-# |count|
#-# +-----+
#-# |  227|
#-# +-----+

#by customerId
subs.groupBy('CustomerID').avg('TotalDiscount').show()
```

```
#-# +----------+------------------+
#-# |CustomerID|avg(TotalDiscount)|
#-# +----------+------------------+
#-# |   1018582|               0.0|
#-# |    951565|         21.957237|
#-# |    501314|               0.0|
#-# |    903182|               0.0|
#-# |    137296|               0.0|
#-# |   1120343|              12.2|
#-# |    308255|               0.0|
#-# |     41098|               0.0|
#-# |    947115|               0.0|
#-# |    722525|               0.0|
#-# |    855148|               0.0|
#-# |    715407|               0.0|
#-# |    971424|             129.0|
#-# |     71010|               0.0|
#-# |    197304|               0.0|
#-# |    671228|               0.0|
#-# |    712777|               0.0|
#-# |     67723|               0.0|
#-# |    594955|               0.0|
#-# |   1004057|               0.0|
#-# +----------+------------------+
#-# only showing top 20 rows
```

```
#by two IDs
subs.groupBy('CustomerID','ProductID').avg('TotalDiscount').show()
```

```
#-# +----------+---------+------------------+
#-# |CustomerID|ProductID|avg(TotalDiscount)|
#-# +----------+---------+------------------+
#-# |   1150307|        6|              56.0|
#-# |    913232|        2|          6.236868|
#-# |    971424|        8|             129.0|
#-# |   1004057|        1|               0.0|
#-# |    868073|        8|               0.0|
#-# |    303500|        8|               0.0|
#-# |    455810|        2|               0.0|
#-# |     53936|        8|               0.0|
#-# |     94618|        8|               0.0|
#-# |     66815|        6|           22.3737|
#-# |    793799|        8|               0.0|
```

```
#-# |     79051|       8|            0.0|
#-# |    812585|       8|            0.0|
#-# |    191542|       8|            0.0|
#-# |   1020508|       8|            0.0|
#-# |    802506|       8|       6.236842|
#-# |      7797|       8|            0.0|
#-# |    905850|       1|            0.0|
#-# |    149524|       8|            0.0|
#-# |     41098|       8|            0.0|
#-# +----------+--------+-----------------+
#-# only showing top 20 rows

#stddev can be accessed as follows:
import pyspark.sql.functions as F

subs.groupBy('ProductID').agg(F.stddev('TotalDiscount')).show()

#-# +---------+---------------------+
#-# |ProductID|stddev(TotalDiscount)|
#-# +---------+---------------------+
#-# |        7|    7.487734568735459|
#-# |        3|                  0.0|
#-# |        8|   26.036006385088974|
#-# |        5|    16.70728604850305|
#-# |        6|     26.8595503381755|
#-# |        1|    6.429876873751685|
#-# |        2|   22.763452891020627|
#-# +---------+---------------------+

####################
#joins

#create toy data
import pandas as pd
import numpy as np


a = pd.DataFrame([[1,'a'],[2,'b'],[3,'c'],[4,'d']], columns = ['id','val'])
a

#-#    id val
#-# 0   1   a
#-# 1   2   b
#-# 2   3   c
```

```
#-# 3    4    d

a = spark.createDataFrame(a)
a.show()

#-# +---+---+
#-# | id|val|
#-# +---+---+
#-# |  1|  a|
#-# |  2|  b|
#-# |  3|  c|
#-# |  4|  d|
#-# +---+---+

b = pd.DataFrame([[2,'g'],[3,'f'],[5,'e']], columns = ['id','val2'])
b

#-#    id val2
#-# 0   2    g
#-# 1   3    f
#-# 2   5    e

b = spark.createDataFrame(b)
b.show()

#-# +---+----+
#-# | id|val2|
#-# +---+----+
#-# |  2|   g|
#-# |  3|   f|
#-# |  5|   e|
#-# +---+----+

#joins
a_b_inner = a.join(b,on='id',how='inner')
a_b_inner.show()

#-# +---+---+----+
#-# | id|val|val2|
#-# +---+---+----+
#-# |  2|  b|   g|
#-# |  3|  c|   f|
#-# +---+---+----+

a_b_left = a.join(b,on='id',how='left_outer')
a_b_left.show()
```

```
#-# +---+---+----+
#-# | id|val|val2|
#-# +---+---+----+
#-# |  1|  a|NULL|
#-# |  2|  b|   g|
#-# |  3|  c|   f|
#-# |  4|  d|NULL|
#-# +---+---+----+

a_b_right = a.join(b,on='id',how='right_outer')
a_b_right.show()

#-# +---+----+----+
#-# | id| val|val2|
#-# +---+----+----+
#-# |  2|   b|   g|
#-# |  3|   c|   f|
#-# |  5|NULL|   e|
#-# +---+----+----+

a_b_full = a.join(b,on='id',how='full_outer')
a_b_full.show()

#-# +---+----+----+
#-# | id| val|val2|
#-# +---+----+----+
#-# |  1|   a|NULL|
#-# |  2|   b|   g|
#-# |  3|   c|   f|
#-# |  4|   d|NULL|
#-# |  5|NULL|   e|
#-# +---+----+----+

#############################################################
#SQL SYNTAX

#Spark also allows us to use pure sql syntax.
#To use sql syntax we need to register our table to
#a catalog, which is an attribute of a session.
#A catalog lists all
#the data available inside the cluster.
#We can use the .listTables() method to return the names of the
#tables as a list.
```

```
# spark.catalog.listTables() #uncomment

subs.createOrReplaceTempView('subs')
#spark.catalog.listTables() #uncomment


spark.sql('select CustomerID, TotalDiscount from subs').show()

#-# +----------+-------------+
#-# |CustomerID|TotalDiscount|
#-# +----------+-------------+
#-# |   1150045|          0.0|
#-# |   1150046|      22.3737|
#-# |     89085|          0.0|
#-# |     89085|          0.0|
#-# |     89087|          0.0|
#-# |     89087|          0.0|
#-# |    325943|          0.0|
#-# |    191542|          0.0|
#-# |     83885|          0.0|
#-# |    309653|         NULL|
#-# |   1111604|    21.957237|
#-# |    809659|          0.0|
#-# |    110573|          0.0|
#-# |    594955|          0.0|
#-# |   1132498|    21.957237|
#-# |   1018582|          0.0|
#-# |    805609|          0.0|
#-# |    892534|    43.914306|
#-# |   1133741|     6.236868|
#-# |    246132|         NULL|
#-# +----------+-------------+
#-# only showing top 20 rows

spark.catalog.dropTempView('subs')

#-# True
```

23.3 PostgreSQL

Given a fixed set of physical computational resources, there are three main ways of improving performance: serialization, tuning usage of computational resources

(RAM and CPU), and tuning queries.

23.3.1 Serialization

Databases are designed to accommodate multiple concurrent sessions (connections) either from different users or a single user. Every active user has at least one session running but a single user can also run multiple concurrent sessions. The latter can be achieved by opening multiple PostgreSQL connections or kernels in our IDE, or running multiple batch sessions in the shell. This means that the possibility exists that multiple sessions try to access the same resource or object at the same time. For some operations that is not a problem. However, some operations cannot happen concurrently in a safe way when they access the same object and therefore need to be serialized. Serialization means that the queries are put in a queue and executed in order. To know when the next query in the queue can be executed, PostgreSQL uses locks. For example, if a query wants to update a record, it first needs to lock the record. The result is that no other query can update the record at the same time and so these other queries are blocked and have to wait until the lock on that record is released. Once the lock is released the next query in the queue will be executed. Concurrent user sessions are important, and are thus automatically supported by the locking mechanism.

However, locks can slow down the processing of our queries to the extent that the combined processing time of two concurrent sessions is longer than the combined processing time of scheduling two sessions serially. For example, if one user always works with the database in the morning, and the other user always in the afternoon, unnecessary blocking can be avoided. Below we discuss the different types of locks, how to detect them, and how to mitigate their negative effects.

Different types of locks

There are two main types of locks: heavyweight locks (table locks, and row locks) and lightweight locks. **Table locks** block reads from and writes to a table when the table is undergoing a specific operation. Table 23.1 contains common queries and whether they can run at the same time on the same table. For example, if a query is in the process of selecting data form a table, the table is locked and cannot be truncated.

Table 23.1: Table locks

Runs concurrently on same table?	select	insert, update, delete	create index	alter table, drop table, truncate
select	yes	yes	yes	no
insert, update, delete	yes	yes	no	no
create index	yes	no	yes	no
alter table, drop table, truncate	no	no	no	no

Row locks serialize concurrent modifications to rows. Table 23.2 contains common queries and whether they can access the same row concurrently. For example, no two records can update the same record at the same time.

Table 23.2: Row locks

Runs concurrently on same row?	select	update, delete
select	yes	yes
update, delete	yes	no

Lightweight locks block queries to protect data in buffers. Most lightweight locks cannot be managed in any meaningful way, but one lock that is very common and can be managed is `WALWriteLock` . The WAL mechanism is discussed in more detail in Section 8.3. A `WALWriteLock` means that the operation is waiting for a write operation from the WAL buffer to the WAL file to complete. Below we explain one possible way to manage `WALWriteLock` s.

Detecting locks

It may be insightful to run the following query to see all running postgres processes. The wait event column will display all operations (including maintenance operations such as vacuuming), not only locks.

```
SELECT pid, wait_event_type, wait_event
FROM pg_stat_activity;
```

Another query that can provide information that is easier to read uses the `pg_locks` view as opposed to the `pg_stat_activity` view. The following query uses the `granted` column in the `pg_locks` view. The `granted` column column indicates true if a lock is held, and false if a lock is awaited. In other words, we are displaying the queries that have not been able to acquire a lock and start processing.

```
select * from pg_locks where not granted;
```

Combining this with the `pg_stat_activity` can result in information that is easier to read:

```
select *
from pg_locks pl left join pg_stat_activity psa on pl.pid = psa.pid
where not pl.granted;
```

We need to remember that locks are not bad; they are necessary to accommodate concurrent operations. However, if certain operations continue to be blocked for extended periods, it may be appropriate to stop our script, and run it when the load on the database is lower. We call this manual serialization. Among other things, this is explained below.

Managing locks

The queries immediately above will return a `pid`, short for process identifier. When we have identified the blocking operation, we may wish to cancel it. We can do that with the following query, where we replace pid with the identifier of the query we want to cancel.

```
select pg_cancel_backend(pid);
```

Once we have canceled our query, we may choose to let the queries of one session finish and run our script later when there is less load on the system. For example, if you have to schedule two scripts that both access the same object in a way that would produce locks, then schedule one in the morning and the other in the afternoon. In that sense serialization happens manually, and overall runtime will be faster.

When it comes to lightweight locks, several of them can be avoided if certain memory components are increased in size. This will make queries go faster, and therefore their locks on objects will be shorter. One specific type of lock, a `WALWriteLock` , is especially hard to avoid. It might be resolved by increasing `wal_buffers` but often that does not improve the incidence of locks. If `WALWriteLock` s continue to slow down your queries, we found that the best course of action is to use unlogged tables. Unlogged tables are just like normal tables in that they persist beyond sessions, unlike temporary tables. The difference between normal tables and unlogged tables is that changes to the latter are not written to the write-ahead-log (WAL) as described in Section 8.3. This means that in the event of a crash or unclean shutdown, unlogged tables are automatically truncated. Unlogged tables are perfect for dynamic data with an expiration date (e.g., they will be truncated regularly or deleted and recreated regularly) and data that can be recreated easily. An unlogged table can be created as follows:

```
drop table if exists a;


create unlogged table a (
    var int
);


--we can also convert existing tables
alter table a set unlogged;


--To see all unlogged tables
select relname from pg_class where relpersistence = 'u';

#-#   relname
#-# 1       a
```

Unlogged tables should not be used for critical data. With critical data we mean unique data that does not have back-ups.

23.3.2 Tuning usage of computational resources

There are two main computational resources: memory and CPU. Section 8.3 explains how to manage memory components. Here we focus on managing the CPU. To speed up queries we can run them in parallel. PostgreSQL has various parameters to manage parallelization. First, the `max_worker_processes`, which is set in the postgres configuration file (see the part on modifying settings in Section 8.3), controls the global maximum number of processes that the system can support. This includes processes for parallel queries and non-parallel queries.

```
show max_worker_processes;

#-#   max_worker_processes
#-# 1                    8
```

The following parameters all take from the pool of `max_worker_processes`. The parameter `max_parallel_workers` controls the maximum number of workers that the system can support for parallel queries. Below we present the query to determine the value of the parameter and how to change the value for the duration of the user session.

```
show max_parallel_workers;

#-#   max_parallel_workers
#-# 1                    8


set max_parallel_workers to 9;


show max_parallel_workers;

#-#   max_parallel_workers
#-# 1                    9
```

Every parallel query has one or more *gather* nodes. A gather node is the process that spawns the parallel processes, and then gathers the results from each individual process into one result. Parallel workers for a gather node are taken from the pool of processes established by `max_worker_processes` and are limited by `max_parallel_workers`. It is important to underscore that parallel queries consume more resources than non-parallel queries because each worker is a separate process. This has to be accounted for when setting memory parameters as discussed in Section 8.3. One has to be especially careful with `work_mem`, as the value of that parameter is applied to each worker. For every parallel worker, Postgres can use `work_mem` more memory. This is also pertinent for disk usage. When running a parallel query, each process will access the disk. This means that the read speeds from the disk will slow down with every additional parallel worker. It is not uncommon to see highly parallel queries spending a lot of time doing input-output (`DataFileRead` and `DataFileWrite`) in `pg_stat_activity` . Below we present the query to determine the value of the parameter and how to change the value for the duration of the user session.

```
show max_parallel_workers_per_gather;

#-#   max_parallel_workers_per_gather
#-# 1                               2


set max_parallel_workers_per_gather to 3;


show max_parallel_workers_per_gather;

#-#   max_parallel_workers_per_gather
#-# 1                               3
```

Index creation (see next subsection) can also be parallelized. Processes related to indices fall under what is called *maintenance*. At the time of this writing, the only maintenance task that supports parallelization is `create index` . The parameter `max_parallel_maintenance_workers` is the number of parallel workers for a single `create index` . Below we present the query to determine the value of the parameter and how to change the value for the duration of the user session.

```
show max_parallel_maintenance_workers;

#-#   max_parallel_maintenance_workers
#-# 1                                2


set max_parallel_maintenance_workers to 3;


show max_parallel_maintenance_workers;

#-#   max_parallel_maintenance_workers
#-# 1                                3
```

Note that all these parameters are maxima. PostgreSQL will compute what the actual optimal value is for each parameter up until the maximum that we have set. The Postgres optimizer uses costs in its algorithm and we can change these costs. If we would want Postgres to use more parallel workers, then we would decrease the values of these parameters: `parallel_tuple_cost`, `parallel_setup_cost`, `min_parallel_table_scan_size`.

```
set parallel_tuple_cost = 0.000025;
set parallel_setup_cost = 10;
set min_parallel_table_scan_size = '5kB';
```

The above is a dramatic decrease from the default values. However, we found that even such a large decrease did not result in what would be the optimal degree of parallelization according to our tests. To force Postgres to use a certain number of cpu cores (say 8), use the following query, where a is the table name.

```
ALTER TABLE a SET (parallel_workers = 8);
```

It is important to note that more cores does not necessarily result in better performance. To benefit from parallelization, additional memory and faster disks such as solid state disks (ssd) are required.

23.3.3 Tuning queries

Perfomance issues often occur when there is a `where` clause or `join` present in the data. The reason is that these queries need to search for subsets of values. Searching for a value in a column - or a combination of values in multiple columns - is slow when the data are not sorted. Without sorting, Postgres needs to traverse all the values in the column, because the value we are looking for might present itself as the last value in the column. To speed up the search, we could sort the data. Given a linear search strategy, this will allow Postgres to stop reading the values of the column that occur after the value we were searching. Figure 23.4 gives a visual overview of the gains that can be realized when data are ordered. In the unordered set, Postgres would have to search all the values, whereas in the ordered set Postgres can stop once it has found the value and the next value is different. In the example, this means that Postgres only has to search 75% of the data. This gain is realized in the case of a linear search. There are much better search algorithms when data are sorted. One example is the binary search algorithm. In this algorithm the sorted values are repeatedly divided in half. The algorithm begins with all the values. If the value of the search key is less than the item in the middle of the values, then the search is narrowed to the lower half of the values. Otherwise the search is narrowed to the upper half. This narrowing is repeatedly executed until the values are found or the result is empty.

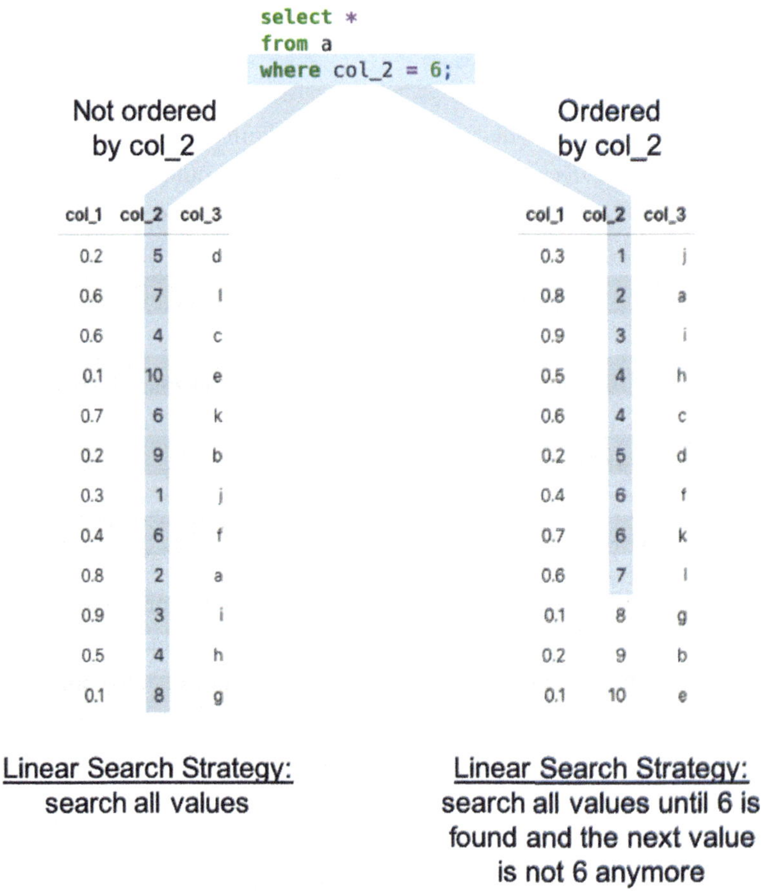

```
select *
from a
where col_2 = 6;
```

Not ordered by col_2

col_1	col_2	col_3
0.2	5	d
0.6	7	l
0.6	4	c
0.1	10	e
0.7	6	k
0.2	9	b
0.3	1	j
0.4	6	f
0.8	2	a
0.9	3	i
0.5	4	h
0.1	8	g

Linear Search Strategy:
search all values

Ordered by col_2

col_1	col_2	col_3
0.3	1	j
0.8	2	a
0.9	3	i
0.5	4	h
0.6	4	c
0.2	5	d
0.4	6	f
0.7	6	k
0.6	7	l
0.1	8	g
0.2	9	b
0.1	10	e

Linear Search Strategy:
search all values until 6 is found and the next value is not 6 anymore

Figure 23.4: Linear search of a sorted vs unsorted table

Given our newly gained understanding of the power of sorting, we might be thinking that the solution to our performance issues is to copy our tables ahead of our queries by using an `order by` clause in the `create table` statement. There are three main reasons not to do that. First, sorting involves moving large amounts of data from one memory location to another and that is a very expensive operation. We would not only move the values in the column that needs to be sorted, but also all the values in all the other columns. Second, if there is an update to the sort column, or we insert a record, then the entire sorting operation would have to be redone. Third, even if we did not care about the sorting cost, Postgres will not exploit this ordering like it does in Figure 23.4. So how do we then exploit the power of sorting? The answer is the use of an index. In the following paragraphs we will explain what an index is.

PostgreSQL creates a hidden system column for every table, called `ctid` , short for tuple (row) identifier. A tuple ID is a pair of identifiers that together identify the physical location of the row on disk and will change if the row is updated or undergoes a `vacuum full` . Postgres stores records on disk in what are called pages or blocks - the smallest storage unit of every database system. Pages for any object are stored in arbitrary order on disk. It are these pages that the `ctid` references along with the row index within the page: `(page number, row index within page)` . Every page is the same size, typically a few kilobytes, and the database fills up each page with records until it is completely full.

On the right side of Figure 23.5 we have created a representation of records in pages (in this case every page is 3 records). One part of the index - the leaf pages, or nodes, as displayed on the left side of Figure 23.5 - contains the ordered column that needed ordering (in this case column 2) for faster search, and the `ctid` . The index pages are not stored sequentially, because if the index needs to be changed (updates, deletions, or inserts) it would be necessary to move large amounts of data, which is too costly. Instead every page has links to two neighboring pages, just like a chain, thereby establishing logical order and allowing the index to read forwards and backwards. The entirety of index pages is called a doubly linked list because of these links. New pages are inserted between two existing pages by updating their links to the new page. Using this mechanism makes it possible to insert new enties without moving large amounts of data. Could Postgres not use a doubly linked list to order the original table? The answer is that this would be suboptimal for two reasons. First, it would have to move the values of all the columns when it is sorting. Second, if there are multiple columns that need to be sorted, then two copies of the table would have to be stored, which is much more expensive than storing two indices.

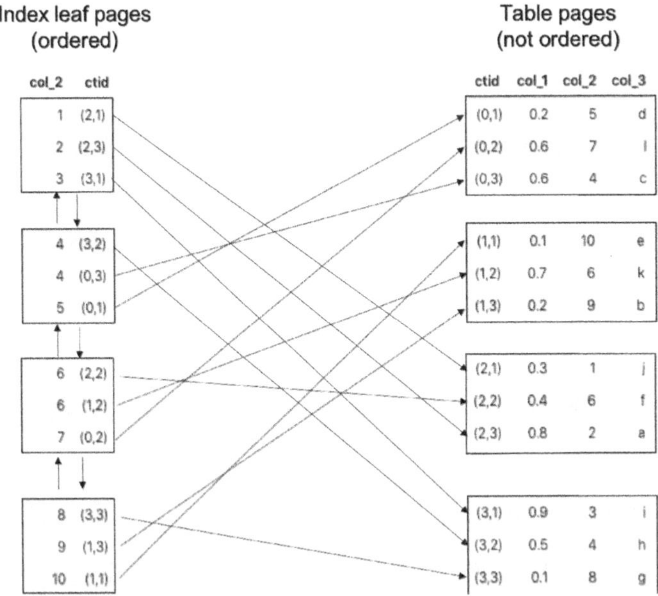

Figure 23.5: Index leaf pages

To make search even faster, indices make use of what is called a b-tree, short for balanced search tree. A b-tree uses branch nodes (there is only one displayed in Figure 23.6). For large indices, there are typically multiple layers of branch nodes. The term *balanced* refers to the distance between the start of the tree (the root page) and leaf nodes being equal everywhere. To find a value Postgres starts at the root node on the left-hand side of the figure and traverses all values until it finds a value greater than or equal to the search value. It then follows the pointers all the way to the leaf node. Inside the leaf node, it performs a linear search and stops when it has found a value greater than the search value. In Figure 23.6 we provide the traversal path for search value 6.

To summarize, to retrieve data using an index, there are three steps that PostgreSQL needs to do: (i) traverse the tree, (ii) potentially follow the leaf node chain (that would happen if the leaf node in Figure 23.6 would have all 6s, meaning that there could be more 6s in the next leaf node), and (iii) follow the `ctid` pointer to

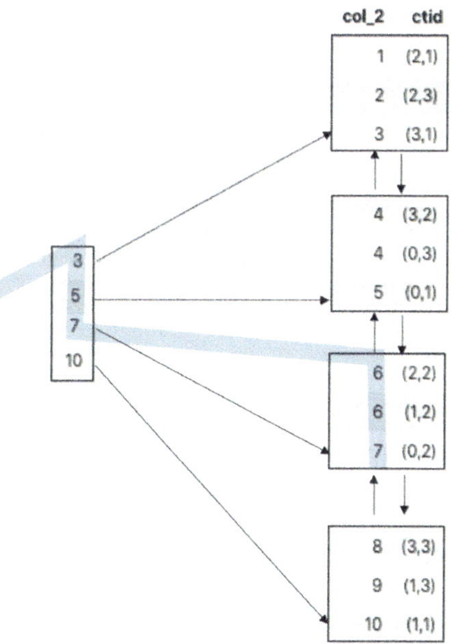

Figure 23.6: Balanced tree traversal

the table and fetch the data. Below we provide an example of how to create an index `my_index` for a column called `col_2` in a table called `a`.

```
create index my_index ON a (col_2);
drop index if exists my_index;
```

Indices can also be created on multiple columns if search need to happen across multiple columns (e.g., `create index my_index ON a (col_2, col_3);`).

Chapter 24

Bonus Chapter: Non-columnar Source Data

Every batch of records that we feed to our machine learning algorithm needs to be organized in a columnar fashion. The same variables need to appear in the same order in each and every batch. In this book we have assumed that our raw - source - data is already columnar and from that perspective we have provided key coding techniques in R, Python, and PostgreSQL to understand and prepare that columnar data for analysis. In other words, the input is columnar data, and the output is columnar data.

Relational databases such as Oracle, and Postgres store data in a normalized fashion and that is the reason why data has a columnar format. One of the main goals of data normalization is ensuring that the data's storage footprint is as small as possible by storing data in separate tables and joining the data when a complete picture is required. In that sense, compute time is sacrified for storage space.

When relational databases were developed, non-columnar data was much less prevalent. With the rise of the internet, and especially social media, source data have become increasingly non-columnar. The reason is that the focus has shifted towards speed. Upon logging into a platform (e.g., Twitter), a user wants to see their personal data immediately. There is no time to do expensive joins between multiple tables to get all the information. Data needs to be displayed as quickly as possible. To accomplish that, data is stored in unnormalized form. For example, each Tweet might include a username and a user identifier, thereby providing fast access to the username without requiring another search. In a relational database, a Tweet would be stored in one table along with the user identifier, and the user identifier and username would be stored in another table. As such, one saves diskspace by not having to store the username for every tweet, but requires compute time to look up the username. Storage in unnormalized form therefore results in faster access. It has to be noted that, if data needs to be updated, it needs to be changed in multiple places. Therefore, this approach is better when reads occur much more frequently than writes.

Document stores are one common type of non-columnar databases. Such a database has *collections* and *documents*, which are considered to be analogous to *tables* and *records* in relational databases. However, while every record in a table has the same sequence of fields, documents in a collection may have fields that are entirely different. MongoDB is one very popular provider of document store software. Table 24.1 shows the main data types in a MongoDB and compares them with PostgreSQL data types. Databases contain collections, which in turn contain documents that are organized by fields.

Table 24.1: Data types in MongoDB

MongoDB	Postgres
Databases	Databases
Collections	Tables
Documents	Records
Fields	Columns

JSON, short for JavaScript Object Notation, is a lightweight text data format, which is easy to read, write and parse. It is language independent and is built on two structures (`https://www.json.org`): Objects and Arrays, where the values in an Object can be an array.

- Objects: unordered key-value pairs: `{'key1':value1, 'key2:value2', ...}`
- Arrays: ordered values: `[value1, value2, ...]`

To install MongoDB Community Edition follow the instructions at the following url: `https://docs.mongodb.com/manual/installation/`. To verify if your installation was successful type `mongosh` in the shell. You should see something similar to this:

```
mb@Michels-MacBook-Pro-2 ~ % mongo
zsh: command not found: mongo
mb@Michels-MacBook-Pro-2 ~ % mongosh
Current Mongosh Log ID: 671952612dd8a13d802bf16d
Connecting to: mongodb://127.0.0.1:27017/?directConnection=
  true&serverSelectionTimeoutMS=2000&appName=mongosh+2.3.2
Using MongoDB: 8.0.1
Using Mongosh: 2.3.2

For mongosh info see: https://www.mongodb.com/docs/mongodb-shell/


To help improve our products, anonymous usage data is collected and sent to MongoDB periodically
(https://www.mongodb.com/legal/privacy-policy).
You can opt-out by running the disableTelemetry() command.

------
   The server generated these startup warnings when booting
   2024-10-23T15:44:17.225-04:00: Access control is not enabled for the database.
   Read and write access to data and configuration is unrestricted
------

test> exit
```

To quit `mongosh` type `exit`. We will use the Python api to MongoDB called `pymongo`, which can be installed as follows in the shell: `pip3 install pymongo`. Next we cover fundamental techniques to set up a new database, make collections, and query the data.

```
#-# <string>:1: ResourceWarning: Unclosed MongoClient opened at:
#-#   File "<string>", line 1, in <module>
#-# Call MongoClient.close() to safely shut down your client and free up resources.


import pymongo

##############################################
#Create a client (dictionary of databases)
#CLient connects to localhost by default
client = pymongo.MongoClient()

##############################################
```

```
#list all the databases
client.list_database_names()

#-# ['admin', 'config', 'local']


#The admin, config and local database are there for internal housekeeping

############################################
#create an empty database called peloton,
#and create handle called db
#A database is a dictionary of collections
db = client['peloton']
#A database can be dropped as follows:
#client.drop_database('peloton')

############################################
#create a collection in the database

#get data from Peloton Inc Twitter account
import requests
response = requests.get('http://hde.onl/tweets_peloton.json')
data = response.json()

#create collection called tweets and insert data
#add 'x =' to prevent printing the list of inserted documents
x = db['tweets'].insert_many(data)


############################################
#list collections inside a database
db.list_collection_names()

#-# ['tweets']

############################################
#Filters

#Many methods (e.g., count the number of documents) in mongodb
#have a filter parameter.

#Filter: A query document specifies a pattern that a document
#must match and works very similar to a where clause
#in sql. The query document can be an empty document to select all
```

```
#documents. An empty filter looks like this: {}.
#Below we will start out with empty filters,
#and gradually build up complexity by adding elements to it.

############################################
#Count all (i.e., empty filter) documents in a collection

db.tweets.count_documents(filter = {})

#-# 3199

#or
db.tweets.count_documents({})

#-# 3199

#or
filter = {}
db.tweets.count_documents(filter)

#-# 3199

############################################
#Display a single document and its fields
#The first in the internal order of the collection:

#All fields and data:
OneRowAllfields = db.tweets.find_one({})

#A single field (e.g., the Tweet text, with field name 'text) (first 50 characters):
OneRowAllfields['text'][0:50]

#-# '@Erin_3lizabeth Hi Erin, please DM us with your or'

#Only the fields (first 3):
list(OneRowAllfields.keys())[0:3]

#-# ['_id', 'user_id', 'status_id']

############################################
#Display more than one document

#To get more than a single document that passes the filter,
#we can use the find() method. This method returns a
#cursor instance, allowing us to iterate over all matching documents,
#with the next() method.
```

```
doc = db.tweets.find(filter)

#print first 50 characters text of next document
doc.next()['text'][0:50]

#-# '@Erin_3lizabeth Hi Erin, please DM us with your or'

#print first 50 characters text of next document
doc.next()['text'][0:50]

#-# '@jbouvier Hi Jordan, thanks for reaching out. Our '

###############################Composing filters (tested with count_documents):

##########
#Create filter that selects tweets where retweet_count is greater than or
#equal to 10.

filter = {'retweet_count': {'$gte': 10}}
#gte stands for greater than or equal
#gt stands for greater than
#lte stands for less than or equal
#lt stands for less than
#eq stands for equal
#ne stands for not equal

db.tweets.count_documents(filter)

#-# 133

##########
#And and Or conditions
#Create a filter to select tweets where retweet_count is greater than or
#equal to 10 AND favorite_count is greater than or equal to 200

#implicit AND:
filter = {'retweet_count': {'$gte': 10},
          'favorite_count': {'$gte': 200}}
db.tweets.count_documents(filter)

#-# 32

#explicit AND:
filter = {'$and': [{'retweet_count': {'$gte': 10}},
                   {'favorite_count': {'$gte': 200}}]}
db.tweets.count_documents(filter)
```

```
#-# 32

#Create a filter to select tweets where retweet_count is greater than or
#equal to 10 OR favorite_count is greater than or equal to 200
#OR
filter = {'$or': [{'retweet_count': {'$gte': 10}},
                  {'favorite_count': {'$gte': 200}}]}
db.tweets.count_documents(filter)

#-# 134

##########
#Create filter that selects tweets for which the source field
#is either 'Twitter Ads' or 'Twitter for iPhone'
filter = {'source': {'$in': ['Twitter Ads','Twitter for iPhone']}}

db.tweets.count_documents(filter)

#-# 98

#not in:
filter = {'source': {'$nin': ['Twitter Ads','Twitter for iPhone']}}

db.tweets.count_documents({})

#-# 3199

##########
#Create filter that selects tweets for which the source field
#is not 'TweetDeck'

filter = {'source': {'$ne':'TweetDeck' }}

db.tweets.count_documents(filter)

#-# 3198

##########
#Create filter that select tweets for which the source field
#is 'Sprout Social'


filter = {'source': {'$eq':'Sprout Social'}}
#or
filter = {'source': 'Sprout Social'}

db.tweets.count_documents(filter)
```

```
#-# 414

##########
#Create a filter that selects tweets for which the 'lang' field exists

filter = {'lang':{'$exists': True}}

db.tweets.count_documents(filter)

#-# 3199

##########
#Reaching into the arrays
#Example of data:
# 'ext_media_expanded_url': [None],
#Suppose we want to select based on the first element (element 0)
#of an array.

filter = {'ext_media_expanded_url.0': {'$ne': None}}
db.tweets.find_one(filter)['ext_media_expanded_url']

#-# ['https://twitter.com/onepeloton/status/1252663024797782017/video/1']

filter = {'ext_media_expanded_url.0': {'$eq': None}}
db.tweets.find_one(filter)['ext_media_expanded_url']

#-# [None]

##########
#What are the distinct values for the source field? Print the first three elements of the
result.

db.tweets.distinct('source')[0:3]

#-# ['Khoros Marketing', 'Percolate', 'Sprout Social']

##########
#How many distinct values are there for the source field?

len(db.tweets.distinct('source'))

#-# 8

#The distinct method also supports filters.
#What are the distinct values for the source field, for
#documents where retweet_count is greater than or
```

```
#equal to 100.

filter = {'retweet_count': {'$gte': 100}}

db.tweets.distinct('source', filter)

#-# ['Khoros Marketing', 'Twitter Web Client', 'Twitter for iPhone']

##########
#Regular expressions
#Note that they are by default case sensitive

#find all documents that have the word 'Twitter'
#***somewhere*** in the 'source' field
filter = {'source': {'$regex': 'Twitter'}}
db.tweets.distinct('source', filter)

#-# ['Twitter Ads', 'Twitter Web App', 'Twitter Web Client', 'Twitter for iPhone']

#for case insensitivity, add '$options': 'i'
#note lower case t in twitter
filter = {'source': {'$regex': 'twitter', '$options': 'i'}}
db.tweets.distinct('source', filter)

#-# ['Twitter Ads', 'Twitter Web App', 'Twitter Web Client', 'Twitter for iPhone']

#find all documents that ***start*** with the word 'Twitter'
#in the 'source' field: ^
filter = {'source': {'$regex': '^Twitter'}}
db.tweets.distinct('source', filter)

#-# ['Twitter Ads', 'Twitter Web App', 'Twitter Web Client', 'Twitter for iPhone']

#find all documents that ***end*** with the word 'Client'
#in the 'source' field: $
filter = {'source': {'$regex': 'Client$'}}
db.tweets.distinct('source', filter)

#-# ['Twitter Web Client']
```

Made in the USA
Coppell, TX
16 February 2025